I0647026

FANTAGRAPHICS BOOKS, 7563 LAKE CITY WAY NE, SEATTLE, WA - 98115
EDITOR, JASON T. MILES | ASSOCIATE PUBLISHER, ERIC REYNOLDS
PUBLISHED BY GARY GROTH & KIM THOMPSON | ALL CONTENTS © 2013 - GRAHAM
CHAFFEE, THIS EDITION COPYRIGHT © 2013 FANTAGRAPHICS BOOKS, INC.
ALL RIGHTS RESERVED. PERMISSION TO REPRODUCE MATERIAL MUST BE
OBTAINED FROM FANTAGRAPHICS BOOKS. | FIRST EDITION: MAY 2013
ISBN: 978-1-60699-636-2 | PRINTED IN CHINA

FOR SOPHIE AND MAX

GONE WHERE GOOD DOGS GO.

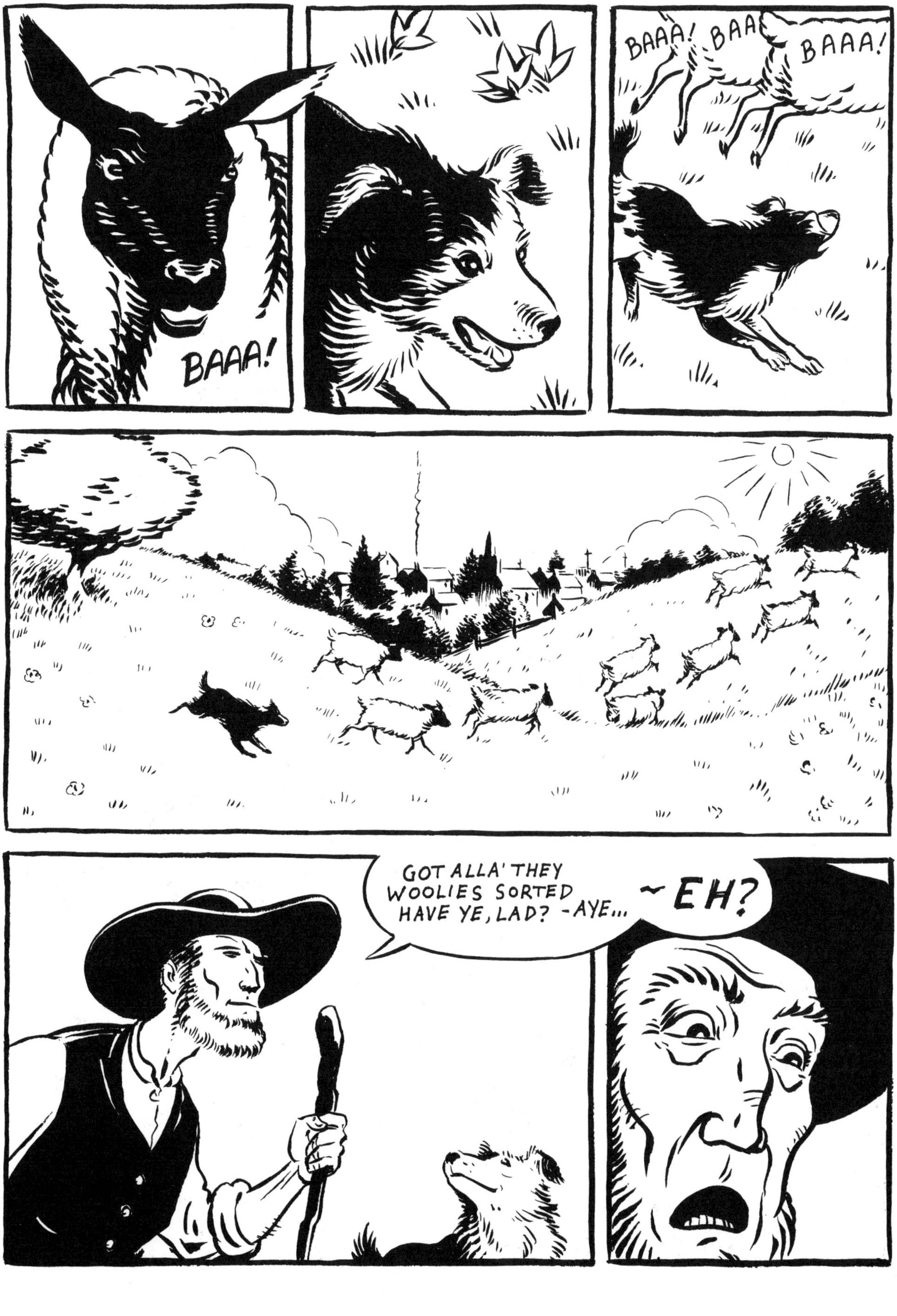
BAAA!
BAAA! BAA BAAA!
GOT ALLA' THEY WOOLIES SORTED HAVE YE, LAD? -AYE...
~EH?

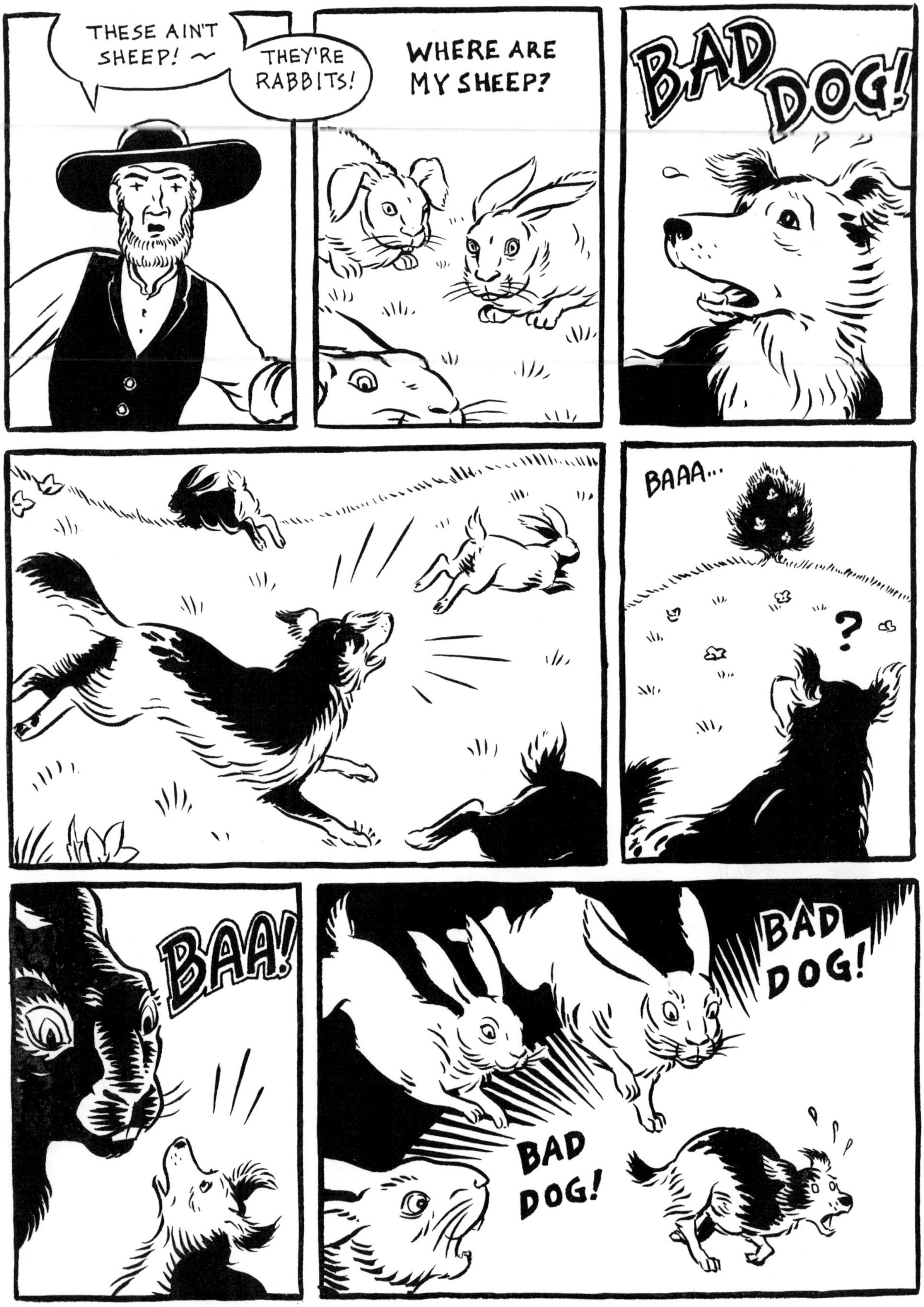
THESE AIN'T SHEEP! ~
THEY'RE RABBITS!
WHERE ARE MY SHEEP?
BAD DOG!
BAAA...
?
BAA!
BAD DOG!
BAD DOG!

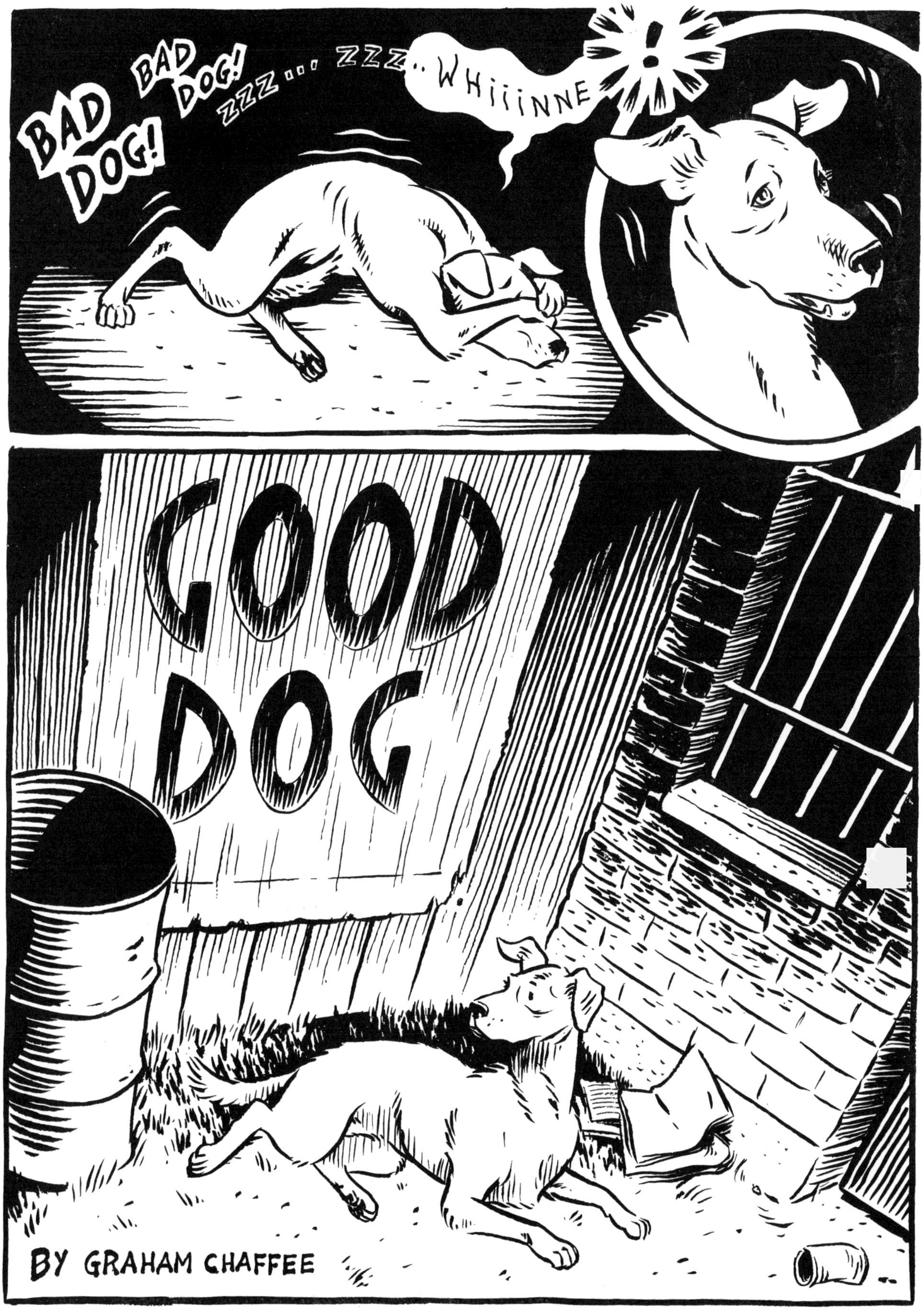
BAD DOG! BAD DOG!
ZZZ... ZZZ... WHiiiNNE
!
GOOD DOG
BY GRAHAM CHAFFEE

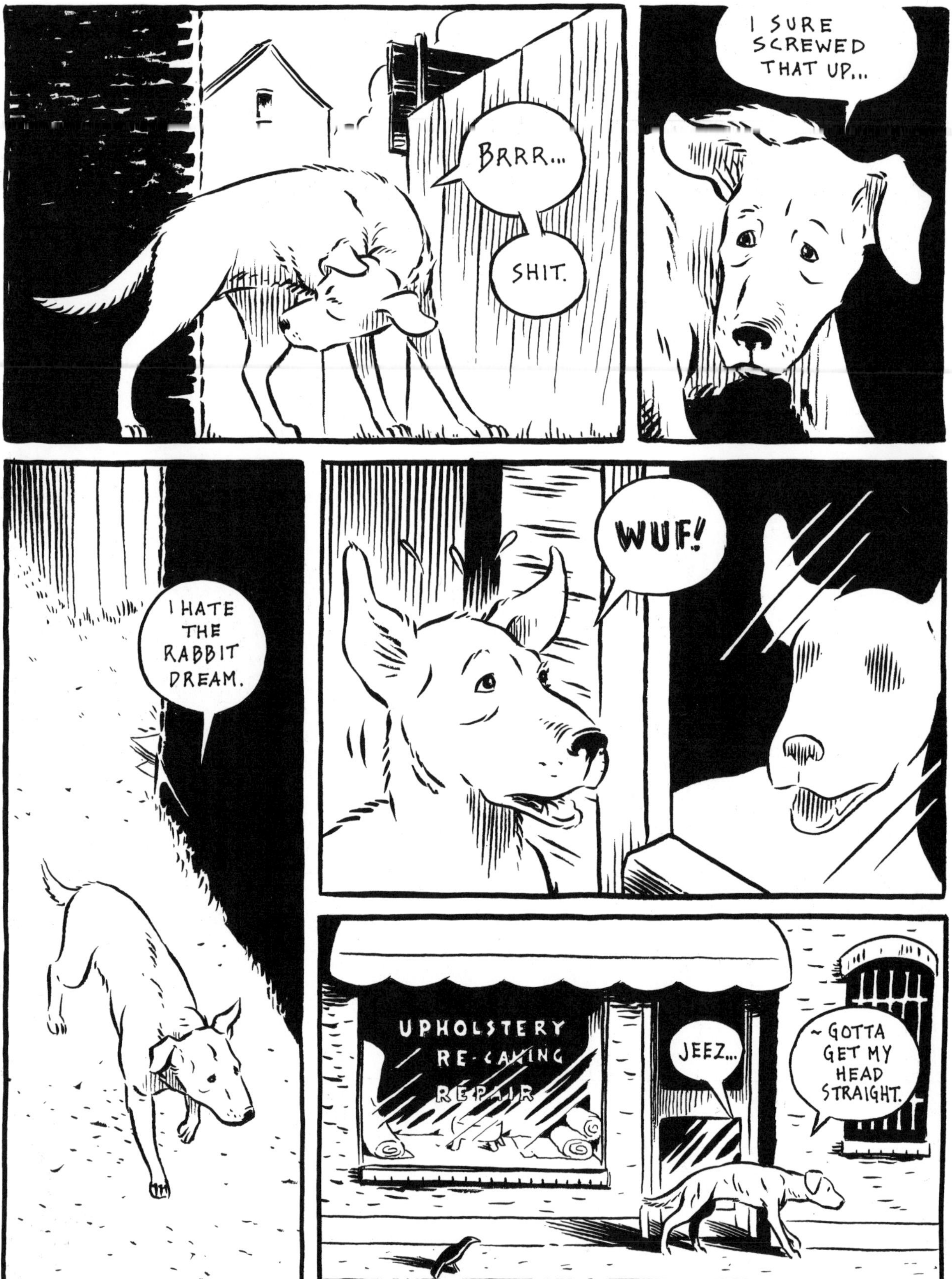
BRRR...
SHIT.
I SURE SCREWED THAT UP...
I HATE THE RABBIT DREAM.
WUF!
UPHOLSTERY
RE-CANING
REPAIR
JEEZ...
~GOTTA GET MY HEAD STRAIGHT.

GRAPH
CHAFFEE

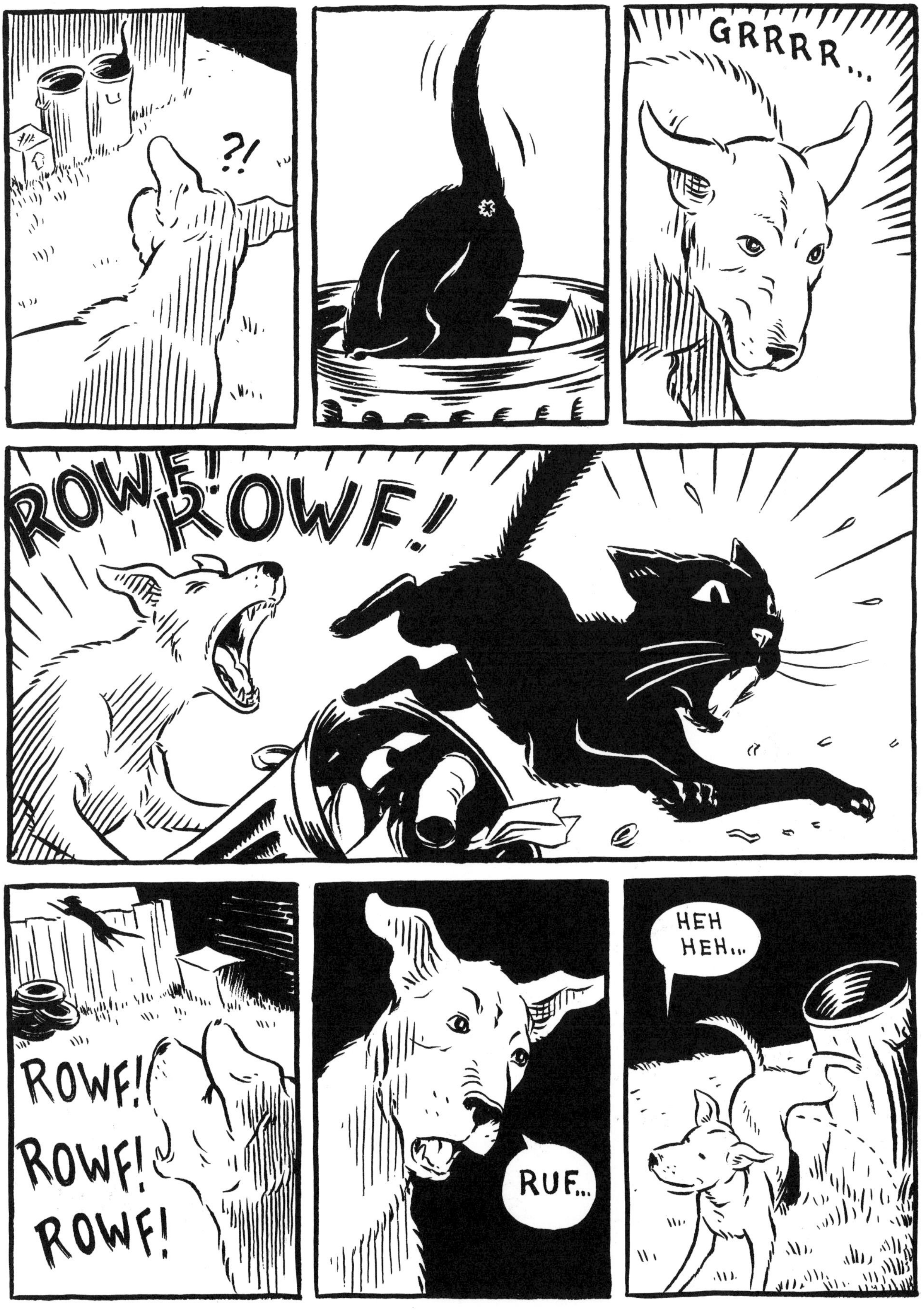
?!
GRRRR...
ROWF! ROWF!
ROWF! ROWF! ROWF!
RUF...
HEH HEH...

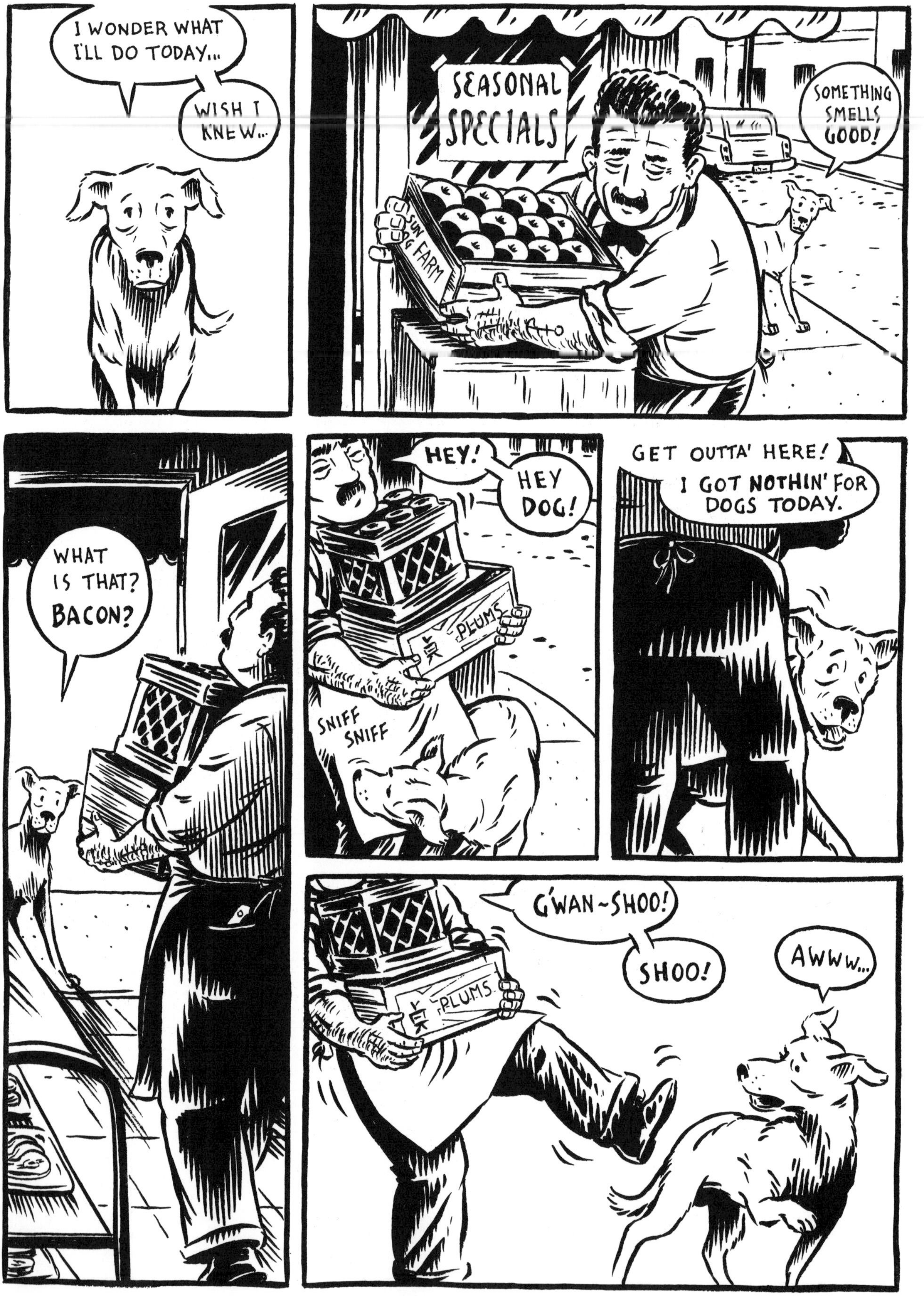
I WONDER WHAT I'LL DO TODAY...
WISH I KNEW...
SEASONAL SPECIALS
SUN DOG FARM
SOMETHING SMELLS GOOD!
WHAT IS THAT? BACON?
HEY!
HEY DOG!
PLUMS
SNIFF SNIFF
GET OUTTA' HERE!
I GOT NOTHIN' FOR DOGS TODAY.
G'WAN~SHOO!
SHOO!
PLUMS
AWWW...

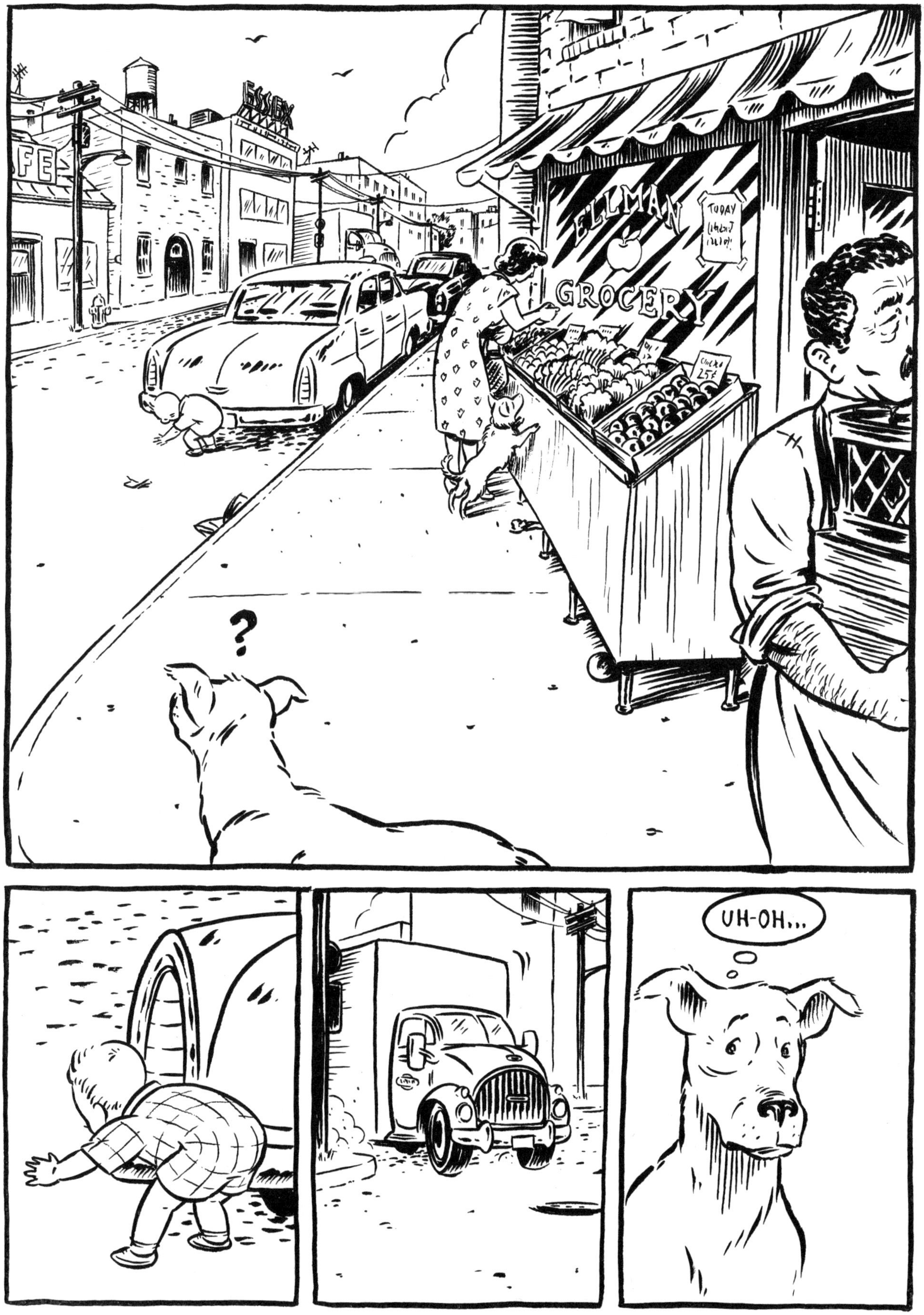
ESSEX
ELLMAN
GROCERY
TODAY
?
UH-OH...

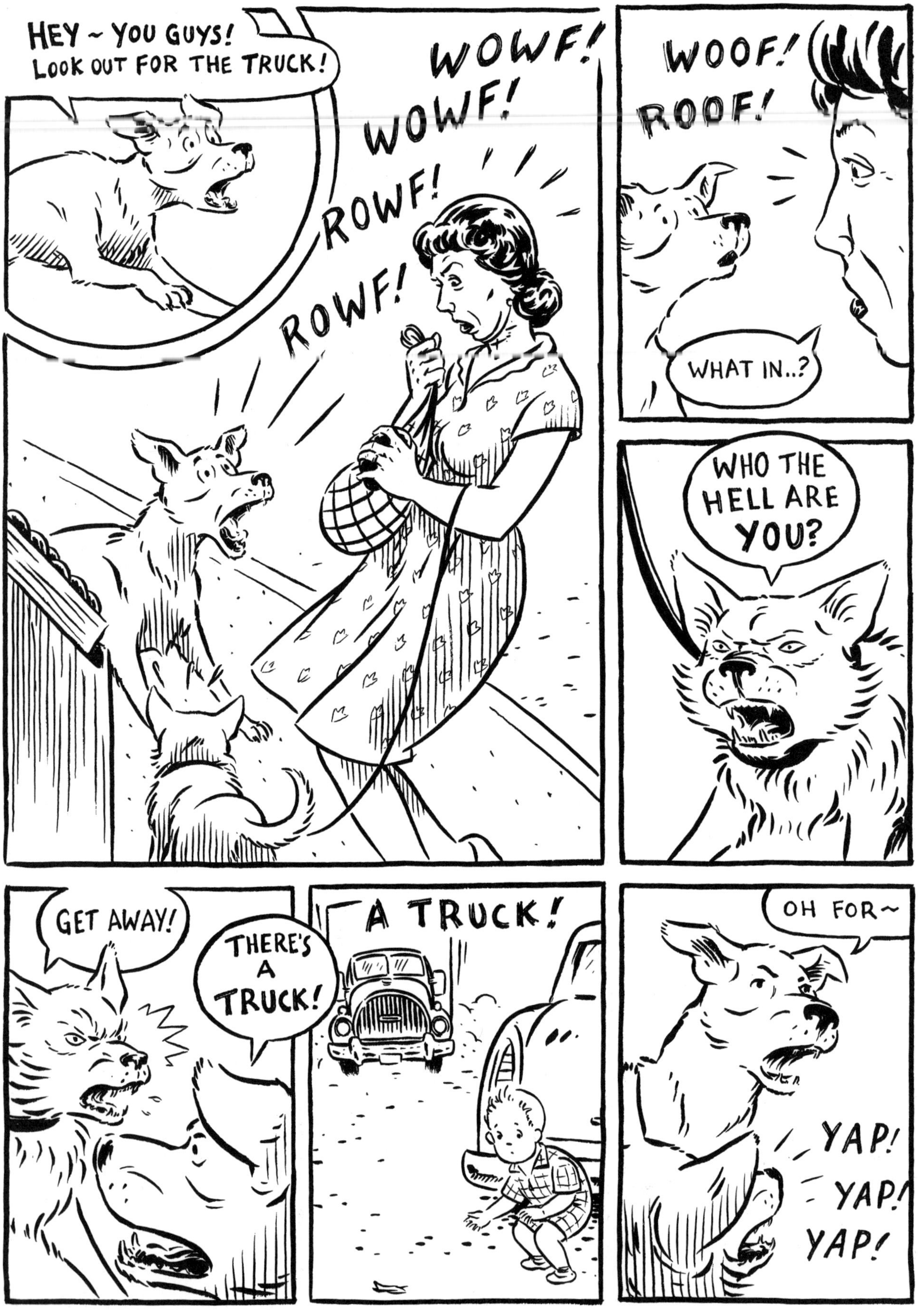
HEY ~ YOU GUYS! LOOK OUT FOR THE TRUCK!
WOWF!
WOWF!
ROWF!
ROWF!
WOOF!
ROOF!
WHAT IN..?
WHO THE HELL ARE YOU?
GET AWAY!
THERE'S A TRUCK!
A TRUCK!
OH FOR~
YAP!
YAP!
YAP!

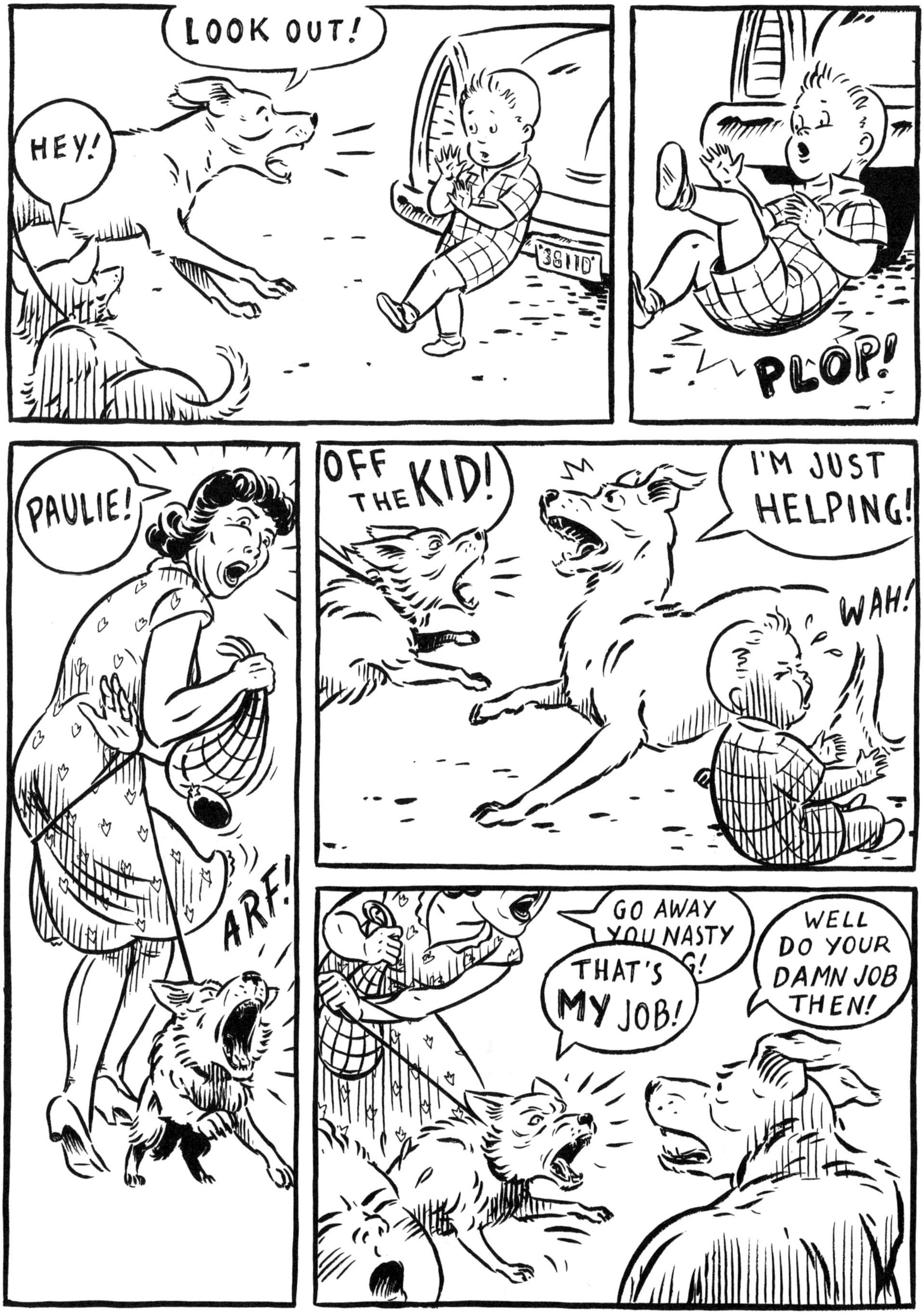
HEY!
LOOK OUT!
PLOP!
PAULIE!
ARF!
OFF THE KID!
I'M JUST HELPING!
WAH!
GO AWAY YOU NASTY
THAT'S MY JOB!
WELL DO YOUR DAMN JOB THEN!

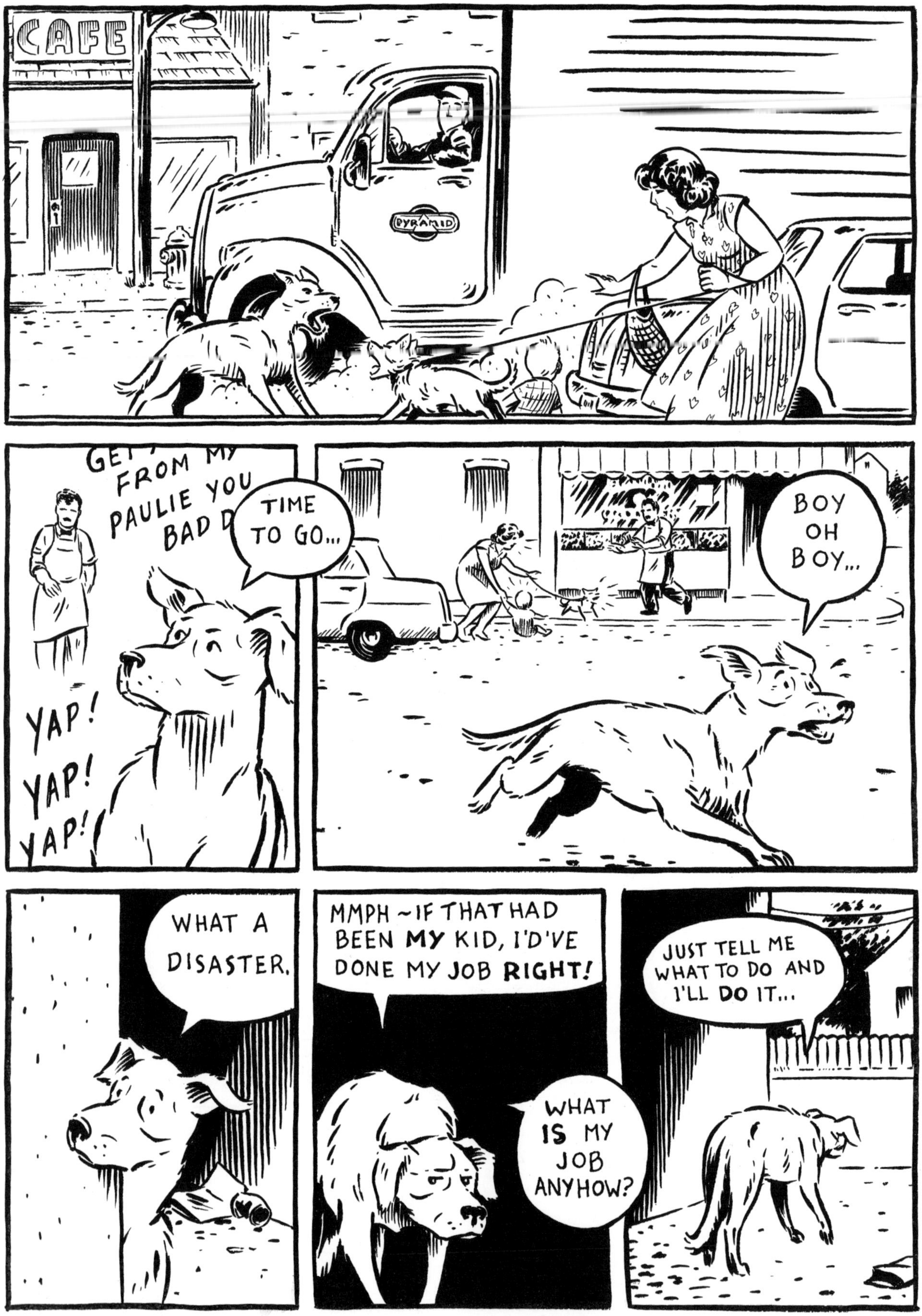
CAFE
PYRAMID
GET FROM MY PAULIE YOU BAD D
TIME TO GO...
YAP! YAP! YAP!
BOY OH BOY...
WHAT A DISASTER.
MMPH ~ IF THAT HAD BEEN MY KID, I'D'VE DONE MY JOB RIGHT!
WHAT IS MY JOB ANYHOW?
JUST TELL ME WHAT TO DO AND I'LL DO IT...

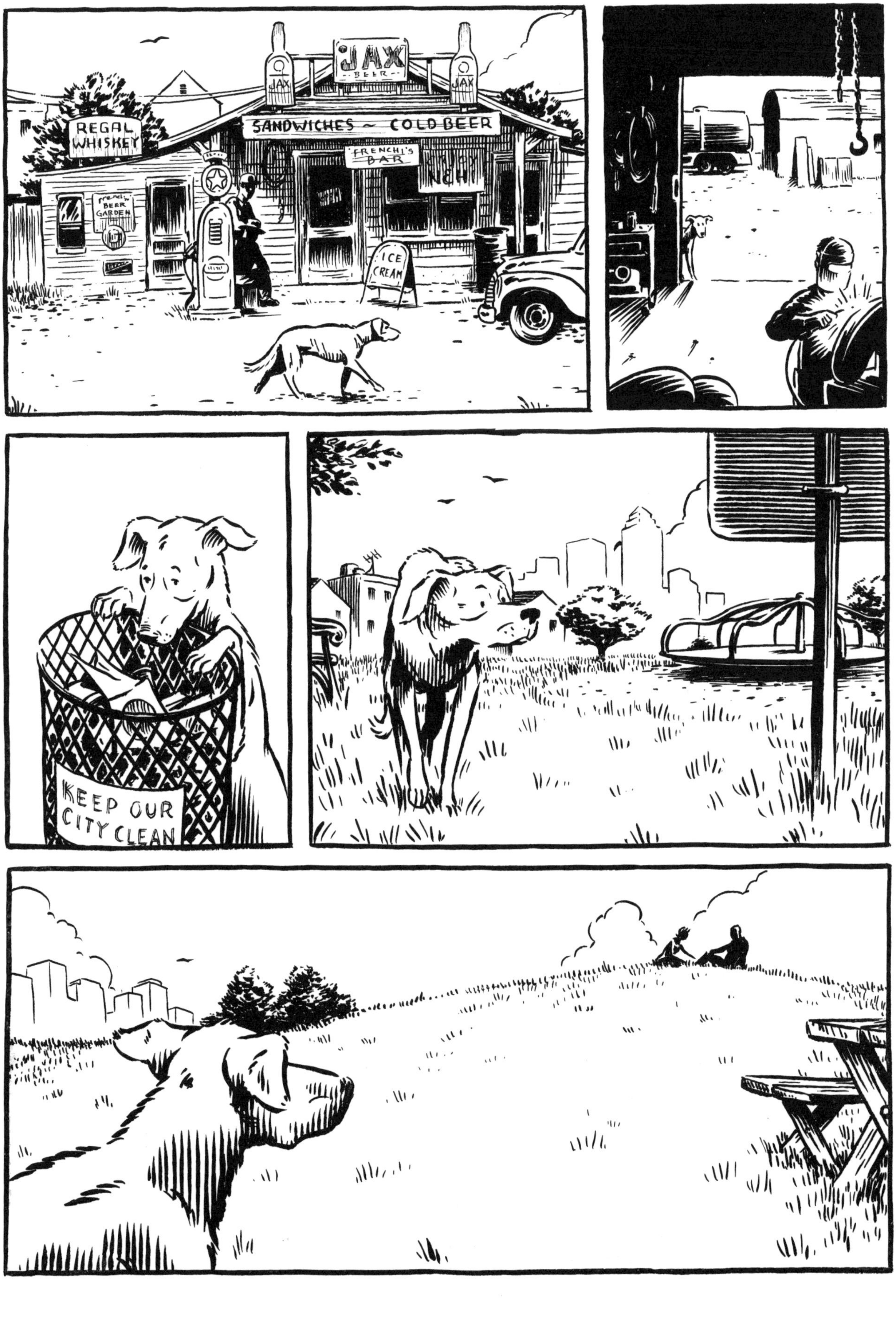

JAX
BEER
JAX
JAX
REGAL WHISKEY
SANDWICHES ~ COLD BEER
FRENCHI'S BAR
ICE CREAM
KEEP OUR CITY CLEAN

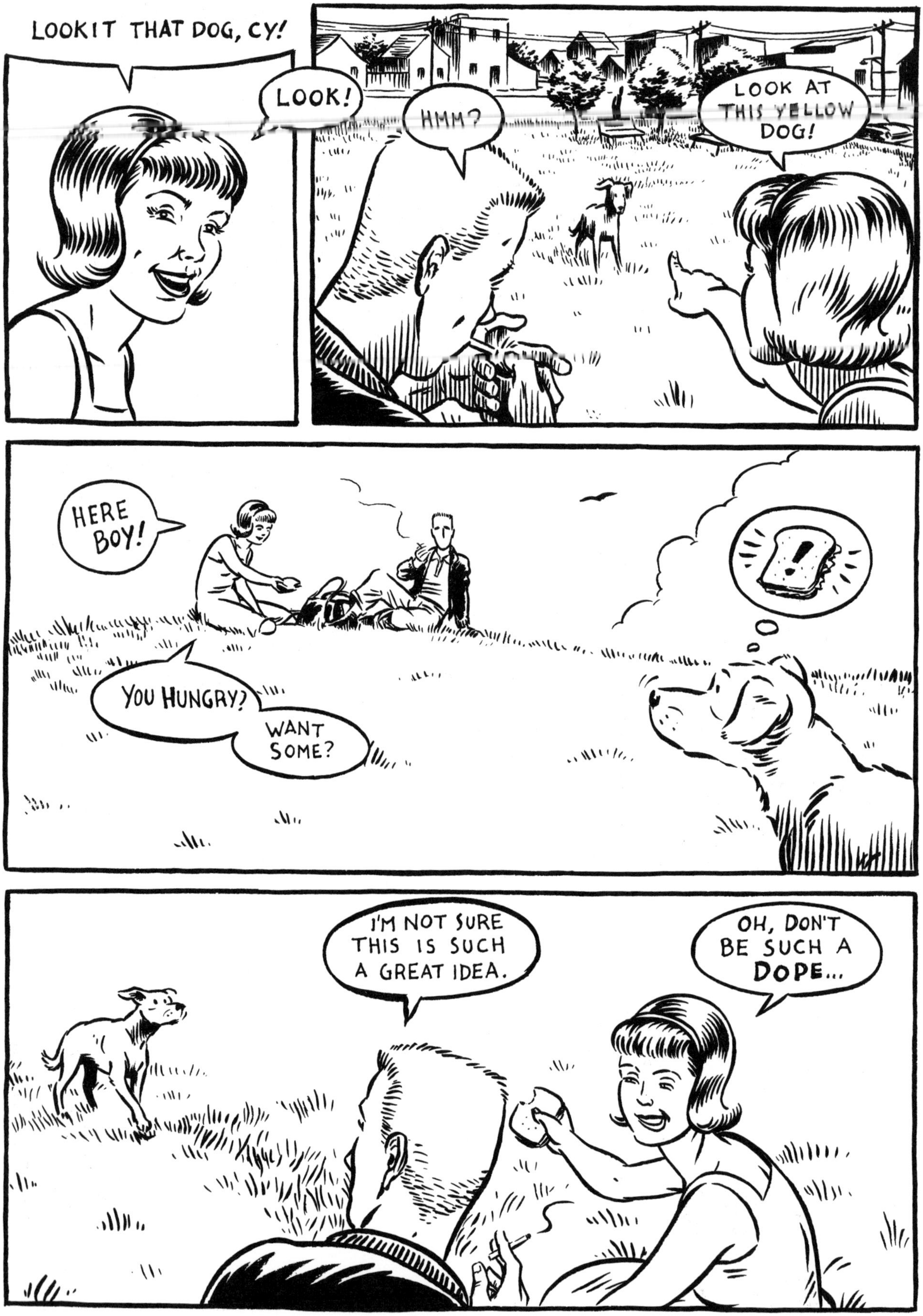
LOOKIT THAT DOG, CY!
LOOK!
HMM?
LOOK AT THIS YELLOW DOG!
HERE BOY!
YOU HUNGRY?
WANT SOME?
I'M NOT SURE THIS IS SUCH A GREAT IDEA.
OH, DON'T BE SUCH A DOPE...

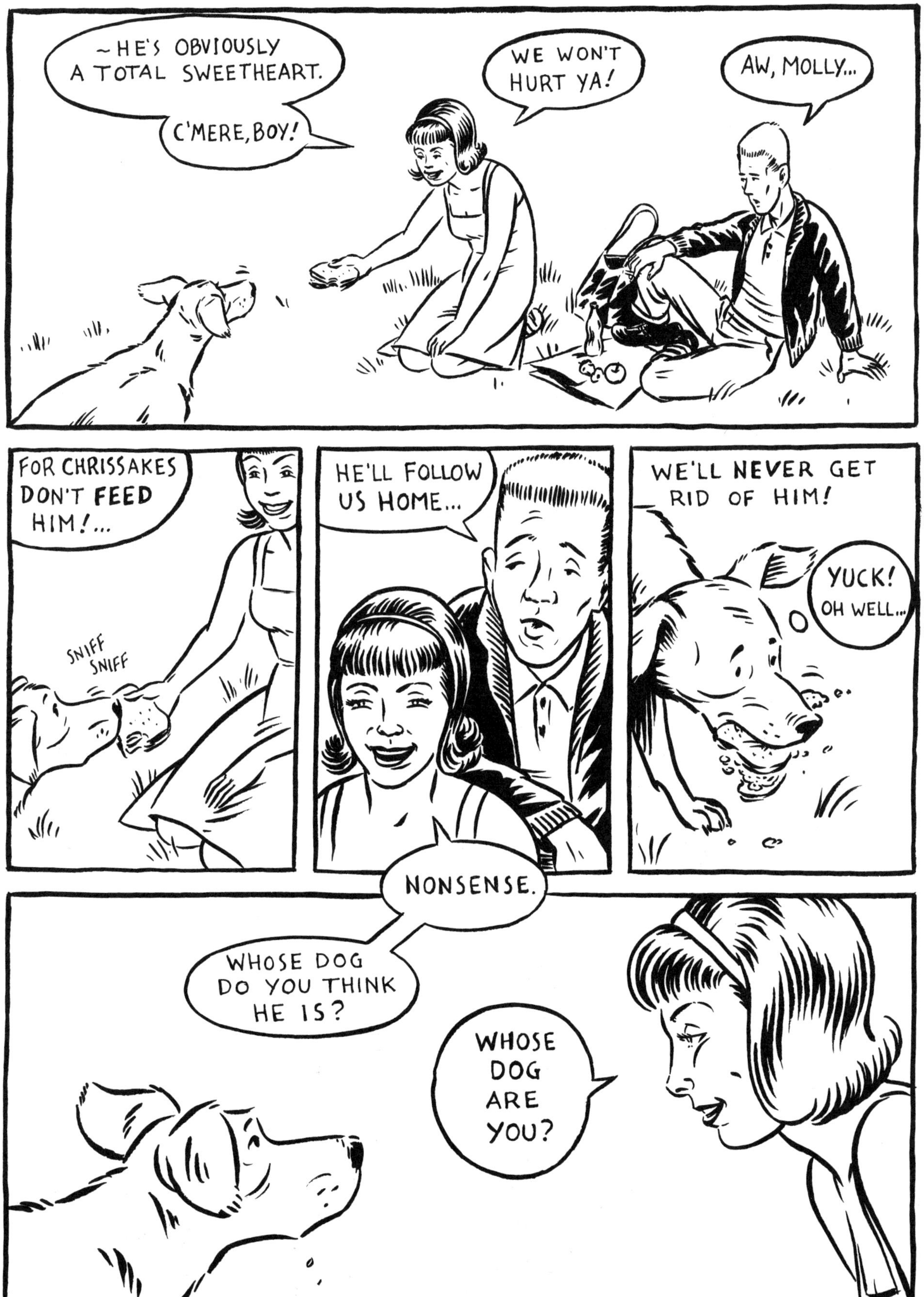
~HE'S OBVIOUSLY A TOTAL SWEETHEART.
C'MERE, BOY!
WE WON'T HURT YA!
AW, MOLLY...
FOR CHRISSAKES DON'T **FEED** HIM!...
SNIFF SNIFF
HE'LL FOLLOW US HOME...
WE'LL **NEVER** GET RID OF HIM!
YUCK! OH WELL...
NONSENSE.
WHOSE DOG DO YOU THINK HE IS?
WHOSE DOG ARE YOU?

LOOKS LIKE A STRAY.
DOESN'T HAVE A COLLAR...
AWW ~ ARE YOU A STRAY?
IS THAT WHAT YOU ARE?
SCRATCH
SCRATCH
SCRATCH
HE'S FILTHY ~ PROBABLY HAS DISEASES.
IS THAT RIGHT? ARE YOU A FILTHY, DISEASEY OL' STRAY?
YEP.
WE SHOULD TAKE OFF...
I GOTTA GET BACK TO WORK.
OKEY-DOKEY, POKEY.
AW, LOOK, CY! HE WANTS TO COME WITH US!
TOLD YOU ~ THAT'S WHAT YOU GET FOR FEEDING A STRAY.

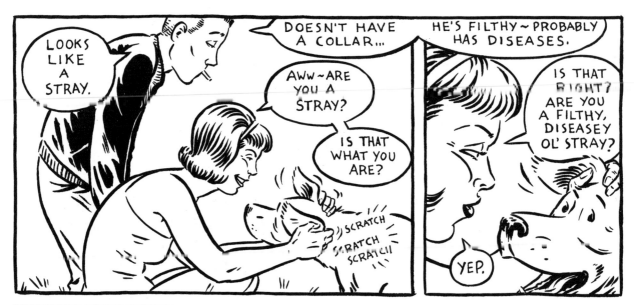

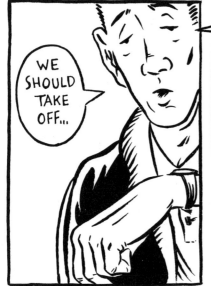

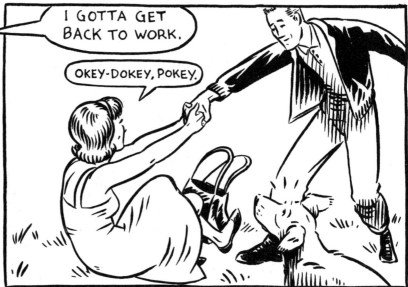

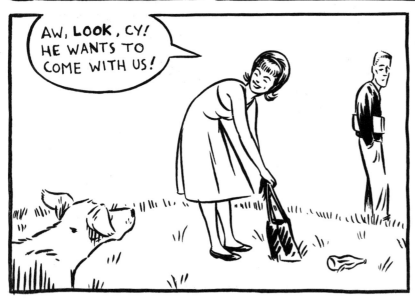

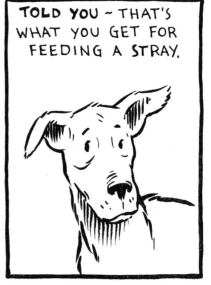

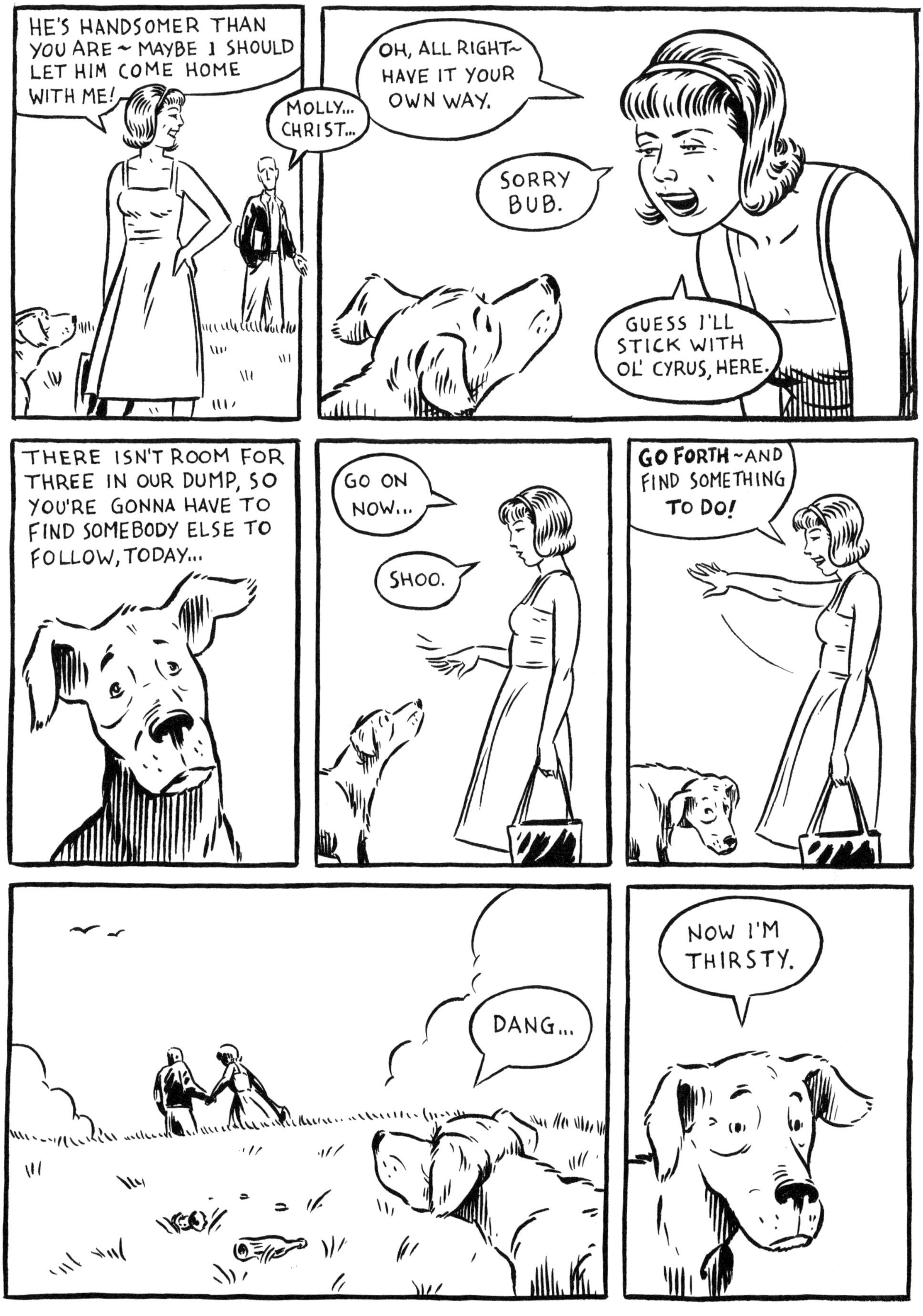
HE'S HANDSOMER THAN YOU ARE ~ MAYBE I SHOULD LET HIM COME HOME WITH ME!
MOLLY... CHRIST...
OH, ALL RIGHT~ HAVE IT YOUR OWN WAY.
SORRY BUB.
GUESS I'LL STICK WITH OL' CYRUS, HERE.
THERE ISN'T ROOM FOR THREE IN OUR DUMP, SO YOU'RE GONNA HAVE TO FIND SOMEBODY ELSE TO FOLLOW, TODAY...
GO ON NOW...
SHOO.
GO FORTH ~AND FIND SOMETHING TO DO!
DANG...
NOW I'M THIRSTY.

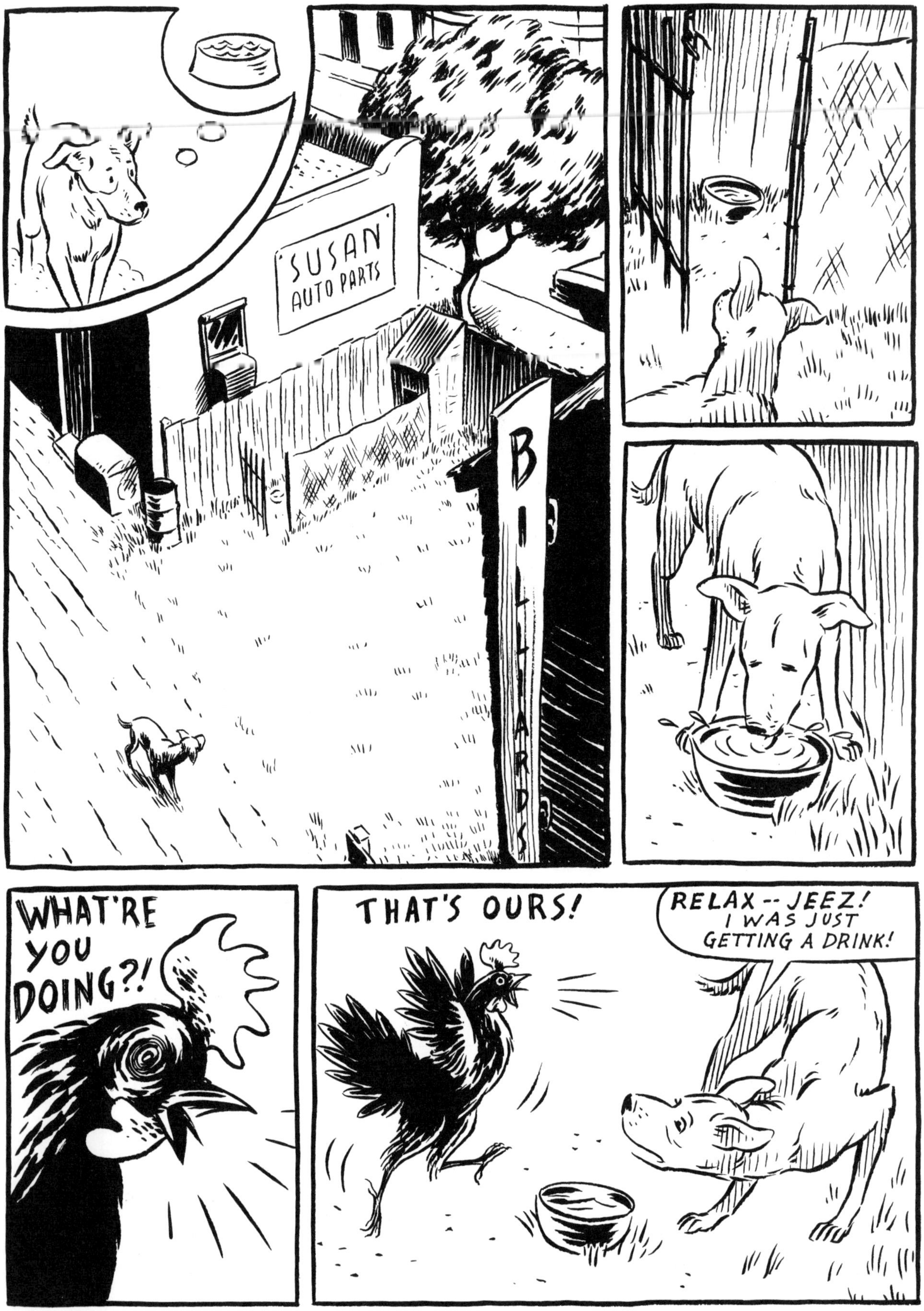
SUSAN AUTO PARTS
BILLIARDS
WHAT'RE YOU DOING?!
THAT'S OURS!
RELAX -- JEEZ! I WAS JUST GETTING A DRINK!

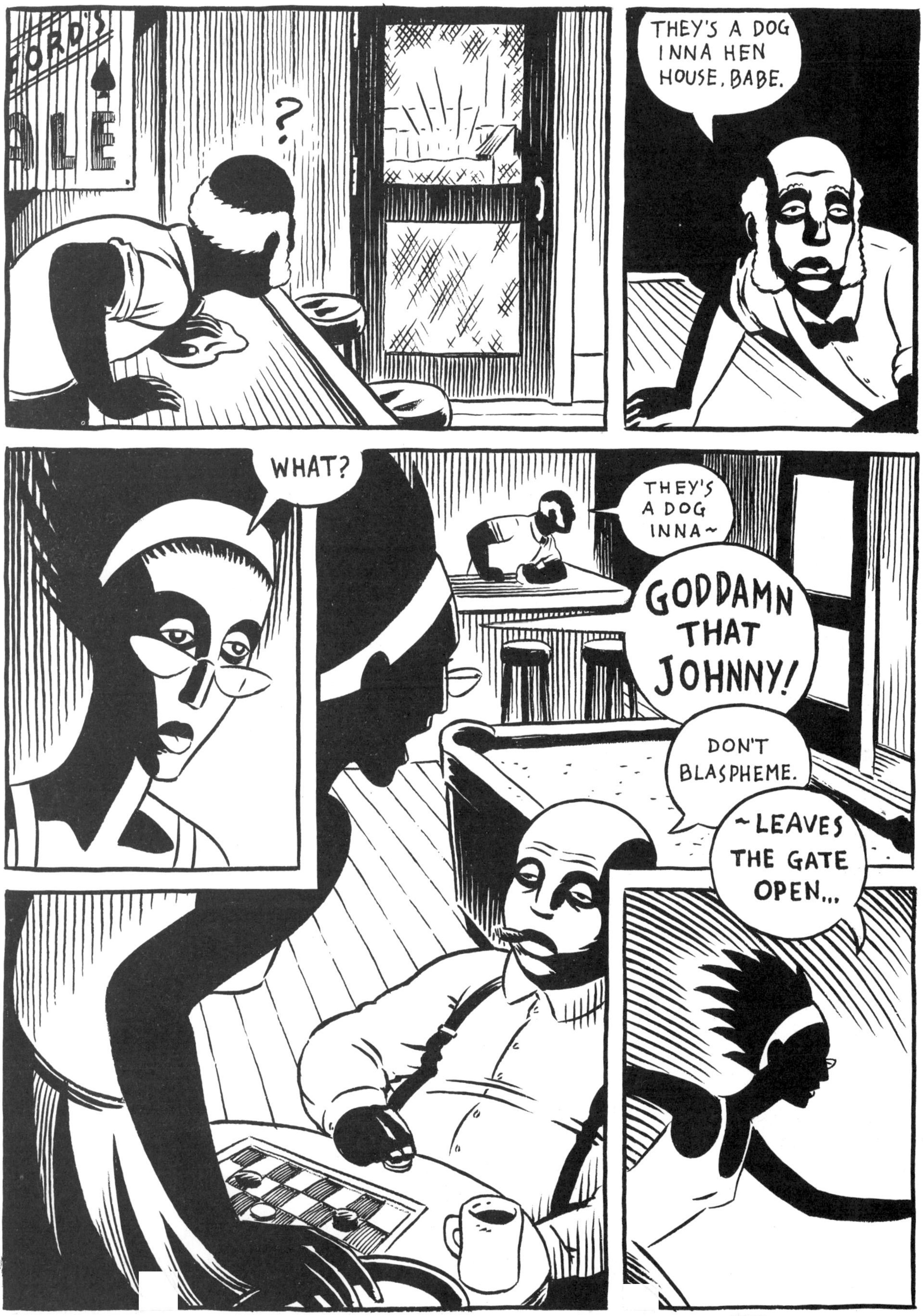
ORD'S
ALE
?
THEY'S A DOG INNA HEN HOUSE, BABE.
WHAT?
THEY'S A DOG INNA~
GODDAMN THAT JOHNNY!
DON'T BLASPHEME.
~LEAVES THE GATE OPEN...

HEY! YOU-DOG!
CRAR
GWAN NOW...
CLINK
GET ANYUM CHICKENS, BABE?
NO.
HE DIDN'T WANT NO CHICKEN...
HE WAS JUST GETTING HIM A DRINK OF WATER ~POOR OLD DOG...
~REMIND ME TO GIVE JOHNNY SOME SHIT ABOUT THAT GATE, THOUGH...

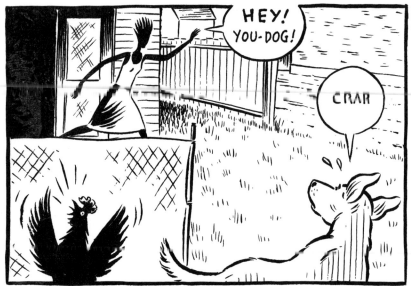

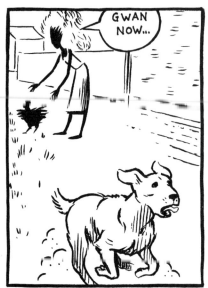

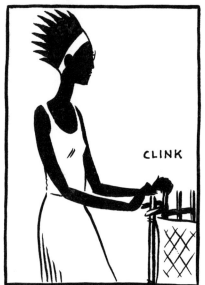

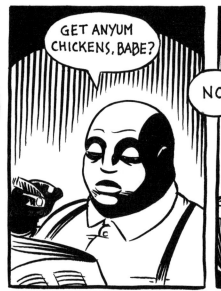

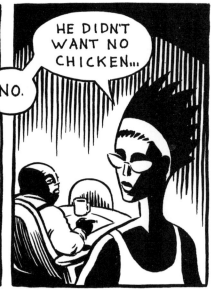

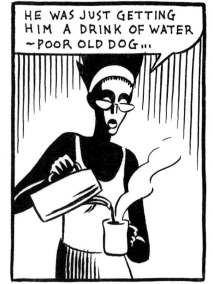

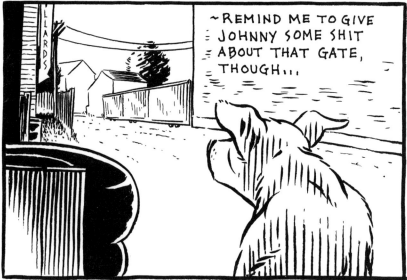

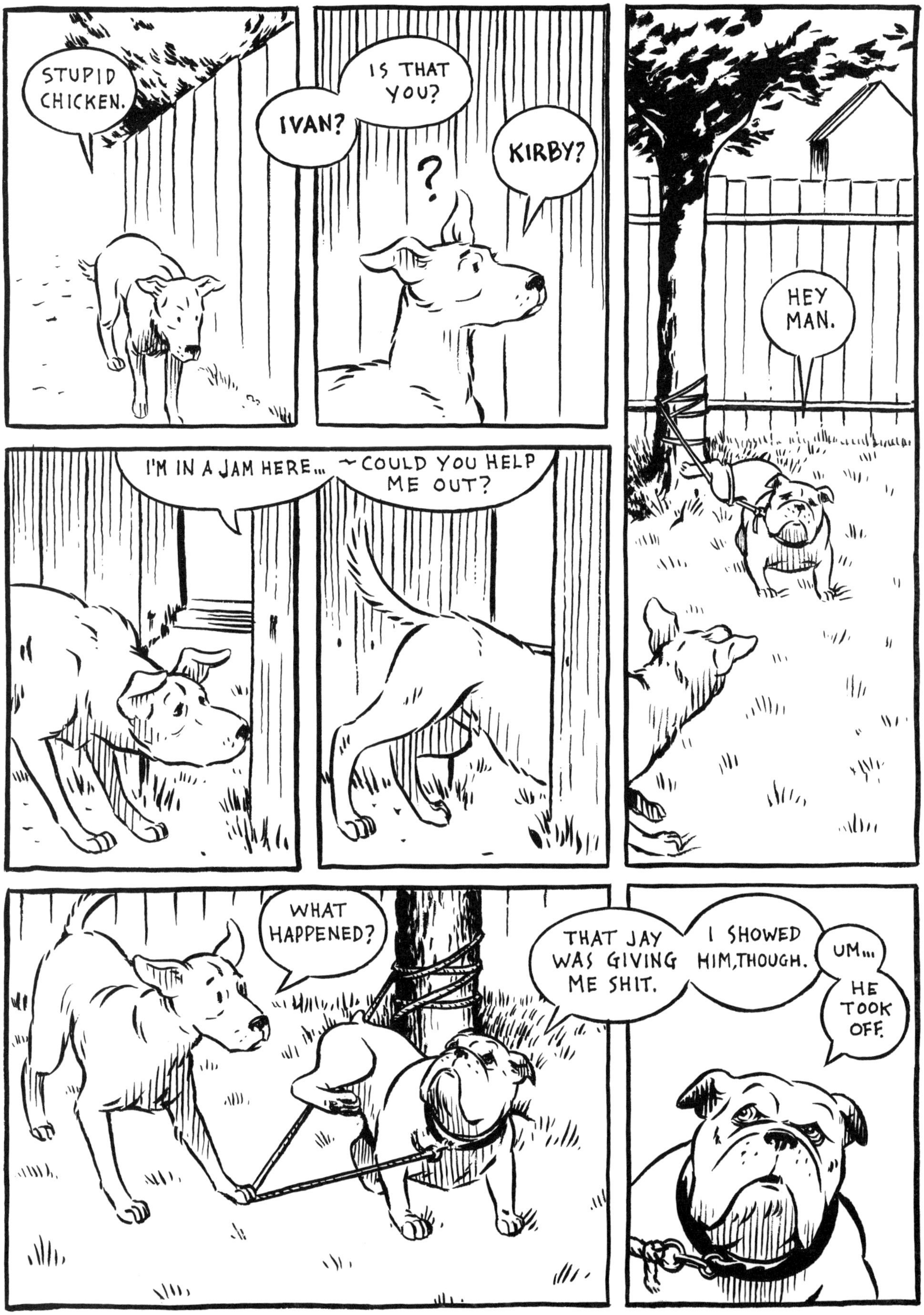

STUPID CHICKEN.
IVAN?
IS THAT YOU?
KIRBY?
?
HEY MAN.
I'M IN A JAM HERE...
~COULD YOU HELP ME OUT?
WHAT HAPPENED?
THAT JAY WAS GIVING ME SHIT.
I SHOWED HIM, THOUGH.
UM...
HE TOOK OFF.

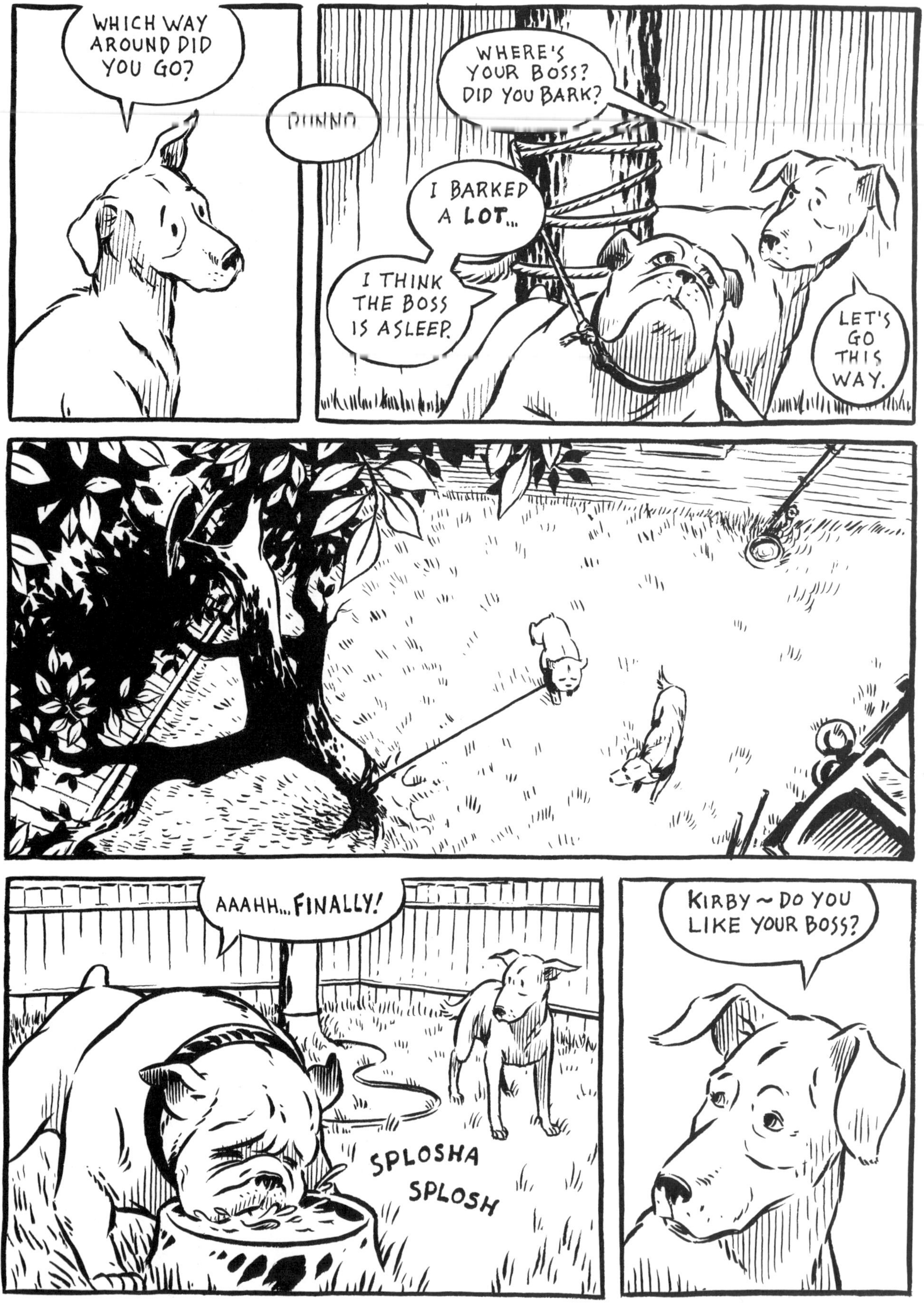
WHICH WAY AROUND DID YOU GO?
DUNNO.
WHERE'S YOUR BOSS? DID YOU BARK?
I BARKED A **LOT**...
I THINK THE BOSS IS ASLEEP.
LET'S GO THIS WAY.
AAAHH... FINALLY!
SPLOSHA
SPLOSH
KIRBY ~ DO YOU LIKE YOUR BOSS?

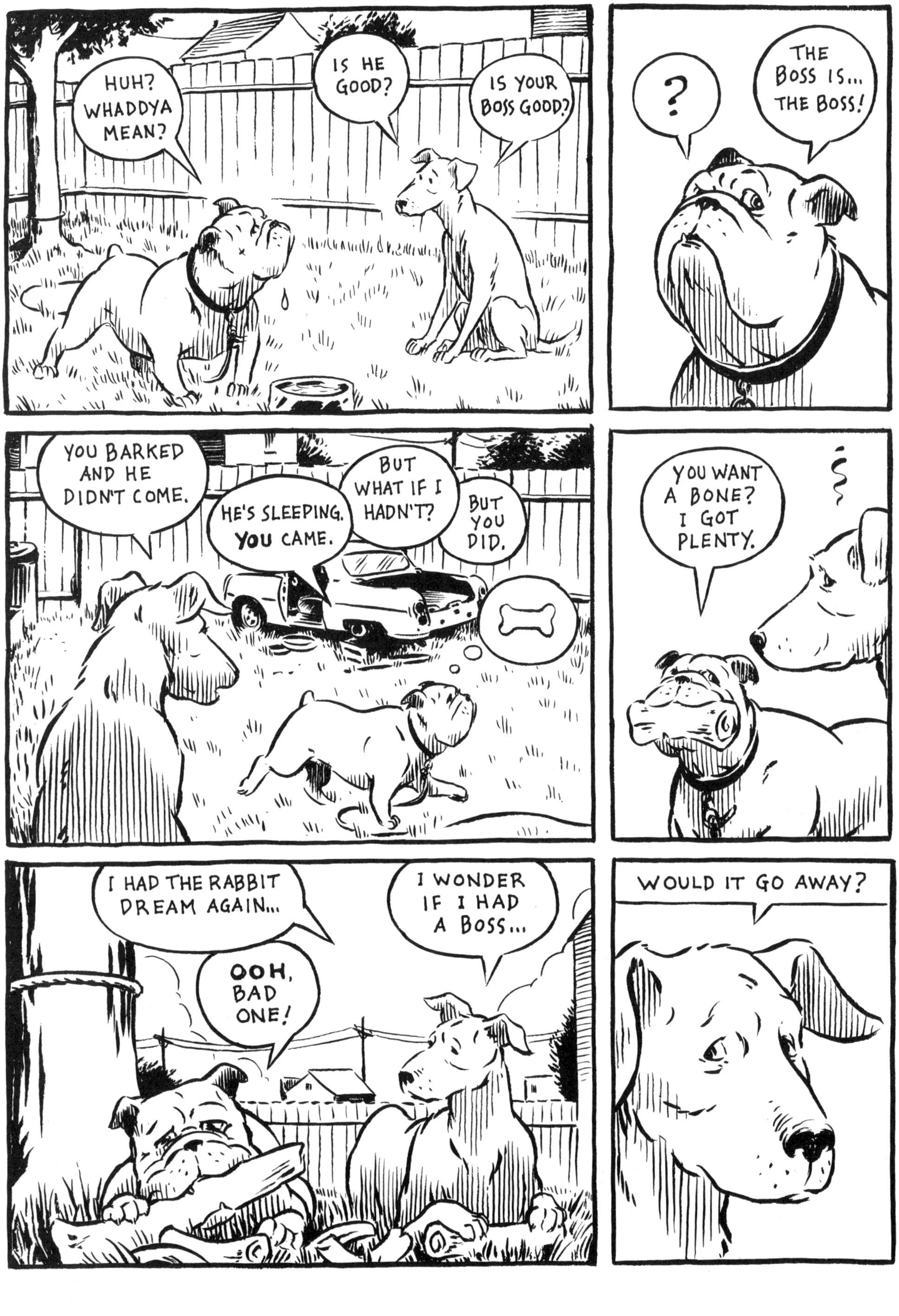
HUH? WHADDYA MEAN?
IS HE GOOD?
IS YOUR BOSS GOOD?
?
THE BOSS IS... THE BOSS!
YOU BARKED AND HE DIDN'T COME.
HE'S SLEEPING. YOU CAME.
BUT WHAT IF I HADN'T?
BUT YOU DID.
YOU WANT A BONE? I GOT PLENTY.
I HAD THE RABBIT DREAM AGAIN...
OOH, BAD ONE!
I WONDER IF I HAD A BOSS...
WOULD IT GO AWAY?

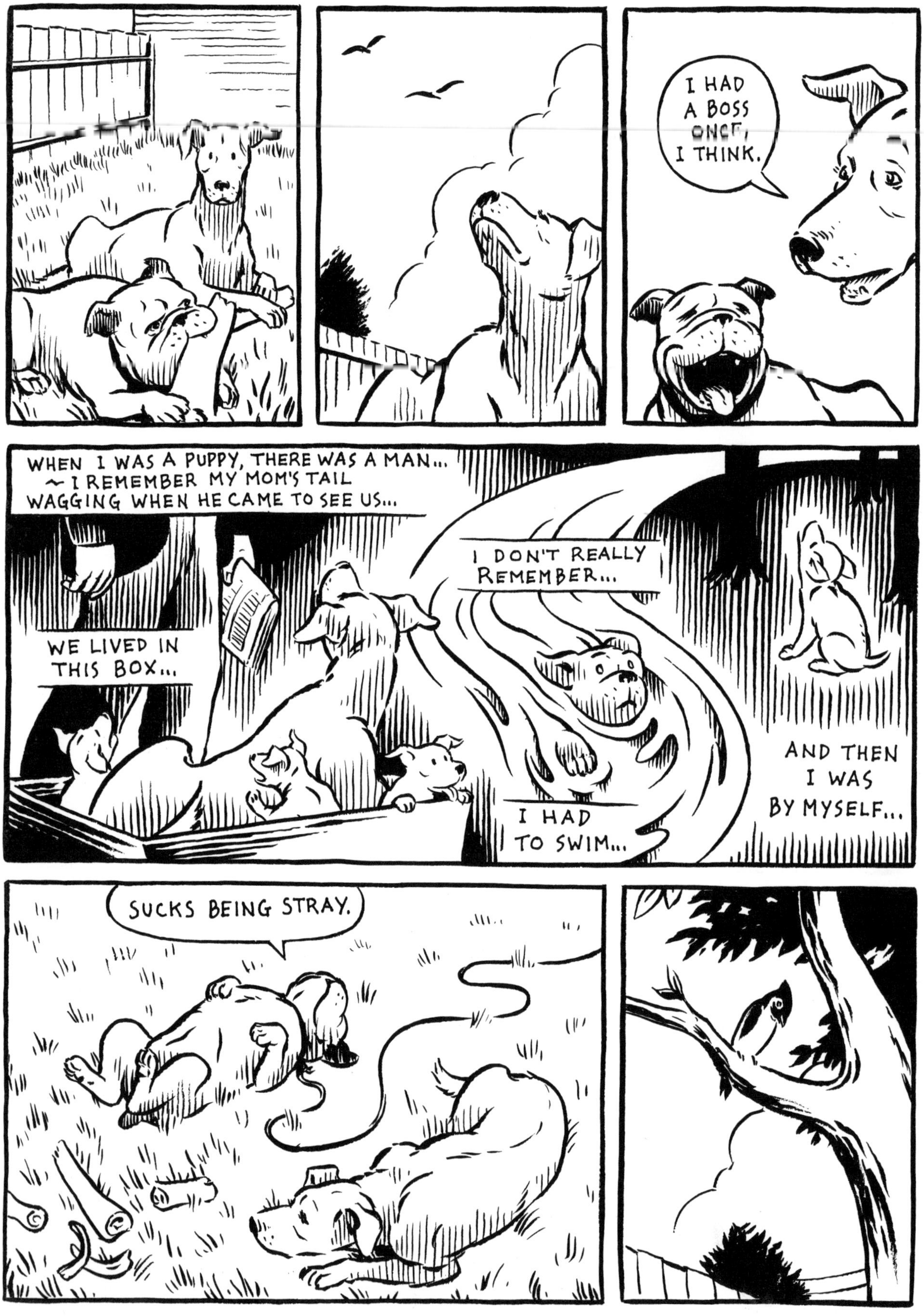
I HAD A BOSS ONCE, I THINK.
WHEN I WAS A PUPPY, THERE WAS A MAN... ~ I REMEMBER MY MOM'S TAIL WAGGING WHEN HE CAME TO SEE US...
WE LIVED IN THIS BOX...
I DON'T REALLY REMEMBER...
I HAD TO SWIM...
AND THEN I WAS BY MYSELF...
SUCKS BEING STRAY.

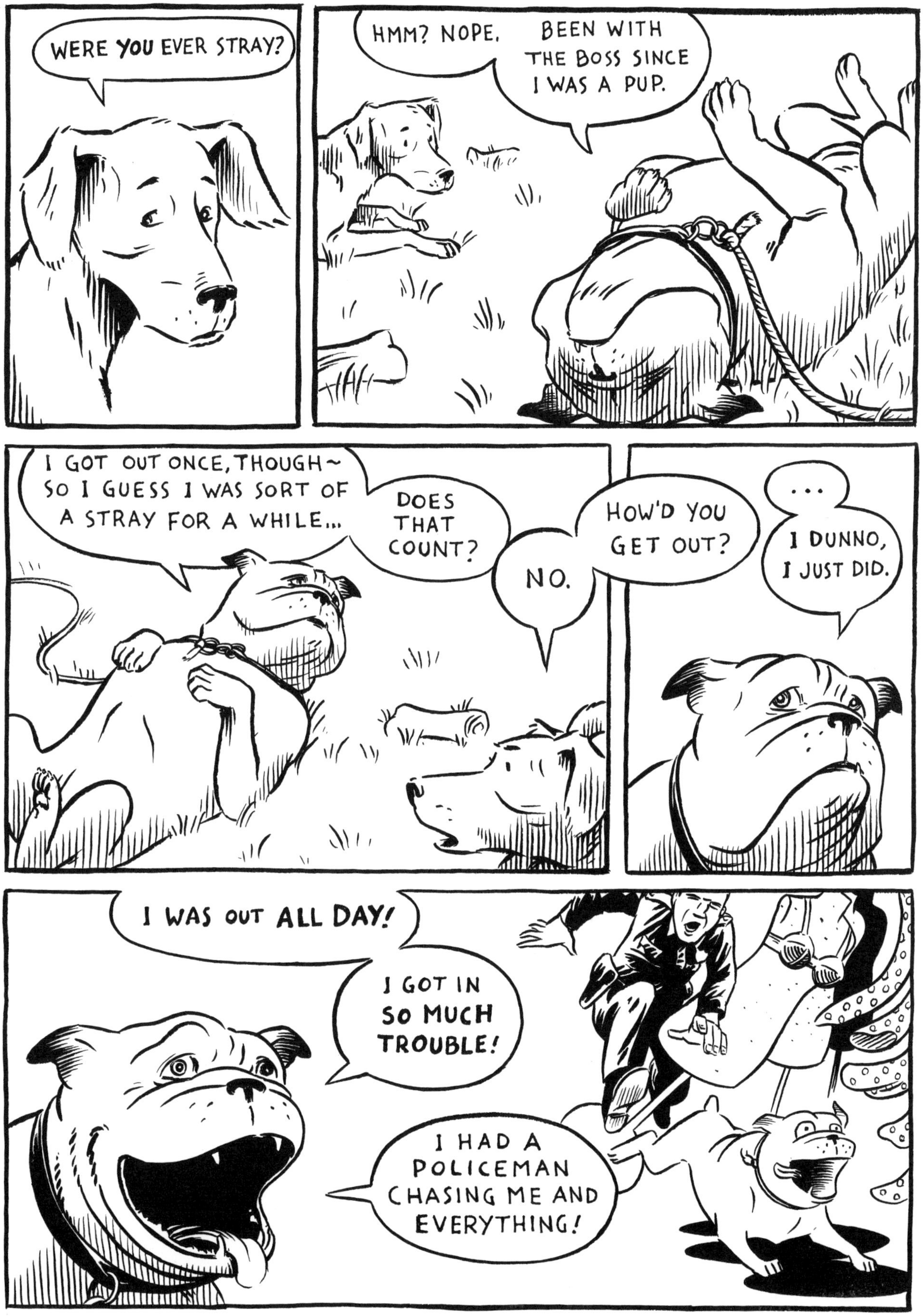
WERE YOU EVER STRAY?
HMM? NOPE.
BEEN WITH THE BOSS SINCE I WAS A PUP.
I GOT OUT ONCE, THOUGH~ SO I GUESS I WAS SORT OF A STRAY FOR A WHILE...
DOES THAT COUNT?
NO.
HOW'D YOU GET OUT?
...
I DUNNO, I JUST DID.
I WAS OUT ALL DAY!
I GOT IN SO MUCH TROUBLE!
I HAD A POLICEMAN CHASING ME AND EVERYTHING!

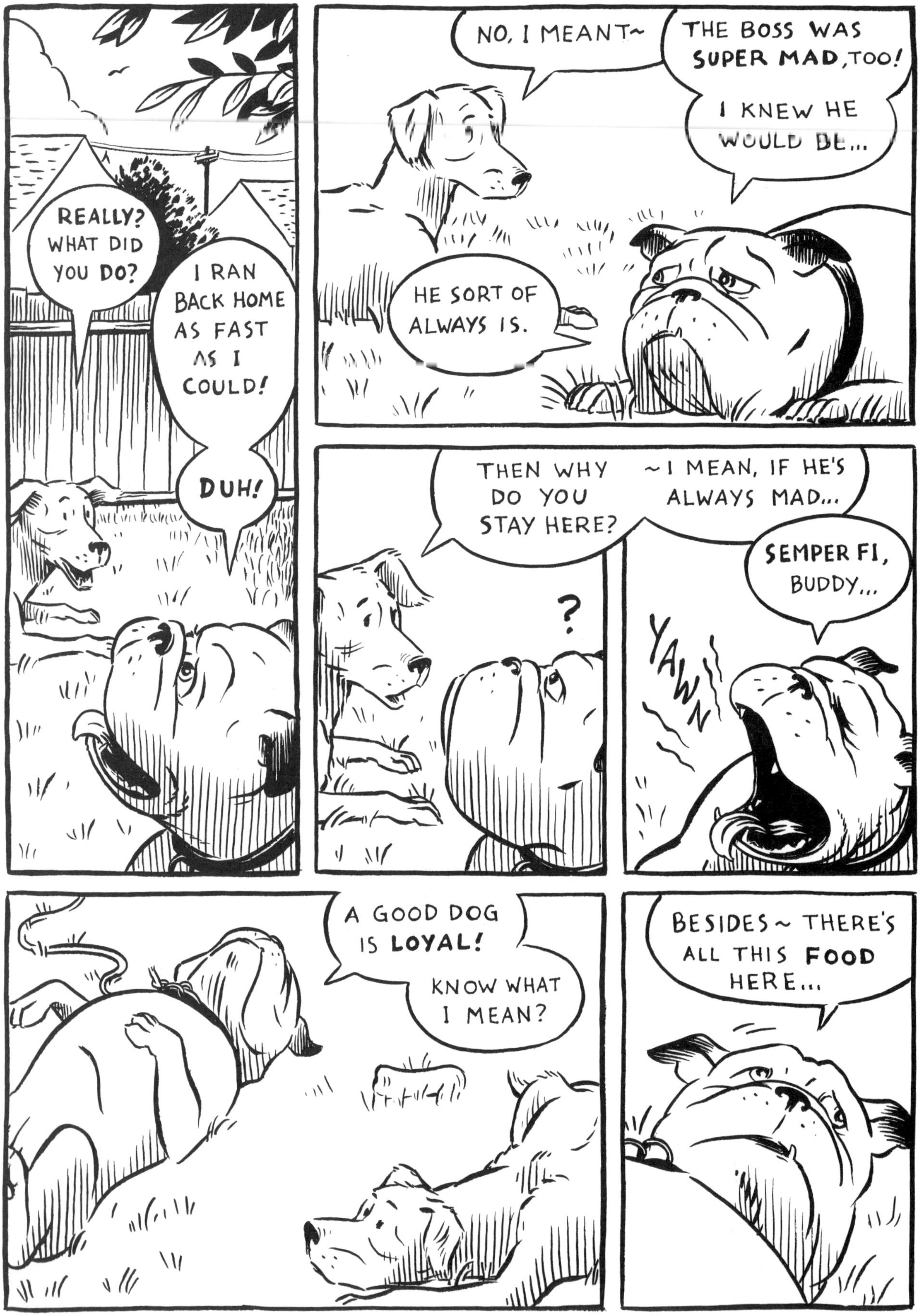
REALLY? WHAT DID YOU DO?
I RAN BACK HOME AS FAST AS I COULD!
DUH!
NO, I MEANT~
THE BOSS WAS SUPER MAD, TOO!
I KNEW HE WOULD BE...
HE SORT OF ALWAYS IS.
THEN WHY DO YOU STAY HERE?
~I MEAN, IF HE'S ALWAYS MAD...
?
SEMPER FI, BUDDY...
YAWN
A GOOD DOG IS LOYAL!
KNOW WHAT I MEAN?
BESIDES~ THERE'S ALL THIS FOOD HERE...

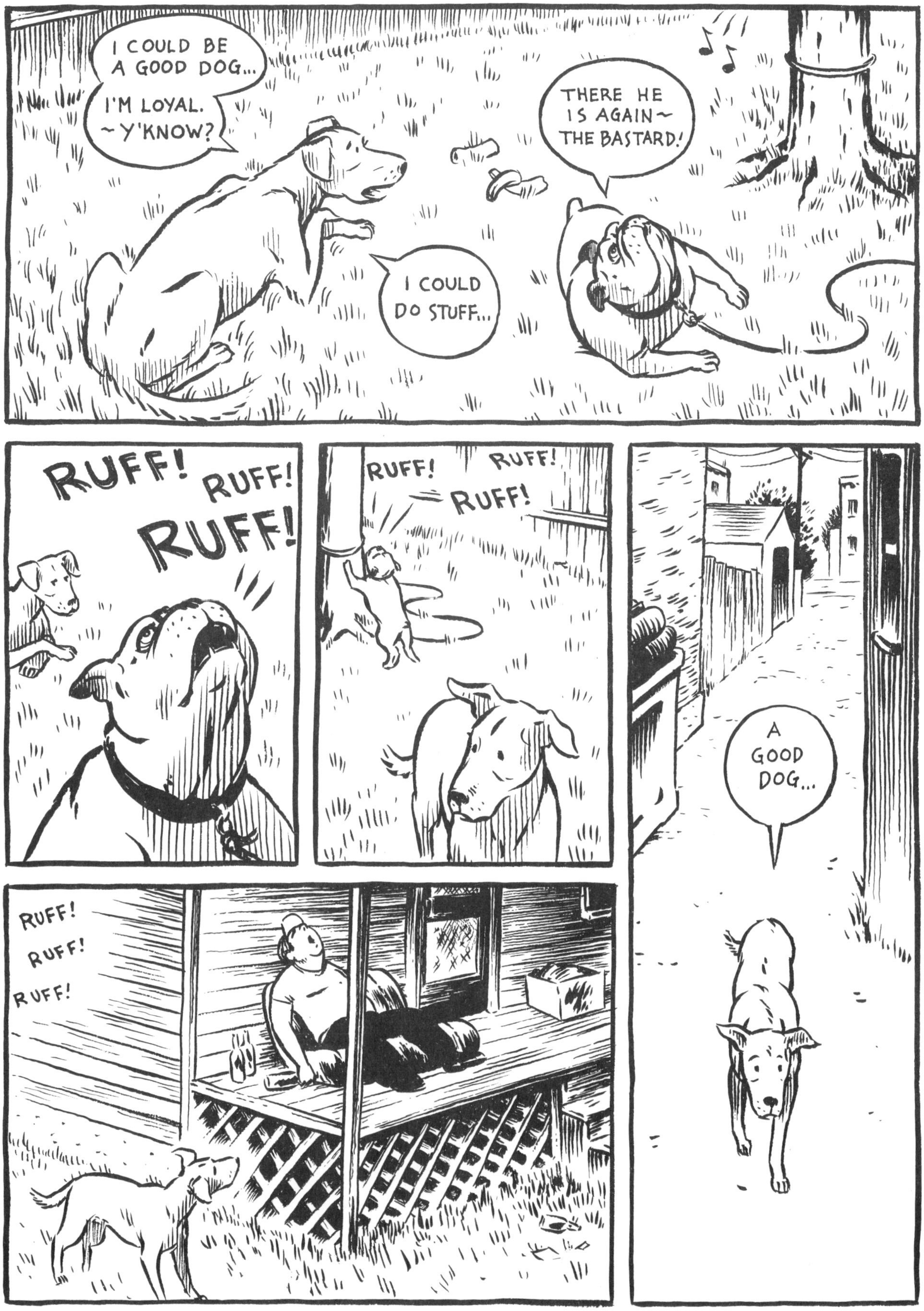
I COULD BE A GOOD DOG...
I'M LOYAL. ~Y'KNOW?
I COULD DO STUFF...
THERE HE IS AGAIN~ THE BASTARD!
RUFF!
RUFF!
RUFF!
RUFF!
RUFF!
RUFF!
A GOOD DOG...
RUFF!
RUFF!
RUFF!

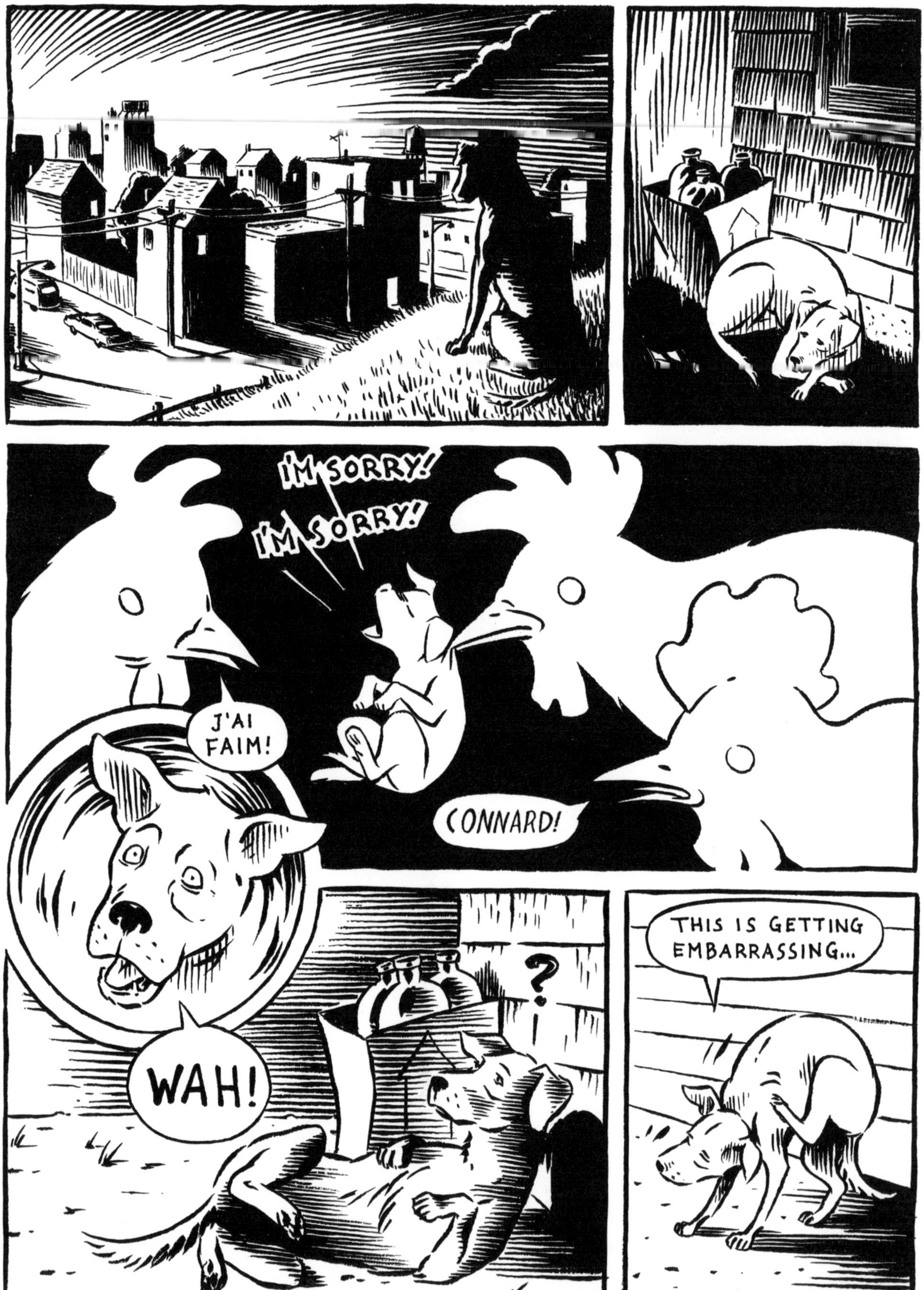
I'M SORRY!
I'M SORRY!
J'AI FAIM!
CONNARD!
WAH!
?
THIS IS GETTING EMBARRASSING...

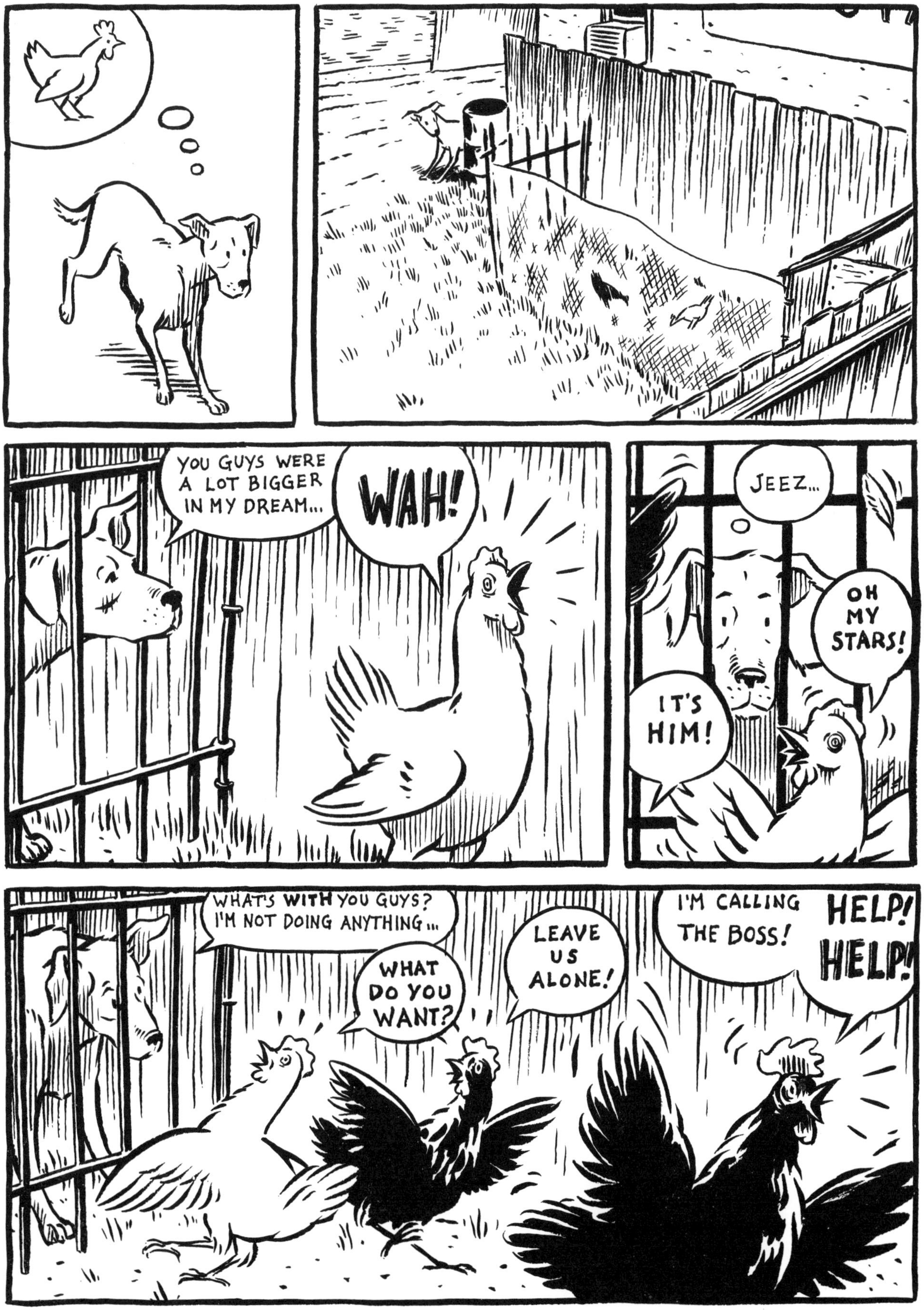
YOU GUYS WERE A LOT BIGGER IN MY DREAM...
WAH!
JEEZ...
OH MY STARS!
IT'S HIM!
WHAT'S WITH YOU GUYS? I'M NOT DOING ANYTHING...
WHAT DO YOU WANT?
LEAVE US ALONE!
I'M CALLING THE BOSS!
HELP! HELP!

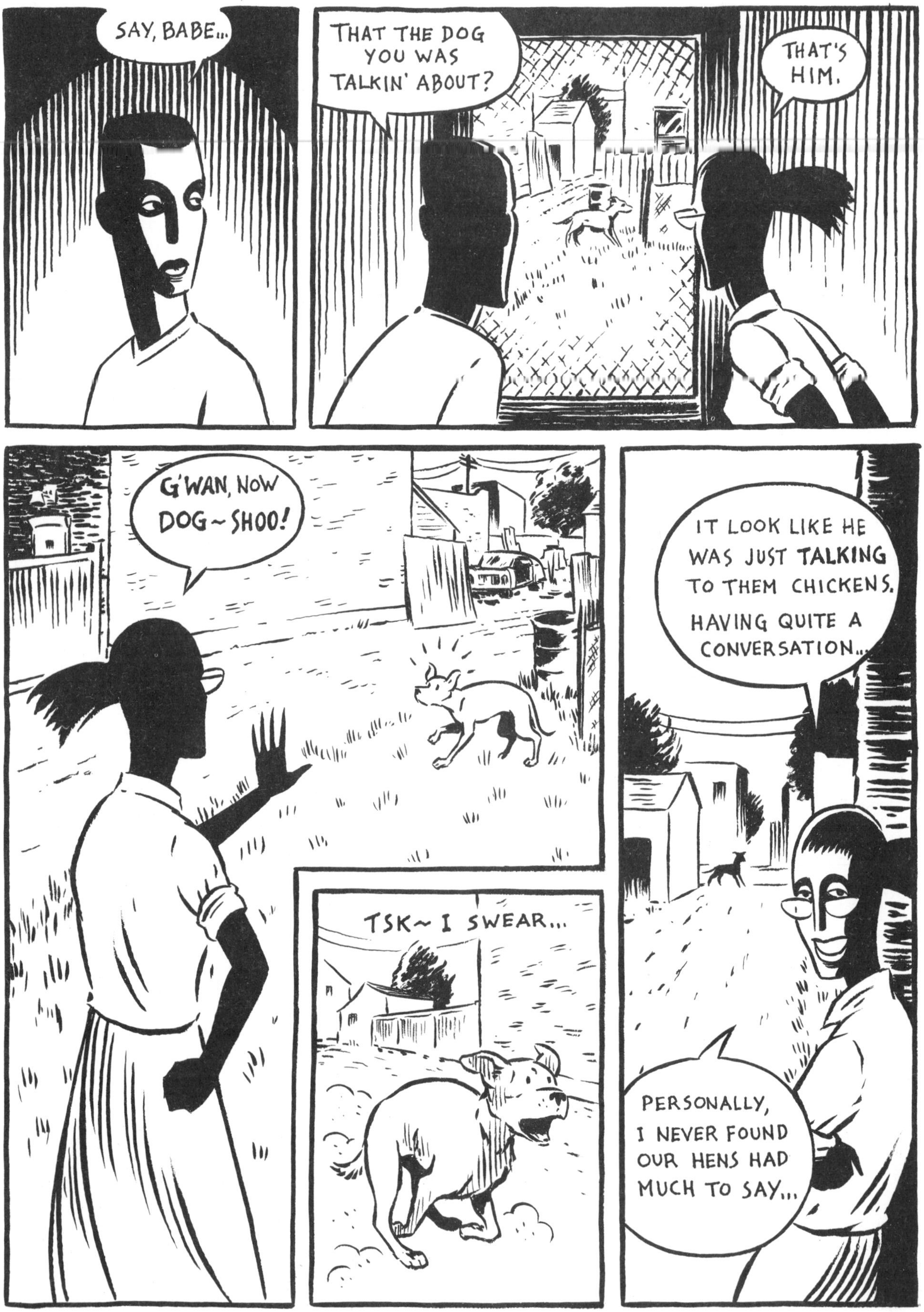
SAY, BABE...
THAT THE DOG YOU WAS TALKIN' ABOUT?
THAT'S HIM.
G'WAN, NOW DOG ~ SHOO!
IT LOOK LIKE HE WAS JUST **TALKING** TO THEM CHICKENS. HAVING QUITE A CONVERSATION...
TSK ~ I SWEAR...
PERSONALLY, I NEVER FOUND OUR HENS HAD MUCH TO SAY...

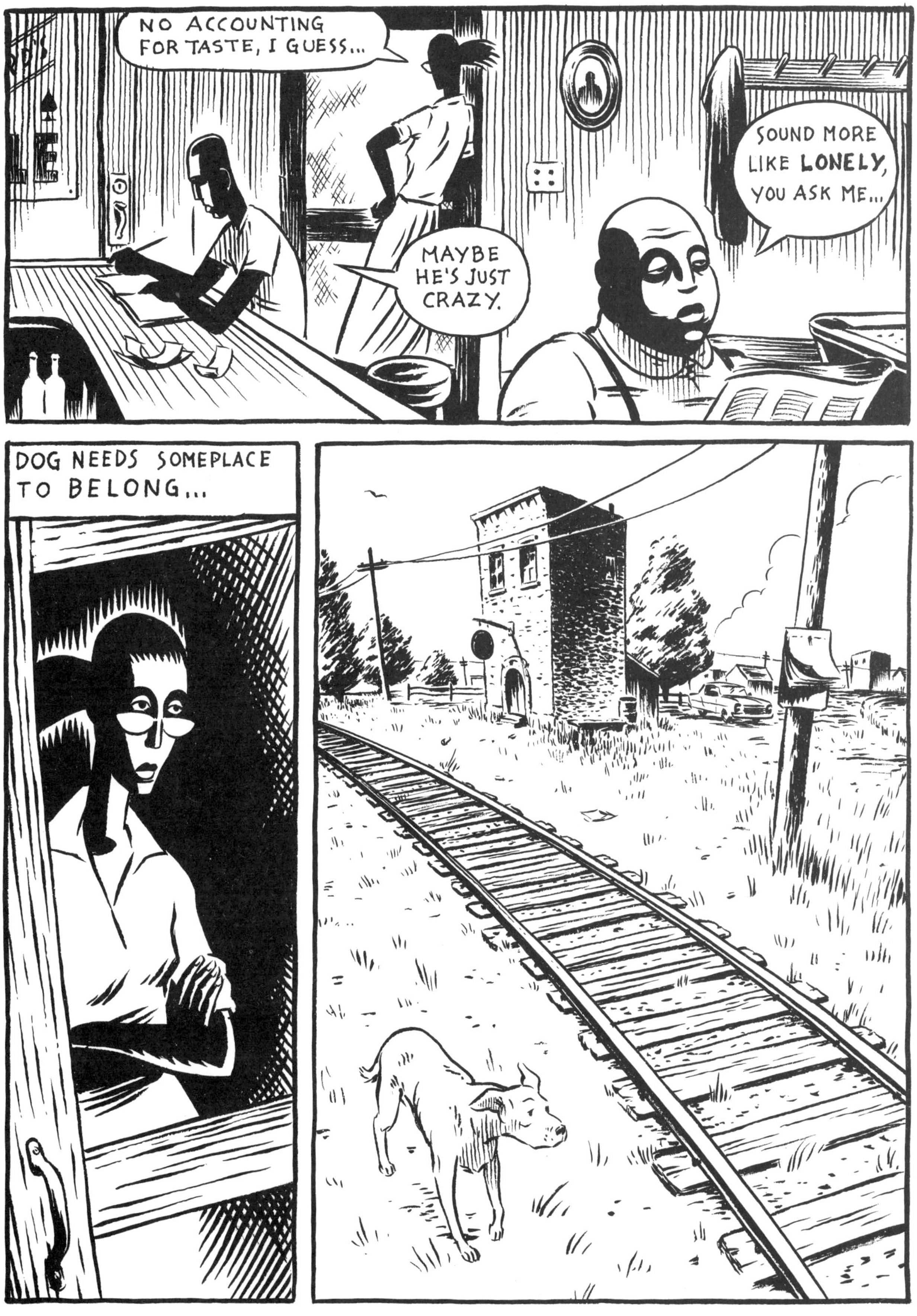
NO ACCOUNTING FOR TASTE, I GUESS...
MAYBE HE'S JUST CRAZY.
SOUND MORE LIKE LONELY, YOU ASK ME...
DOG NEEDS SOMEPLACE TO BELONG...

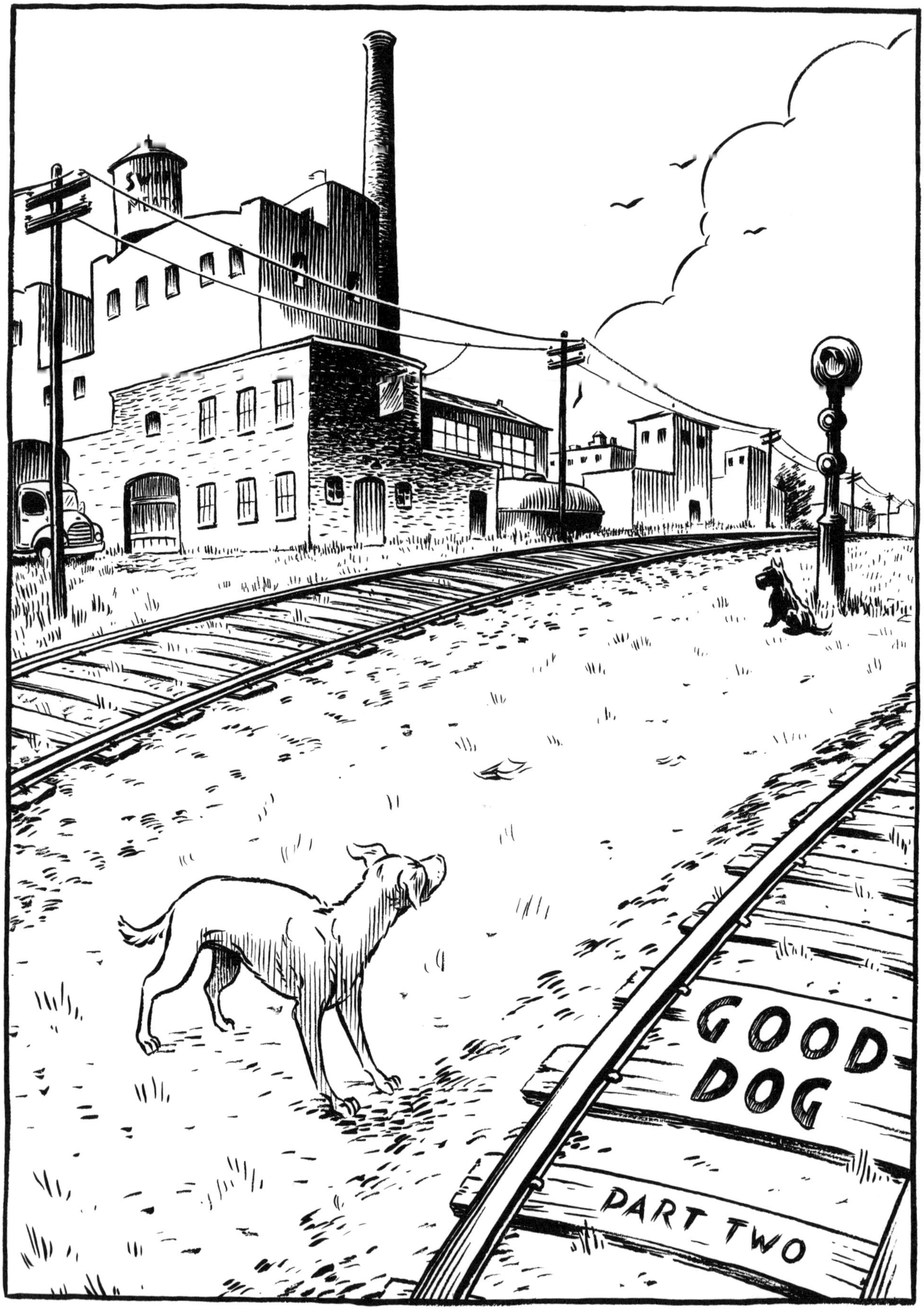
GOOD DOG
PART TWO

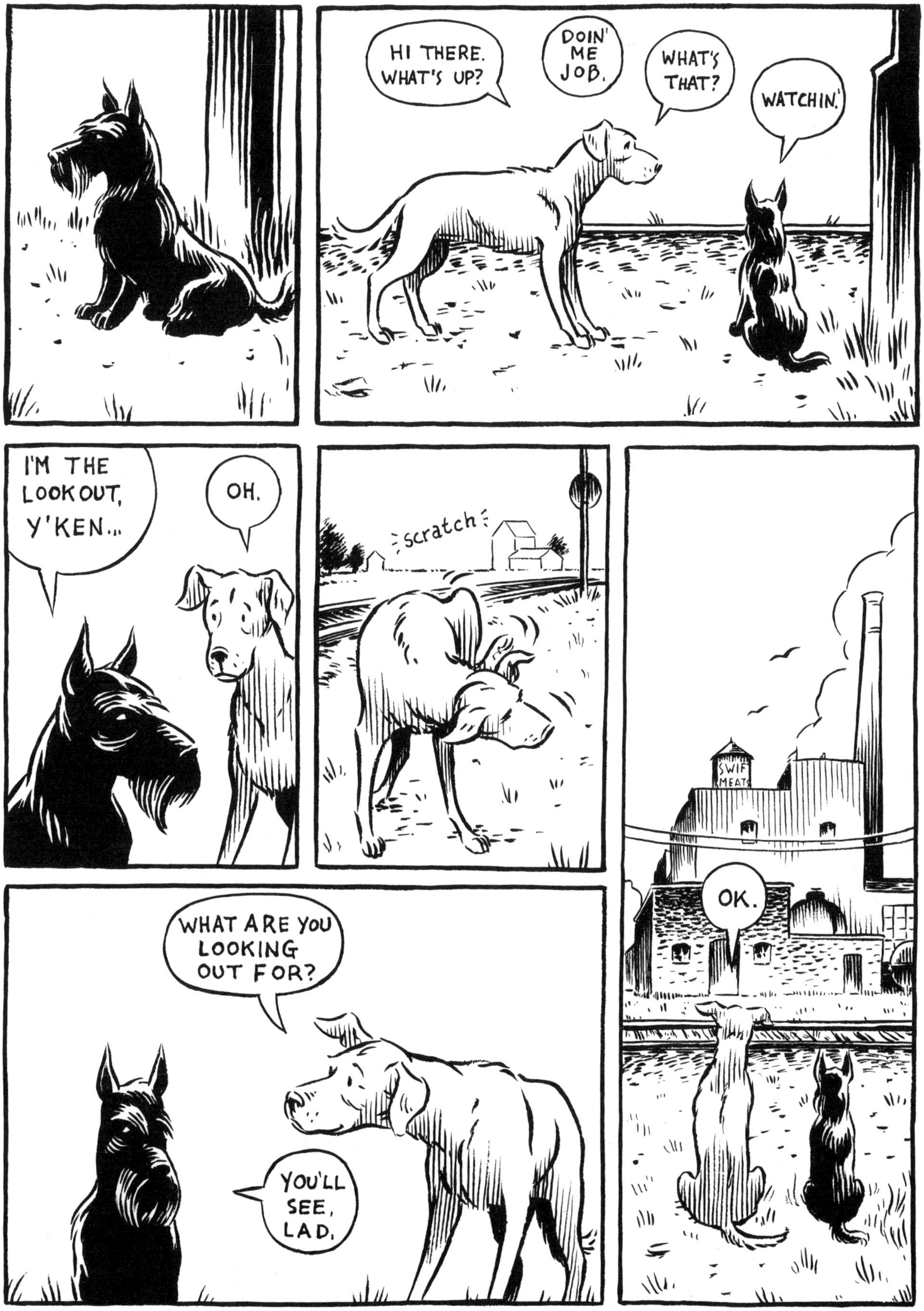
HI THERE. WHAT'S UP?
DOIN' ME JOB.
WHAT'S THAT?
WATCHIN'.
I'M THE LOOKOUT, Y'KEN...
OH.
scratch
WHAT ARE YOU LOOKING OUT FOR?
YOU'LL SEE, LAD.
OK.

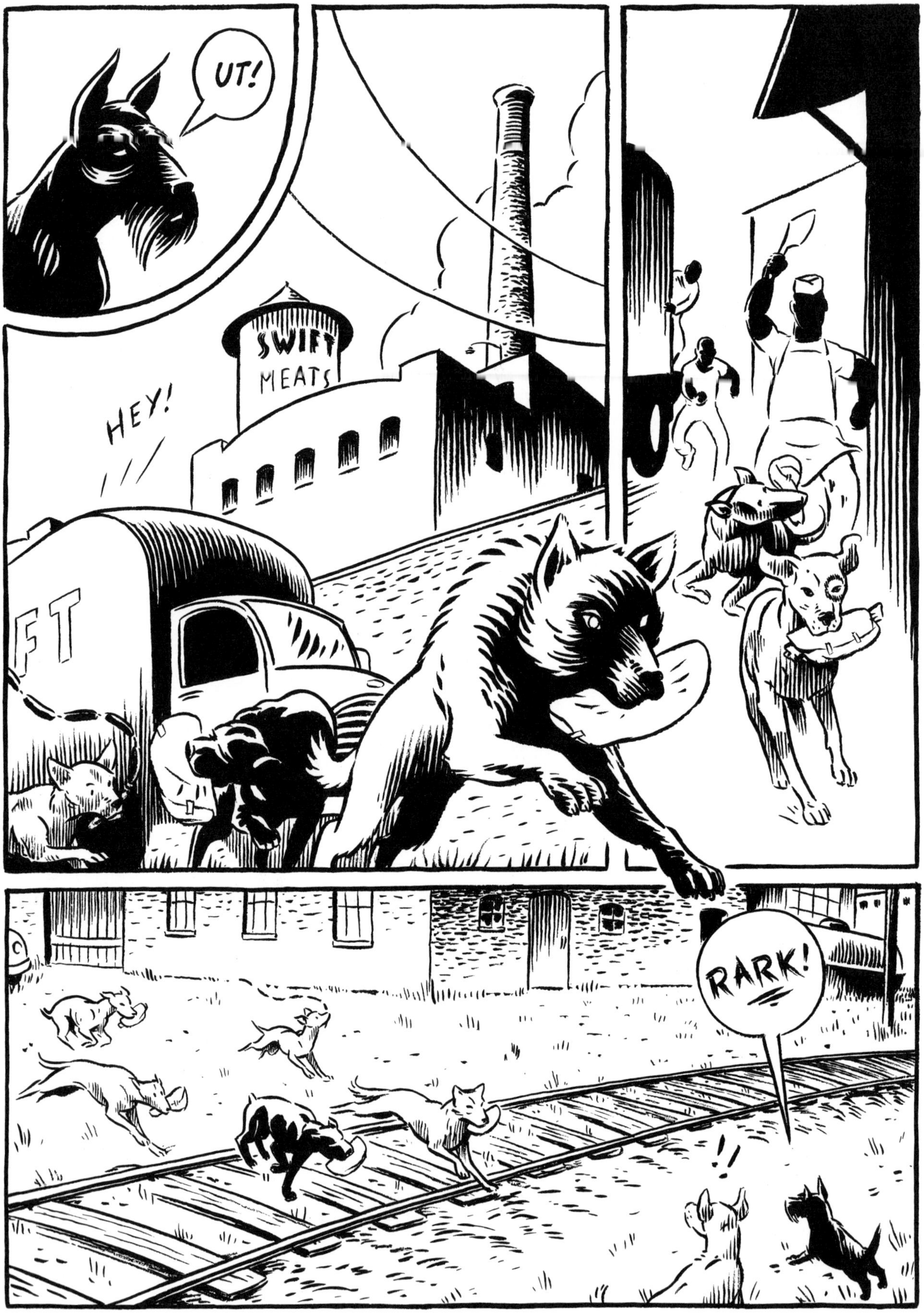
UT!
SWIFT MEATS
HEY!
FT
RARK!
!!

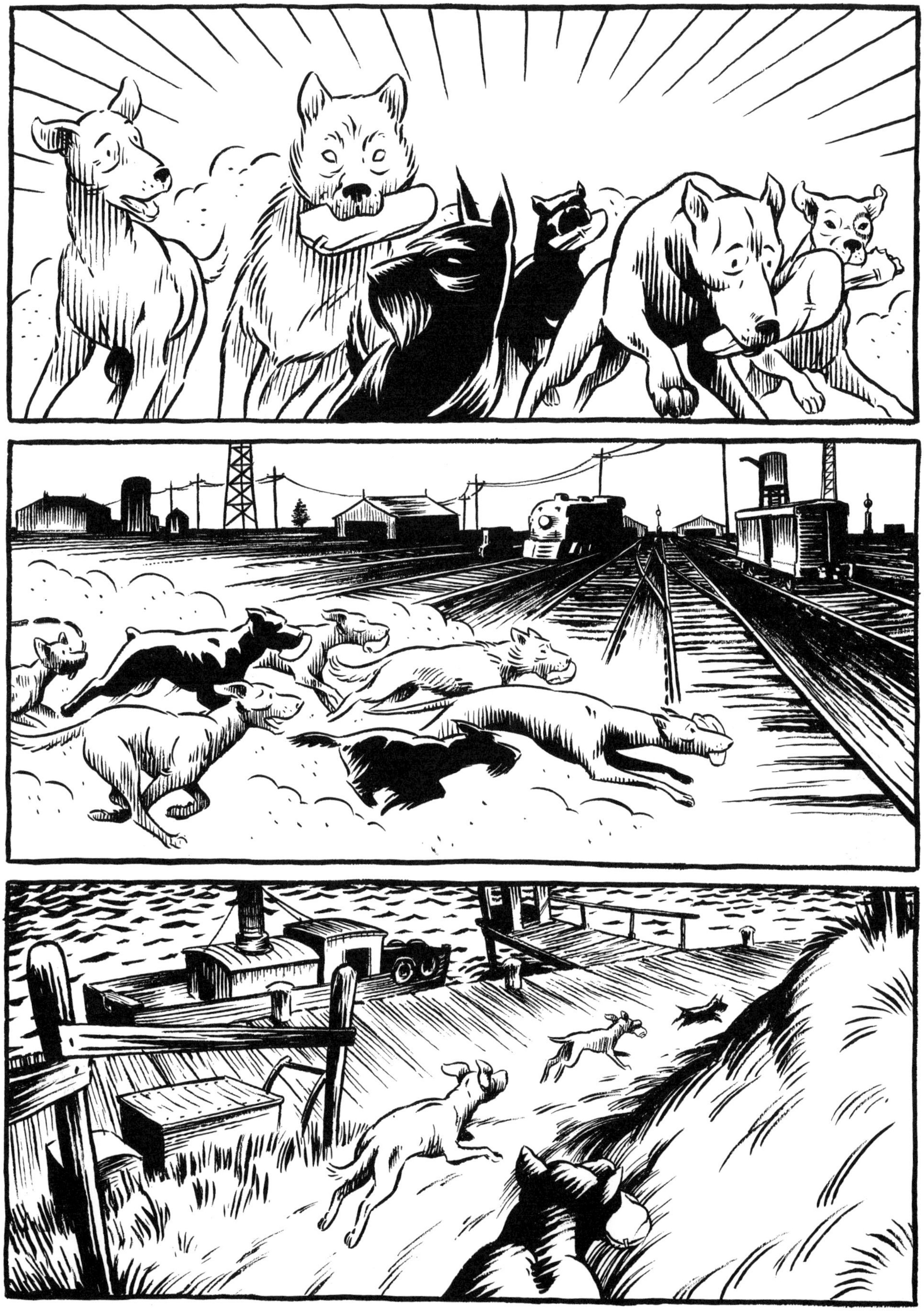

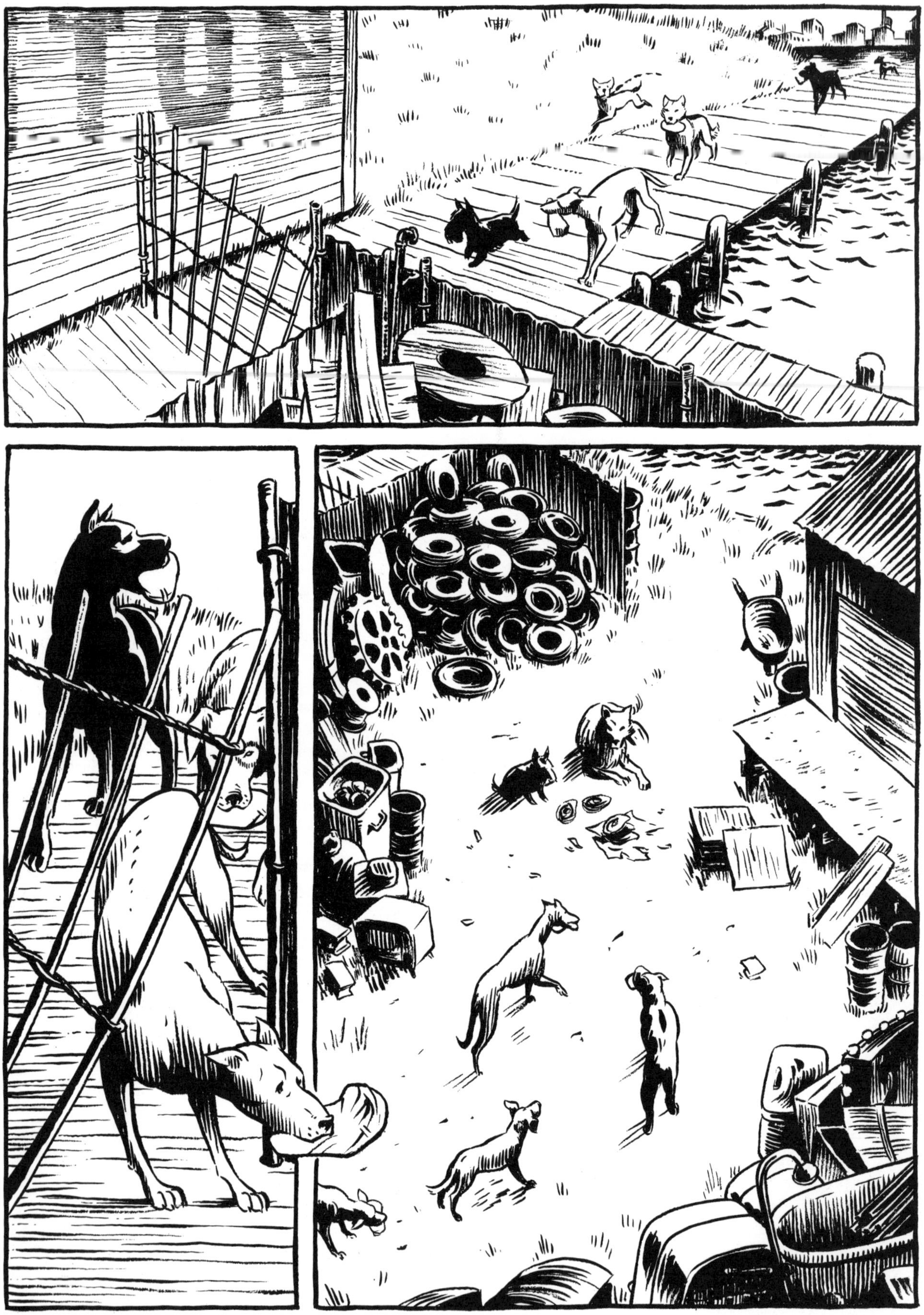

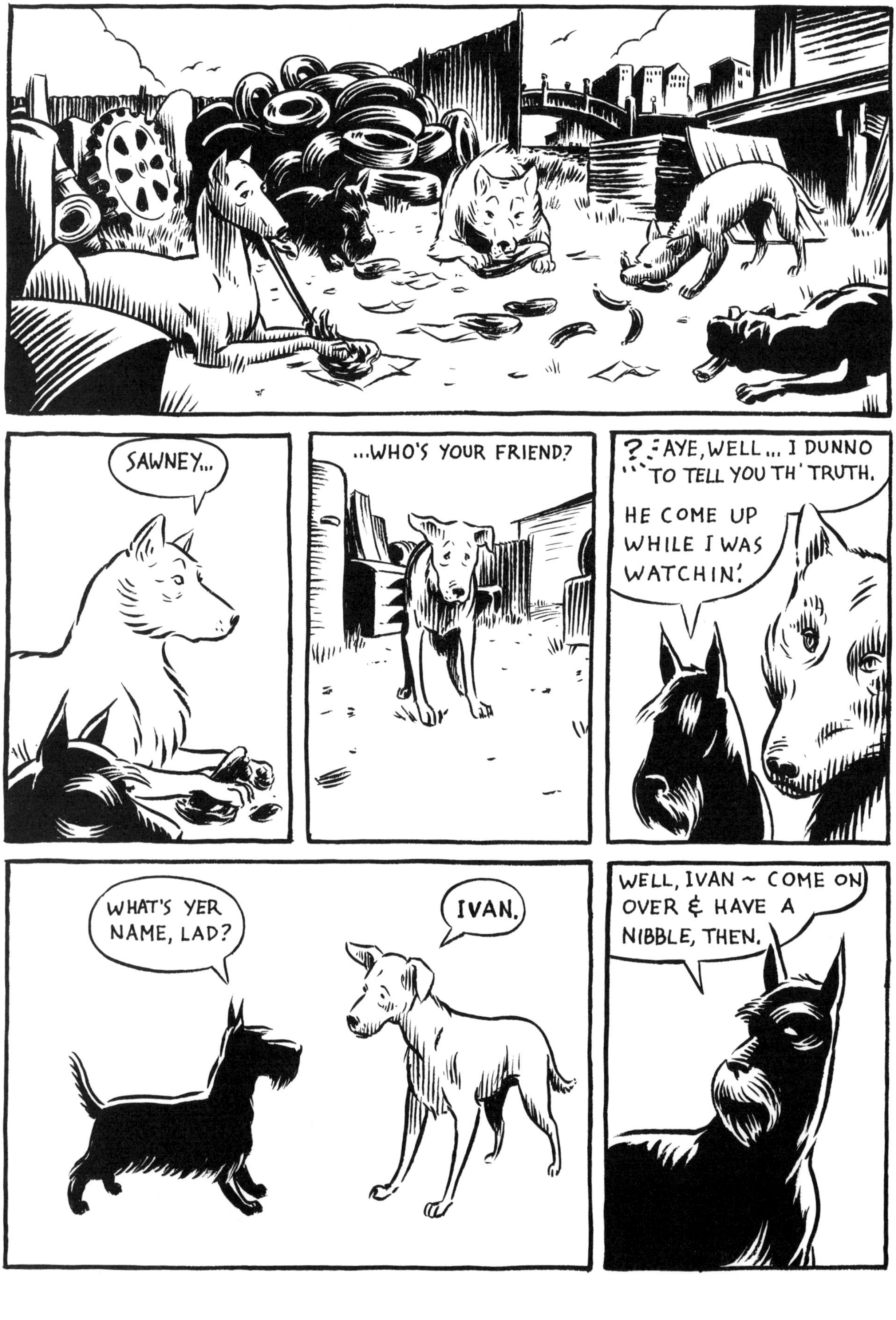
SAWNEY...
...WHO'S YOUR FRIEND?
?
AYE, WELL... I DUNNO TO TELL YOU TH' TRUTH.
HE COME UP WHILE I WAS WATCHIN'.
WHAT'S YER NAME, LAD?
IVAN.
WELL, IVAN ~ COME ON OVER & HAVE A NIBBLE, THEN.

NEVER SEEN YOU GUYS AROUND HERE, BEFORE.
HUH.
WELL WE'RE HERE **NOW**...
DIDN'T KNOW WE NEEDED YER DAMN **PERMISSION**.
?
WHAT'S YOUR PROBLEM?
JEEZ, I DUNNO... ~MAYBE I JUST DON'T LIKE YER **STUPID FACE!**
RRRRRRRR
RRGRRRRRRRRRRRR
GRRR
RRRRRR
GRRRRRRR
SAWNEY...
AYE.

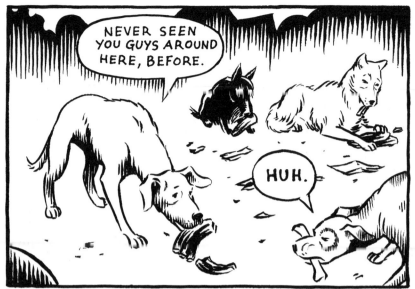

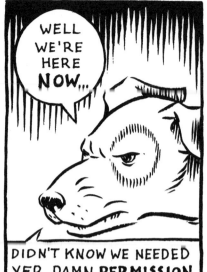

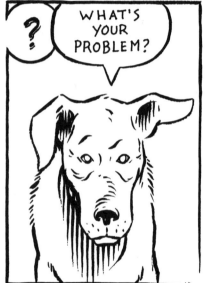

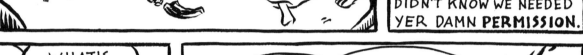

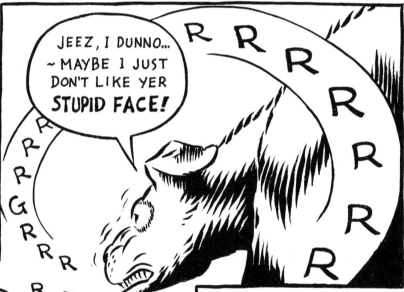

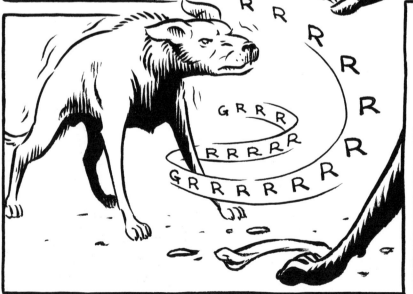

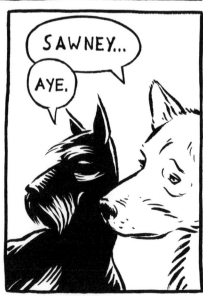

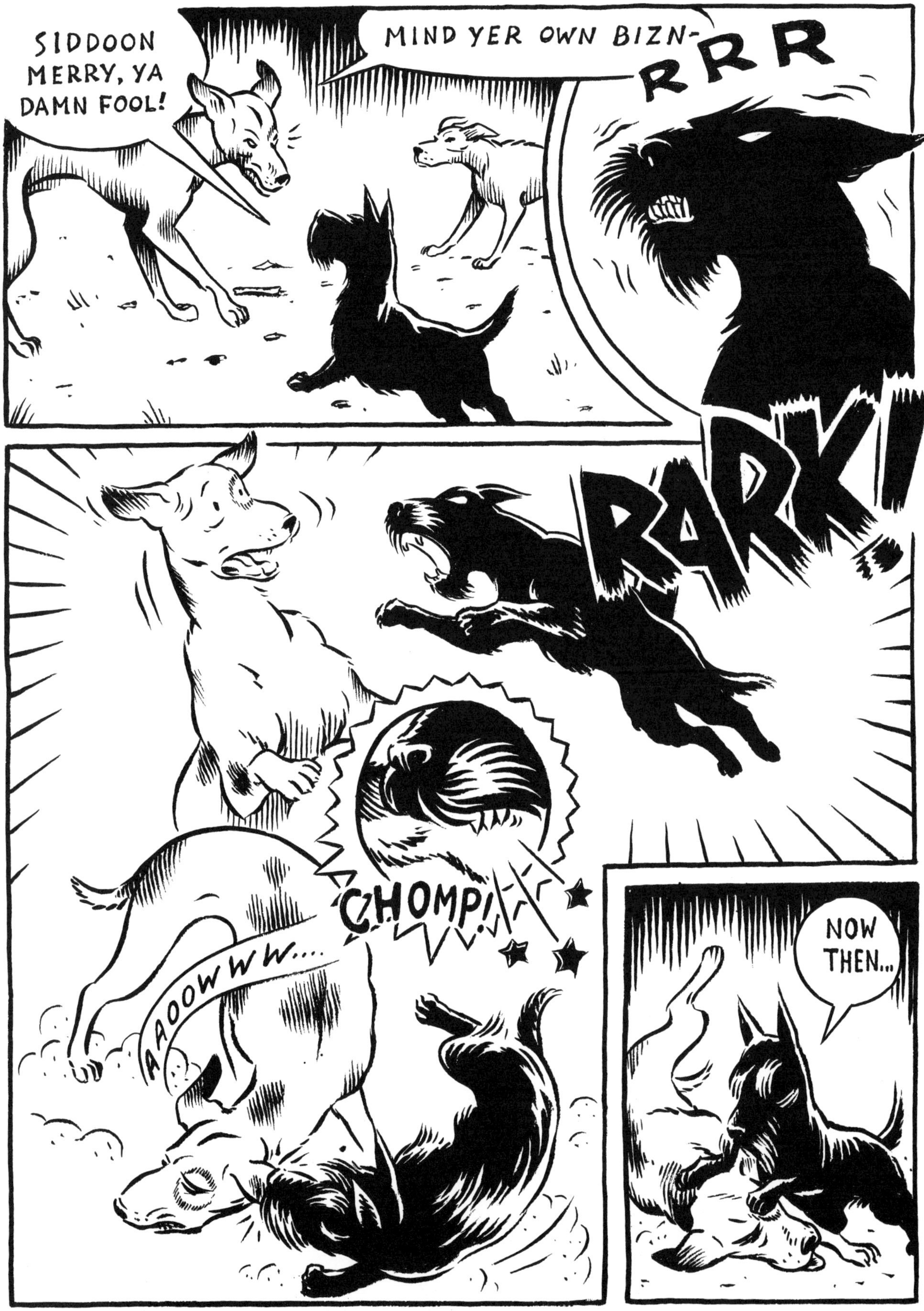
SIDDOON MERRY, YA DAMN FOOL!
MIND YER OWN BIZN-RRR
RARK!
CHOMP!
AAOOWWW....
NOW THEN...

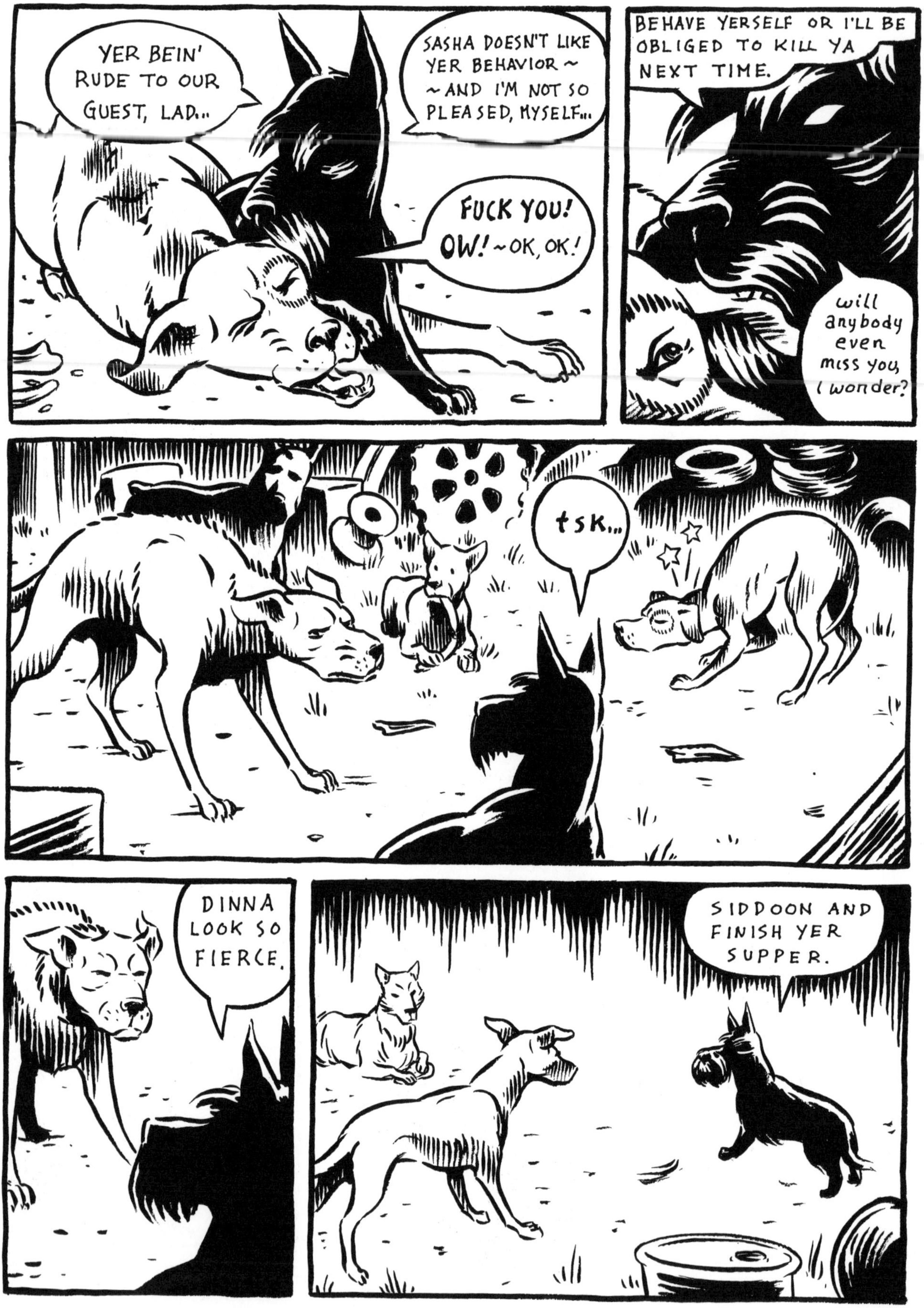
YER BEIN' RUDE TO OUR GUEST, LAD...
SASHA DOESN'T LIKE YER BEHAVIOR ~
~ AND I'M NOT SO PLEASED, MYSELF...
FUCK YOU! OW! ~ OK, OK!
BEHAVE YERSELF OR I'LL BE OBLIGED TO KILL YA NEXT TIME.
will anybody even miss you, I wonder?
tsk...
DINNA LOOK SO FIERCE.
SIDDOON AND FINISH YER SUPPER.

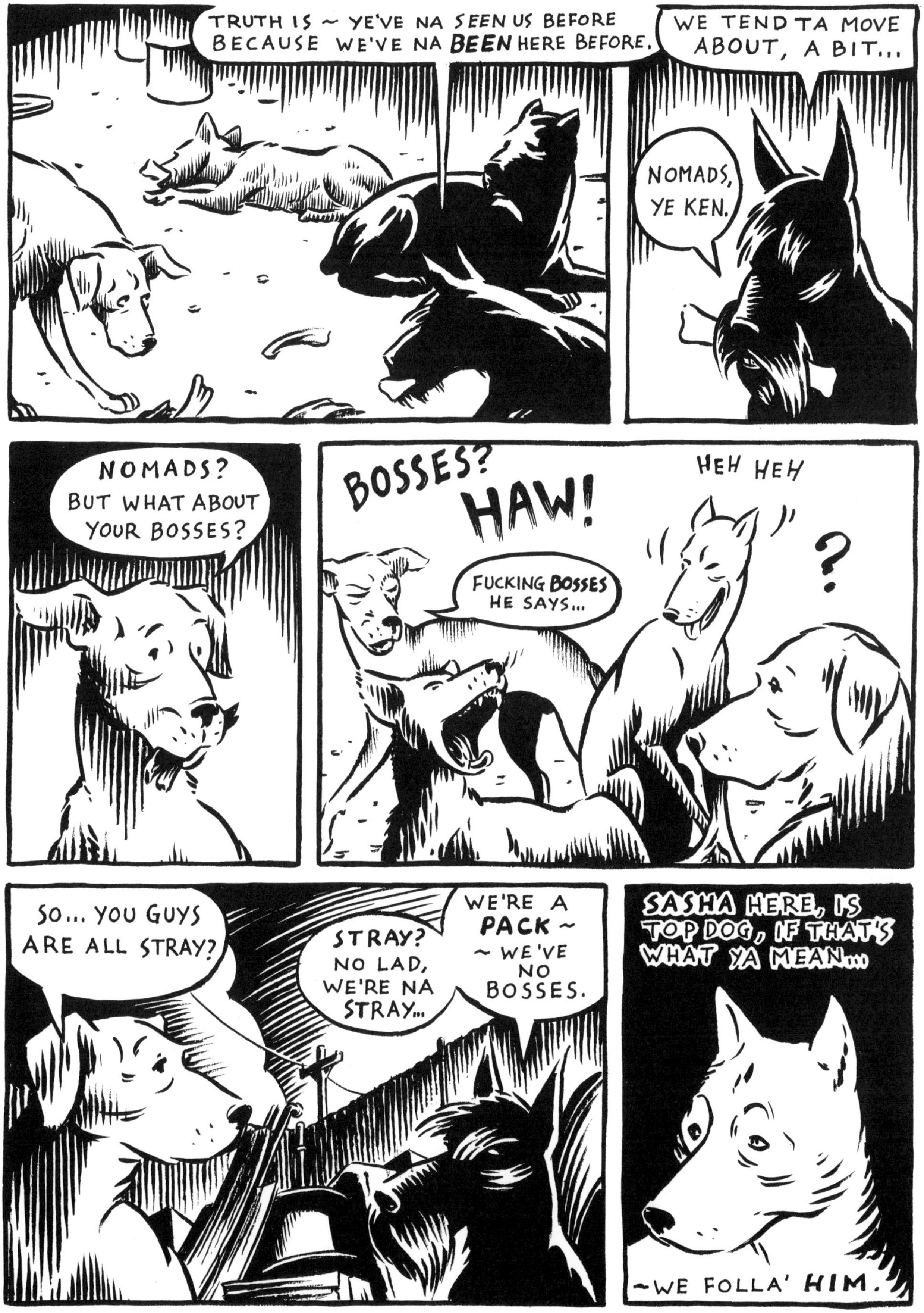
TRUTH IS ~ YE'VE NA SEEN US BEFORE BECAUSE WE'VE NA **BEEN** HERE BEFORE.
WE TEND TA MOVE ABOUT, A BIT...
NOMADS, YE KEN.
NOMADS? BUT WHAT ABOUT YOUR BOSSES?
BOSSES? HAW!
FUCKING **BOSSES** HE SAYS...
HEH HEH
?
SO... YOU GUYS ARE ALL STRAY?
STRAY? NO LAD, WE'RE NA STRAY...
WE'RE A **PACK** ~ ~ WE'VE NO BOSSES.
SASHA HERE, IS TOP DOG, IF THAT'S WHAT YA MEAN...
~WE FOLLA' **HIM**.

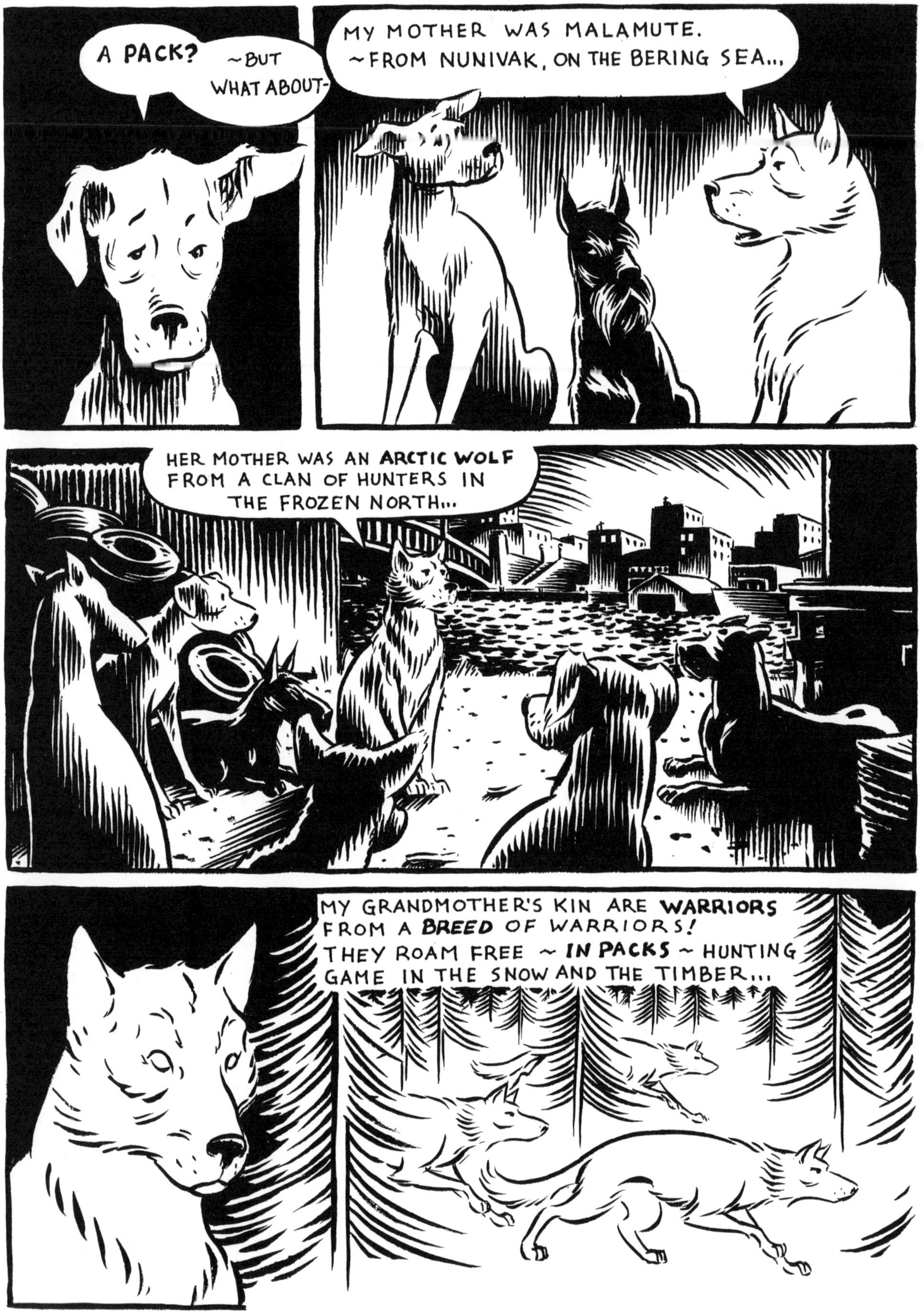
A PACK? ~BUT WHAT ABOUT-
MY MOTHER WAS MALAMUTE. ~FROM NUNIVAK, ON THE BERING SEA...
HER MOTHER WAS AN ARCTIC WOLF FROM A CLAN OF HUNTERS IN THE FROZEN NORTH...
MY GRANDMOTHER'S KIN ARE WARRIORS FROM A BREED OF WARRIORS! THEY ROAM FREE ~ IN PACKS ~ HUNTING GAME IN THE SNOW AND THE TIMBER...

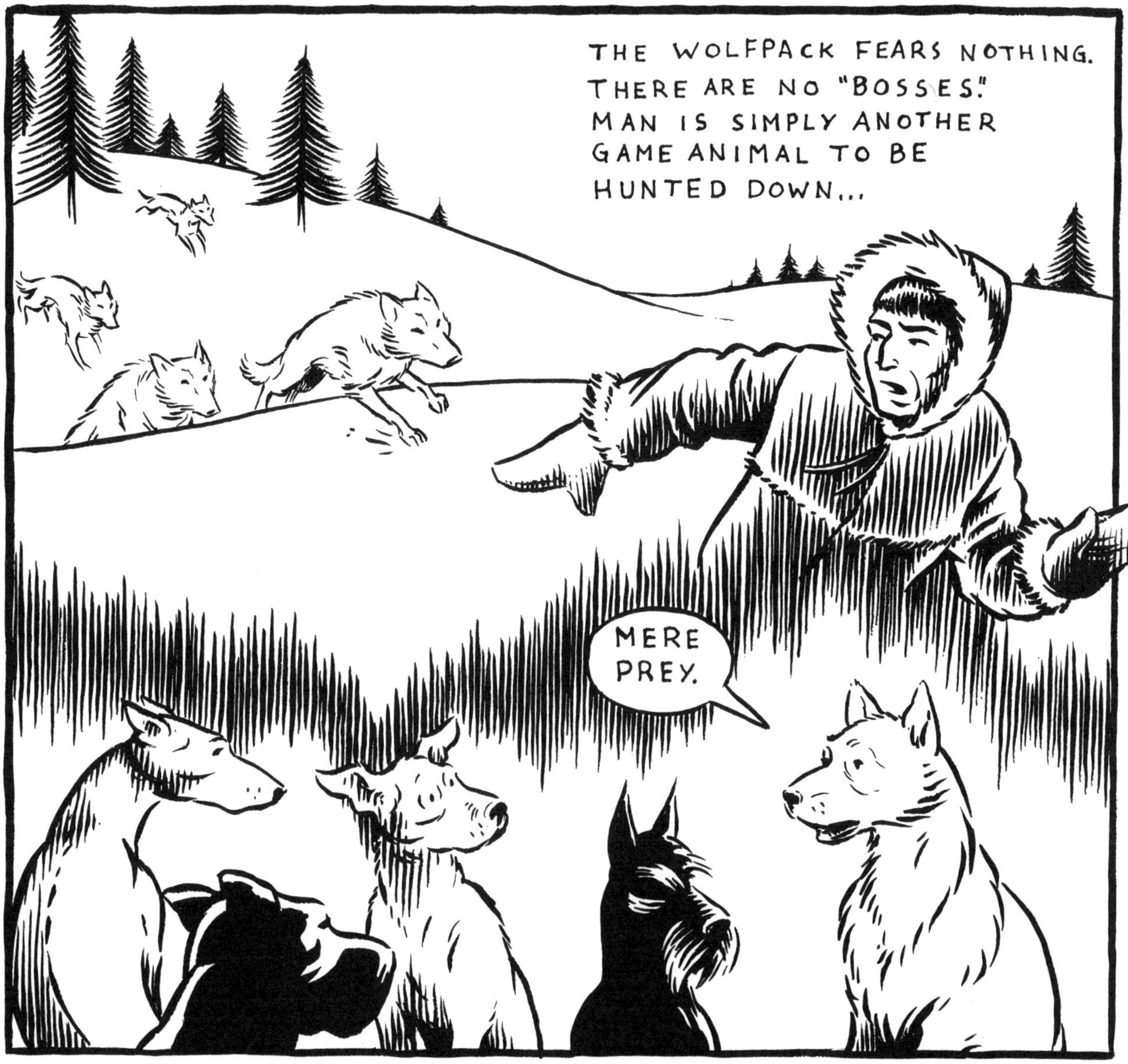
THE WOLFPACK FEARS NOTHING. THERE ARE NO "BOSSES." MAN IS SIMPLY ANOTHER GAME ANIMAL TO BE HUNTED DOWN...
MERE PREY.

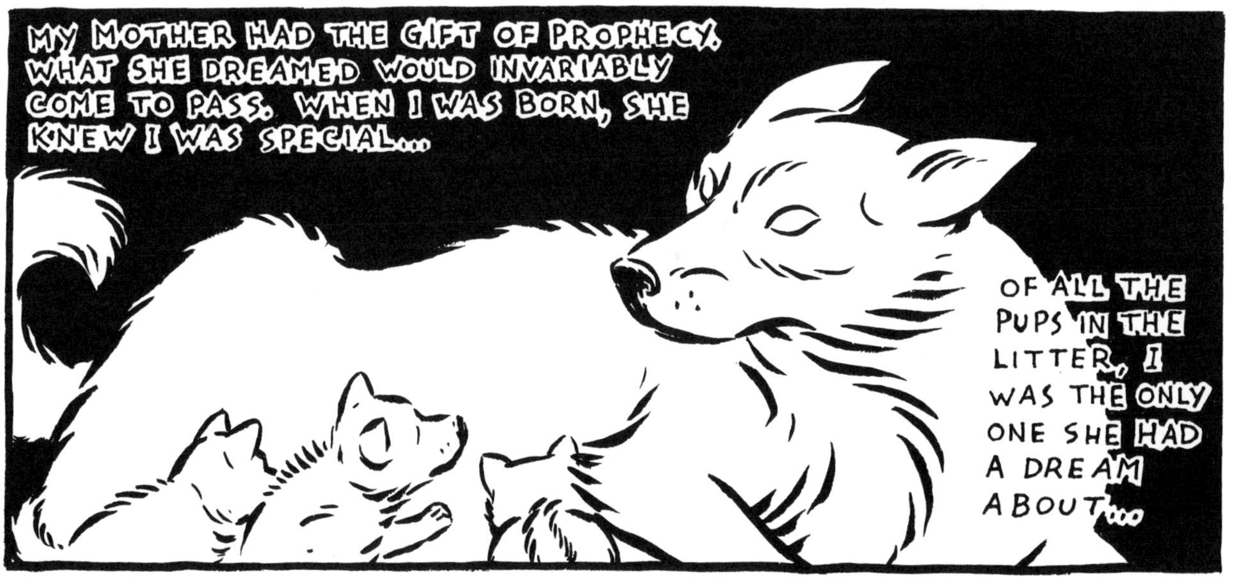
MY MOTHER HAD THE GIFT OF PROPHECY. WHAT SHE DREAMED WOULD INVARIABLY COME TO PASS. WHEN I WAS BORN, SHE KNEW I WAS SPECIAL...
OF ALL THE PUPS IN THE LITTER, I WAS THE ONLY ONE SHE HAD A DREAM ABOUT...

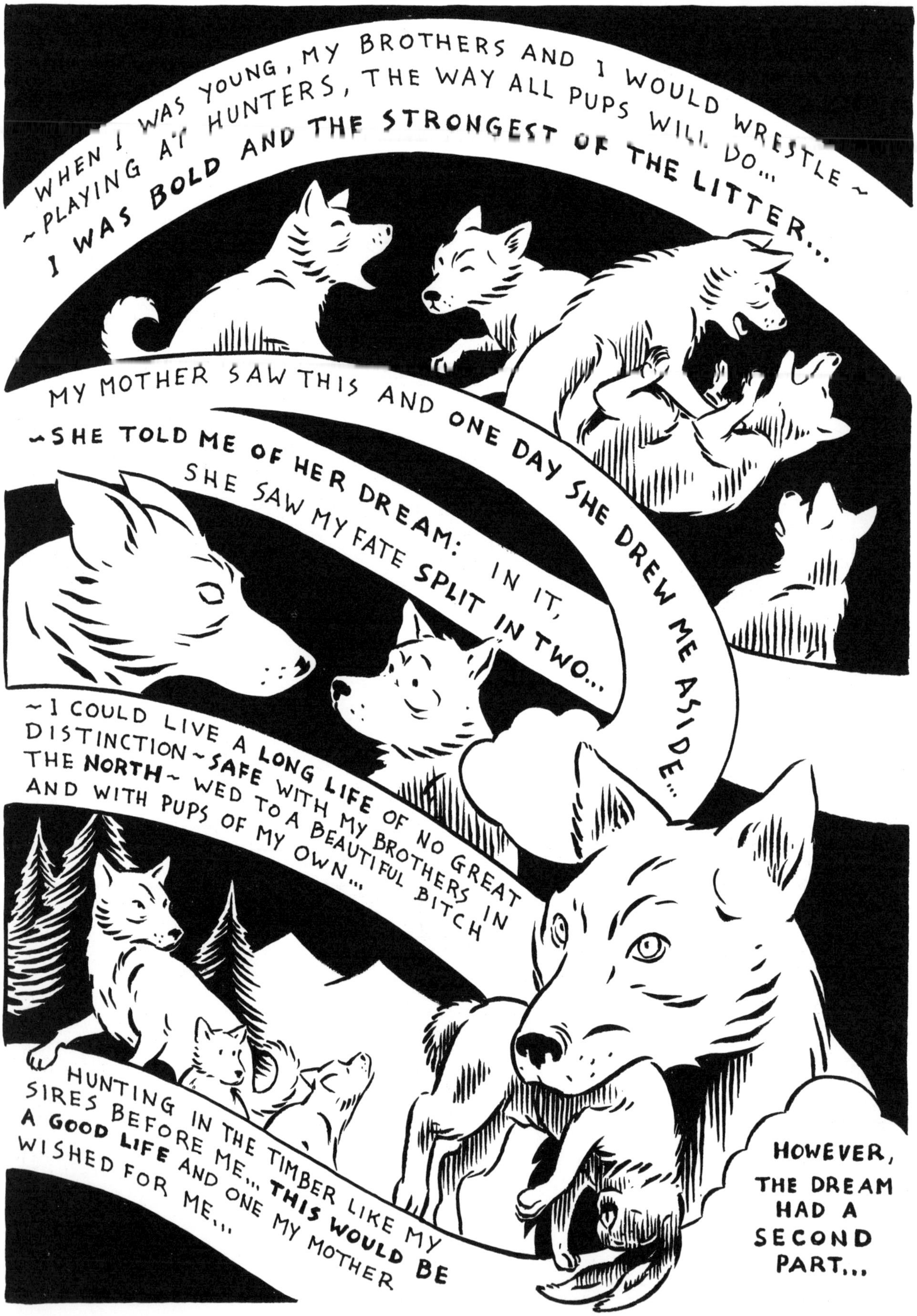

WHEN I WAS YOUNG, MY BROTHERS AND I WOULD WRESTLE ~PLAYING AT HUNTERS, THE WAY ALL PUPS WILL DO...
I WAS BOLD AND THE STRONGEST OF THE LITTER...
MY MOTHER SAW THIS AND ONE DAY SHE DREW ME ASIDE...
~SHE TOLD ME OF HER DREAM: IN IT, SHE SAW MY FATE SPLIT IN TWO...
~I COULD LIVE A LONG LIFE OF NO GREAT DISTINCTION~SAFE WITH MY BROTHERS IN THE NORTH~ WED TO A BEAUTIFUL BITCH AND WITH PUPS OF MY OWN...
HUNTING IN THE TIMBER LIKE MY SIRES BEFORE ME... THIS WOULD BE A GOOD LIFE AND ONE MY MOTHER WISHED FOR ME...
HOWEVER, THE DREAM HAD A SECOND PART...

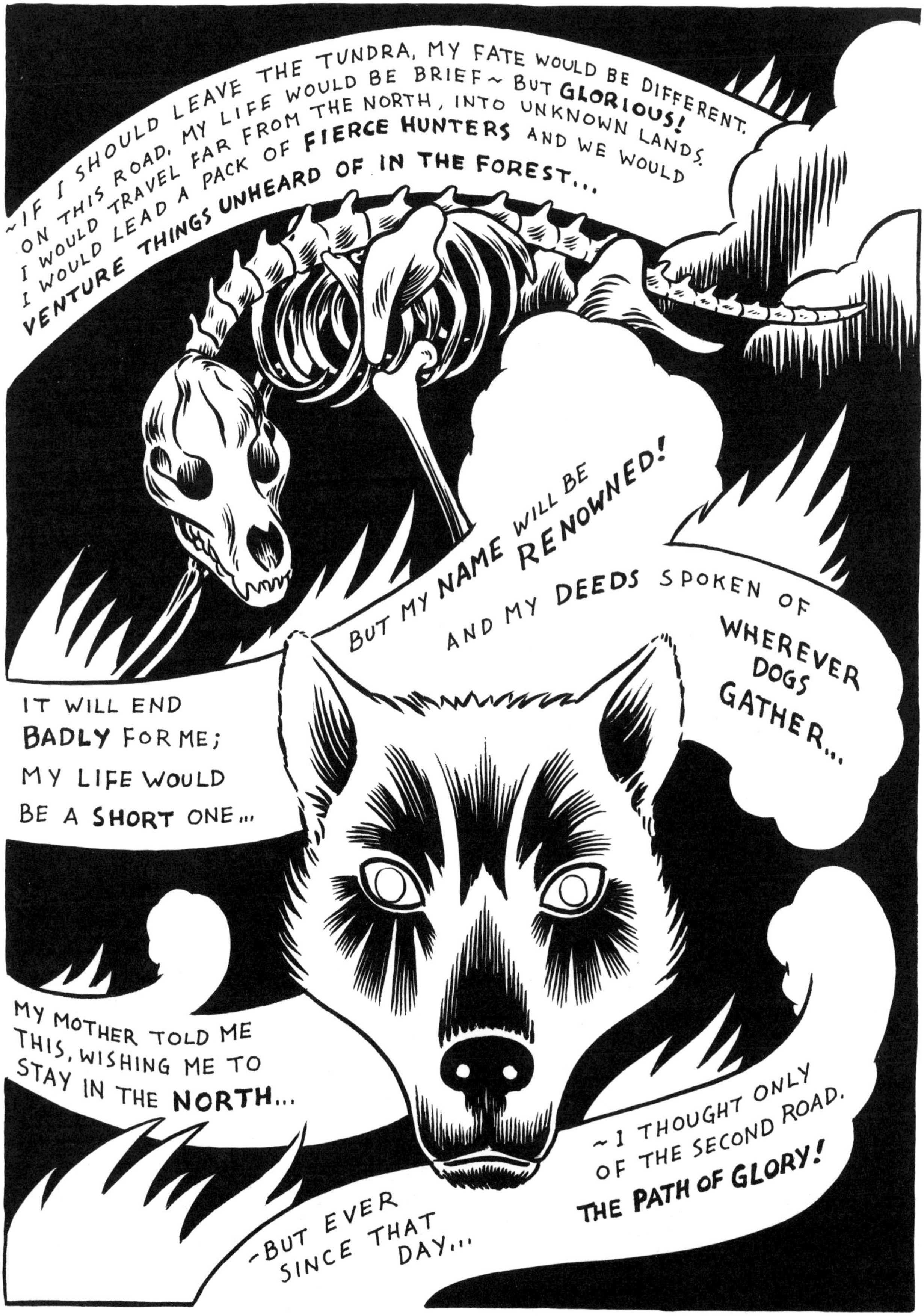
~IF I SHOULD LEAVE THE TUNDRA, MY FATE WOULD BE DIFFERENT. ON THIS ROAD, MY LIFE WOULD BE BRIEF~ BUT GLORIOUS! I WOULD TRAVEL FAR FROM THE NORTH, INTO UNKNOWN LANDS. I WOULD LEAD A PACK OF FIERCE HUNTERS AND WE WOULD VENTURE THINGS UNHEARD OF IN THE FOREST...
IT WILL END BADLY FOR ME; MY LIFE WOULD BE A SHORT ONE...
BUT MY NAME WILL BE RENOWNED!
AND MY DEEDS SPOKEN OF
WHEREVER DOGS GATHER...
MY MOTHER TOLD ME THIS, WISHING ME TO STAY IN THE NORTH...
~BUT EVER SINCE THAT DAY...
~I THOUGHT ONLY OF THE SECOND ROAD. THE PATH OF GLORY!

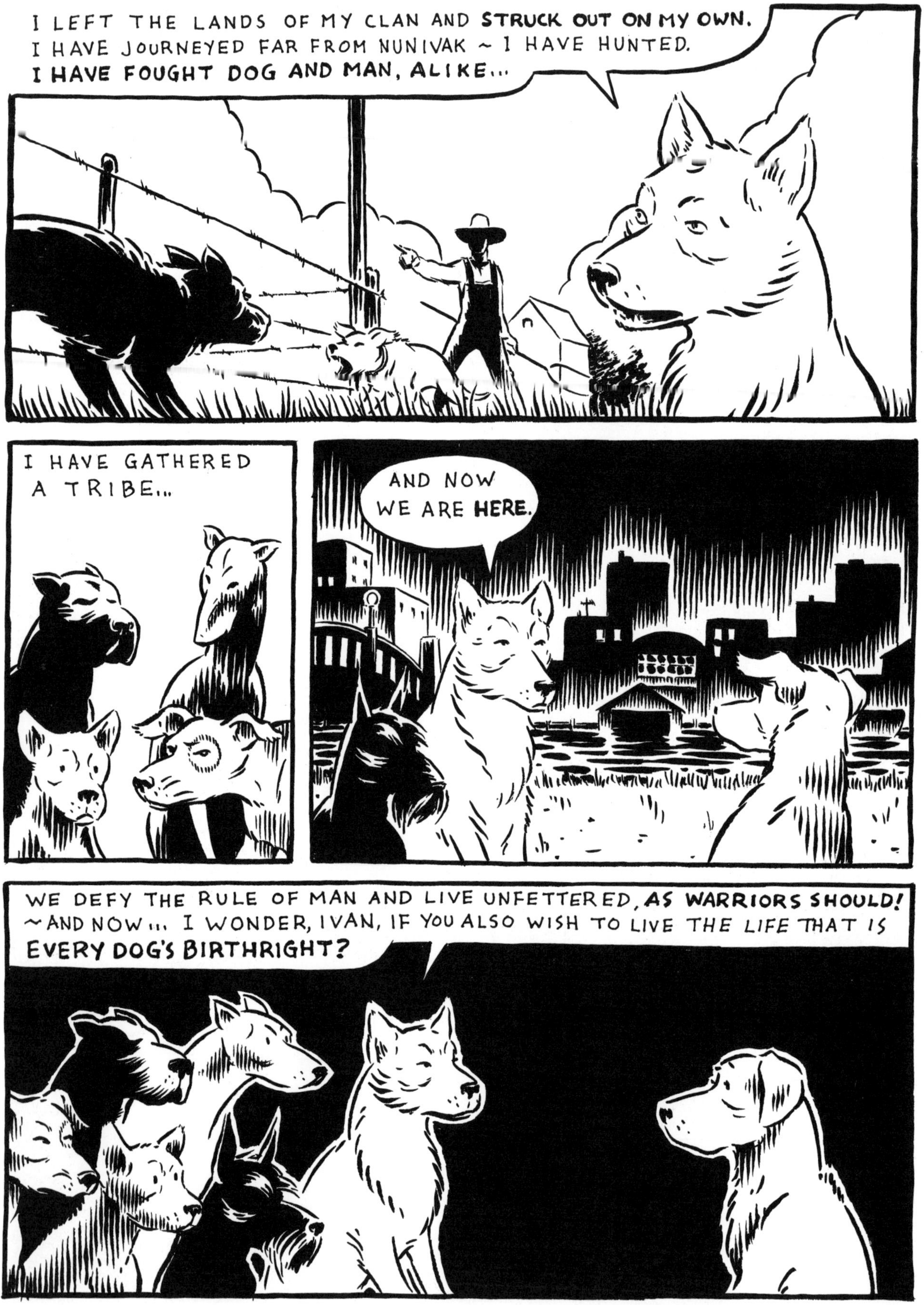
I LEFT THE LANDS OF MY CLAN AND STRUCK OUT ON MY OWN. I HAVE JOURNEYED FAR FROM NUNIVAK ~ I HAVE HUNTED. I HAVE FOUGHT DOG AND MAN, ALIKE...
I HAVE GATHERED A TRIBE...
AND NOW WE ARE HERE.
WE DEFY THE RULE OF MAN AND LIVE UNFETTERED, AS WARRIORS SHOULD! ~AND NOW... I WONDER, IVAN, IF YOU ALSO WISH TO LIVE THE LIFE THAT IS EVERY DOG'S BIRTHRIGHT?

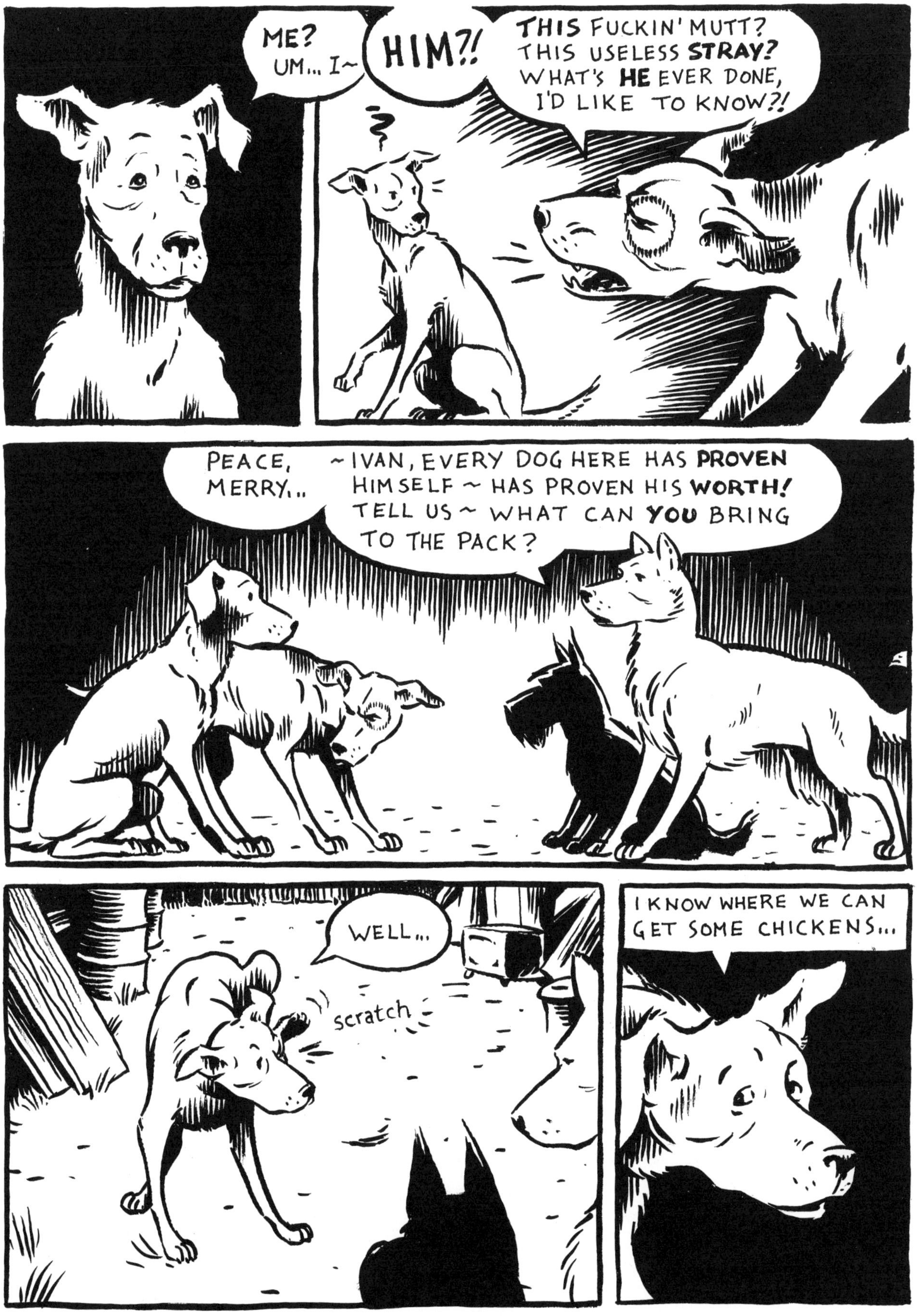

ME? UM... I~
HIM?!
THIS FUCKIN' MUTT? THIS USELESS STRAY? WHAT'S HE EVER DONE, I'D LIKE TO KNOW?!
PEACE, MERRY...
~IVAN, EVERY DOG HERE HAS PROVEN HIMSELF ~ HAS PROVEN HIS WORTH! TELL US ~ WHAT CAN YOU BRING TO THE PACK?
WELL...
scratch
I KNOW WHERE WE CAN GET SOME CHICKENS...

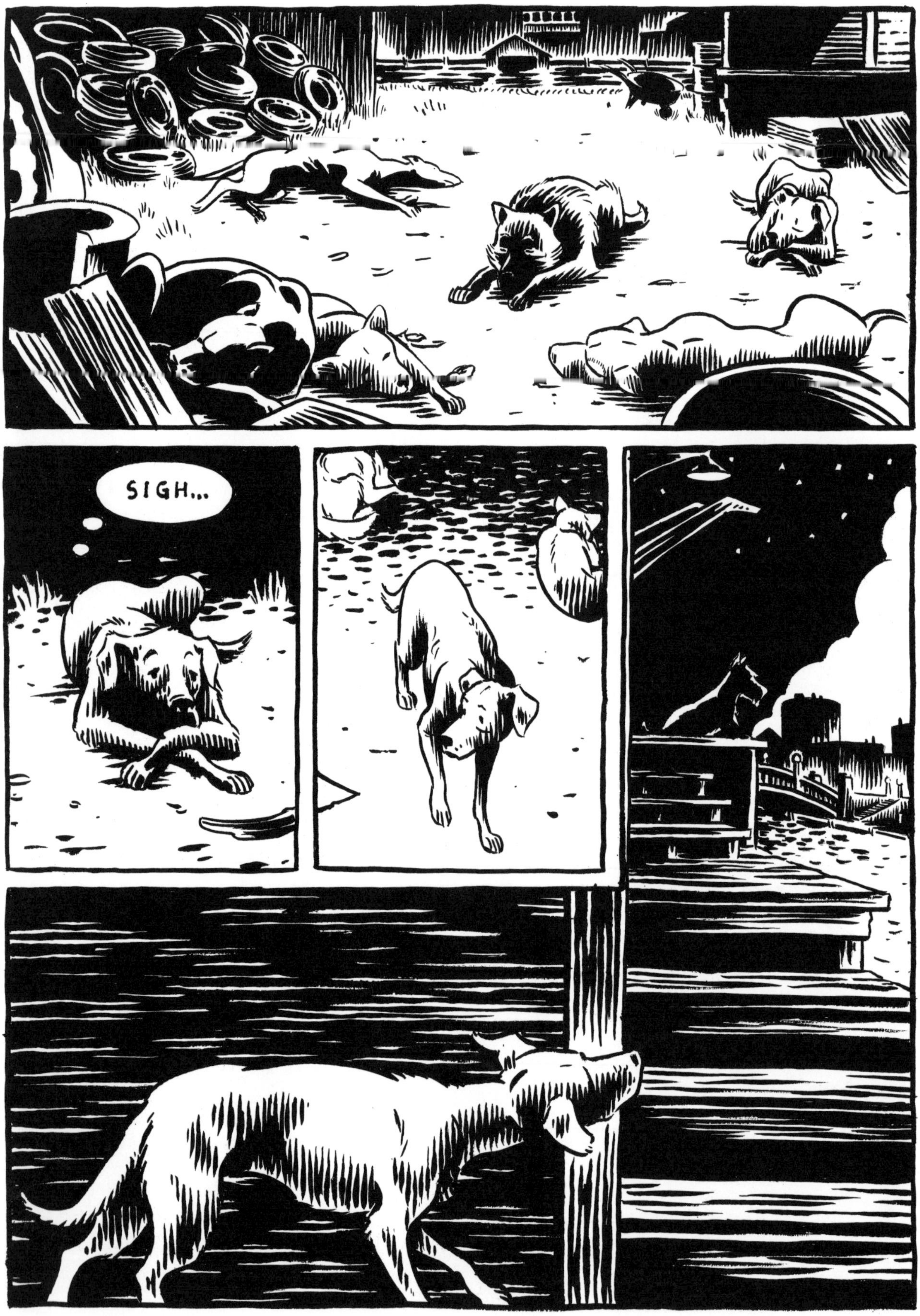
SIGH...

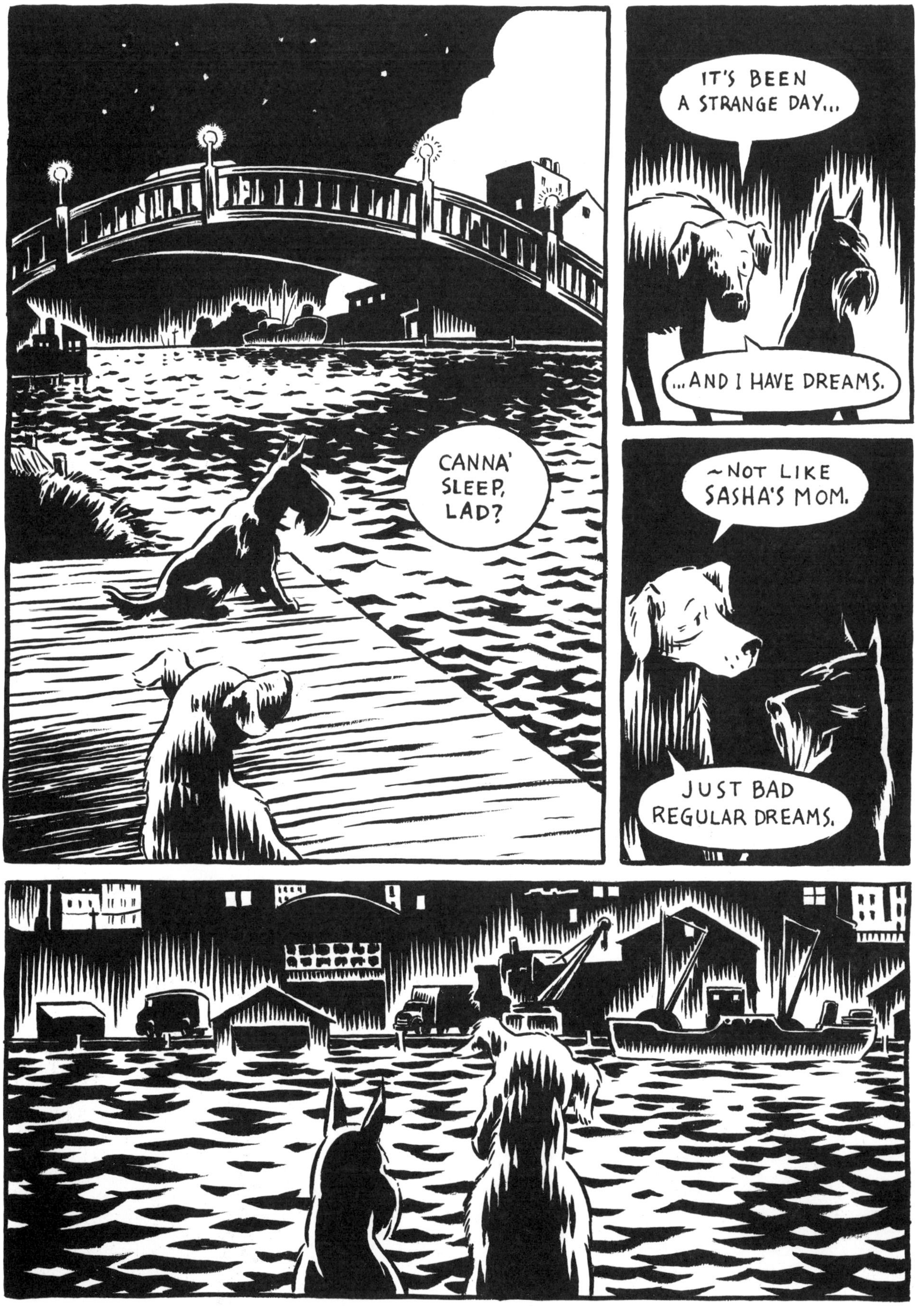
CANNA' SLEEP, LAD?
IT'S BEEN A STRANGE DAY...
...AND I HAVE DREAMS.
~NOT LIKE SASHA'S MOM.
JUST BAD REGULAR DREAMS.

SAWNEY? IS ALL THAT TRUE? SASHA'S STORY ABOUT HIS MOTHER'S DREAMS AND ALL THAT?

WEEL...

BETWEEN YOU AND ME, LAD, I DINNA PUT MUCH STOCK IN DREAMS. ~ BUT THERE'S NO DOUBT THAT SASHA'S THE FINEST DOG I EVER SAW. BRAVE ~ FIERCE, LIKE HE SAYS...

HE GOT ME OUT'VE A JAM, WENT FOR A MAN WHO WAS ON ME WITH A STICK ~ FAIRLY TORE HIM UP...

~ I'VE STUCK BY HIM EVER SINCE.

A WATCHDOG, IF Y'LIKE.

LOYALTY, MIND ~ BUT ALSO TO LOOK OUT FOR HIM. HE'S FAIR FEARLESS ~ ACTS A BIT RASH, SOMETIMES. HE NEEDS A BODY WITH ALL FOUR FEET ON THE GROUND...

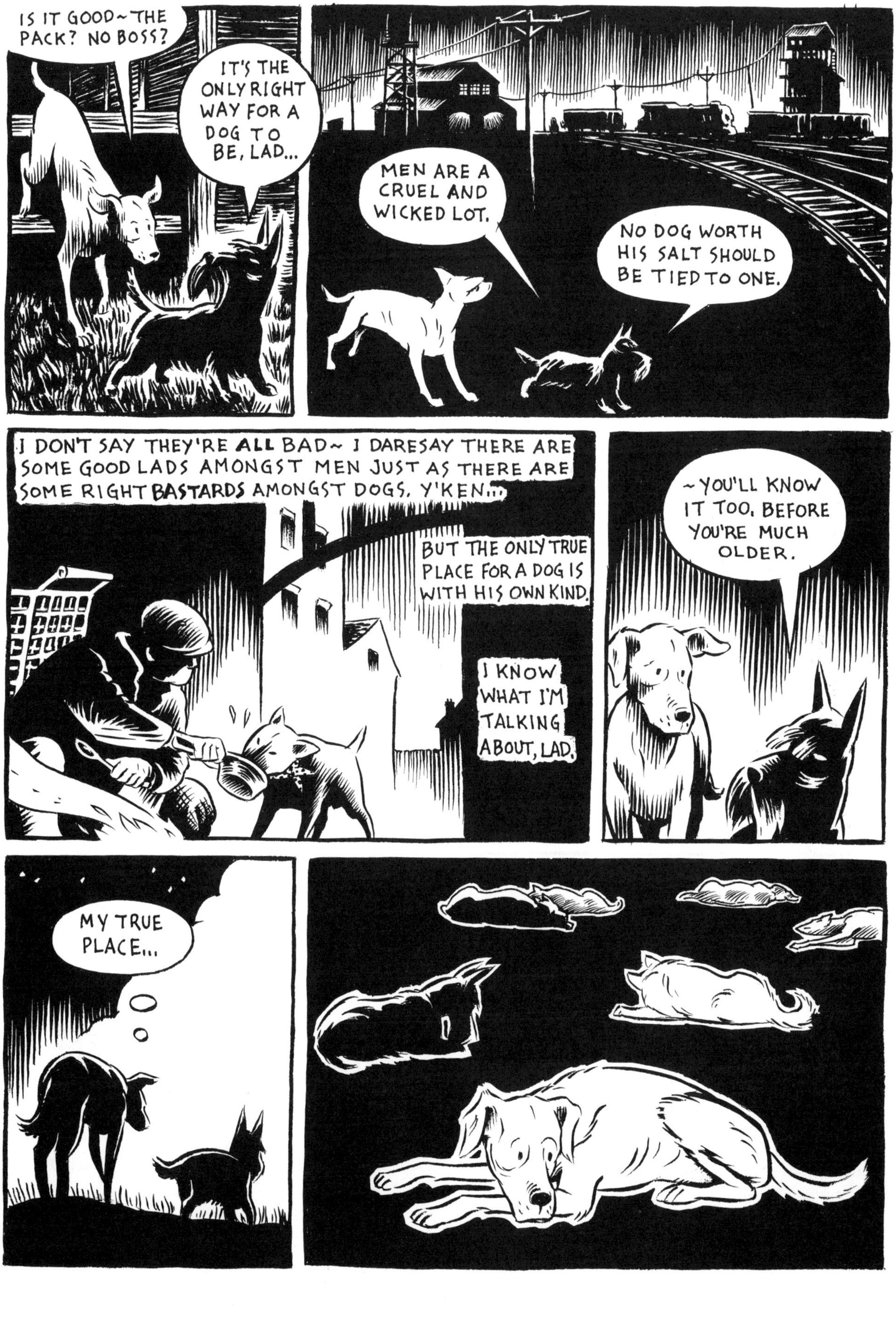
IS IT GOOD~ THE PACK? NO BOSS?
IT'S THE ONLY RIGHT WAY FOR A DOG TO BE, LAD...
MEN ARE A CRUEL AND WICKED LOT.
NO DOG WORTH HIS SALT SHOULD BE TIED TO ONE.
I DON'T SAY THEY'RE **ALL** BAD~ I DARESAY THERE ARE SOME GOOD LADS AMONGST MEN JUST AS THERE ARE SOME RIGHT **BASTARDS** AMONGST DOGS, Y'KEN...
BUT THE ONLY TRUE PLACE FOR A DOG IS WITH HIS OWN KIND.
I KNOW WHAT I'M TALKING ABOUT, LAD.
~YOU'LL KNOW IT TOO, BEFORE YOU'RE MUCH OLDER.
MY TRUE PLACE...

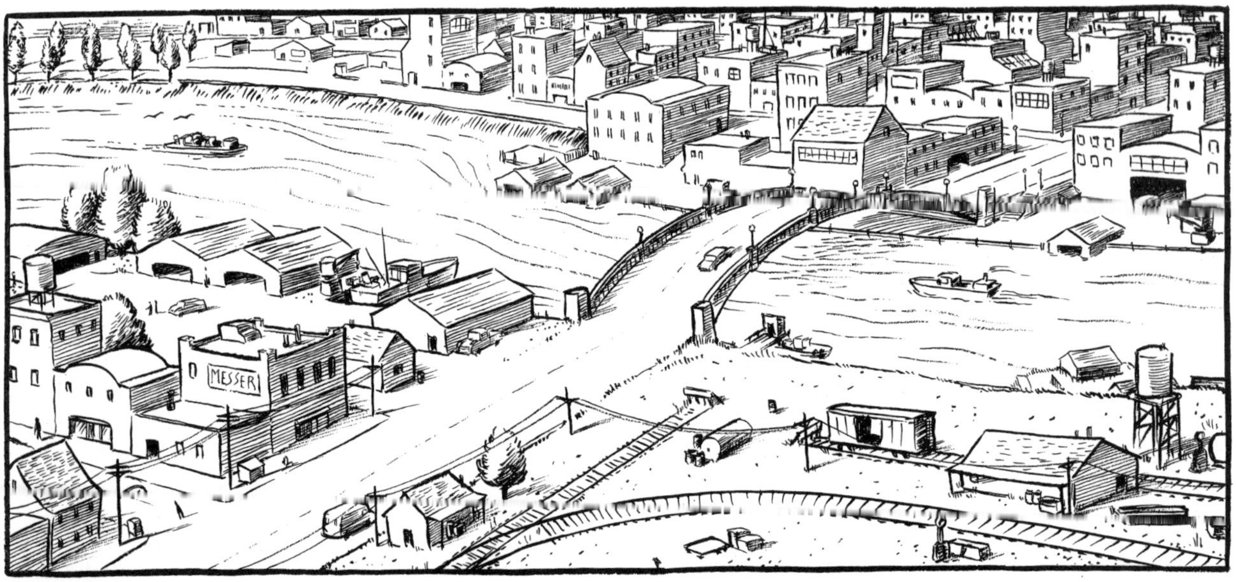
MESSER

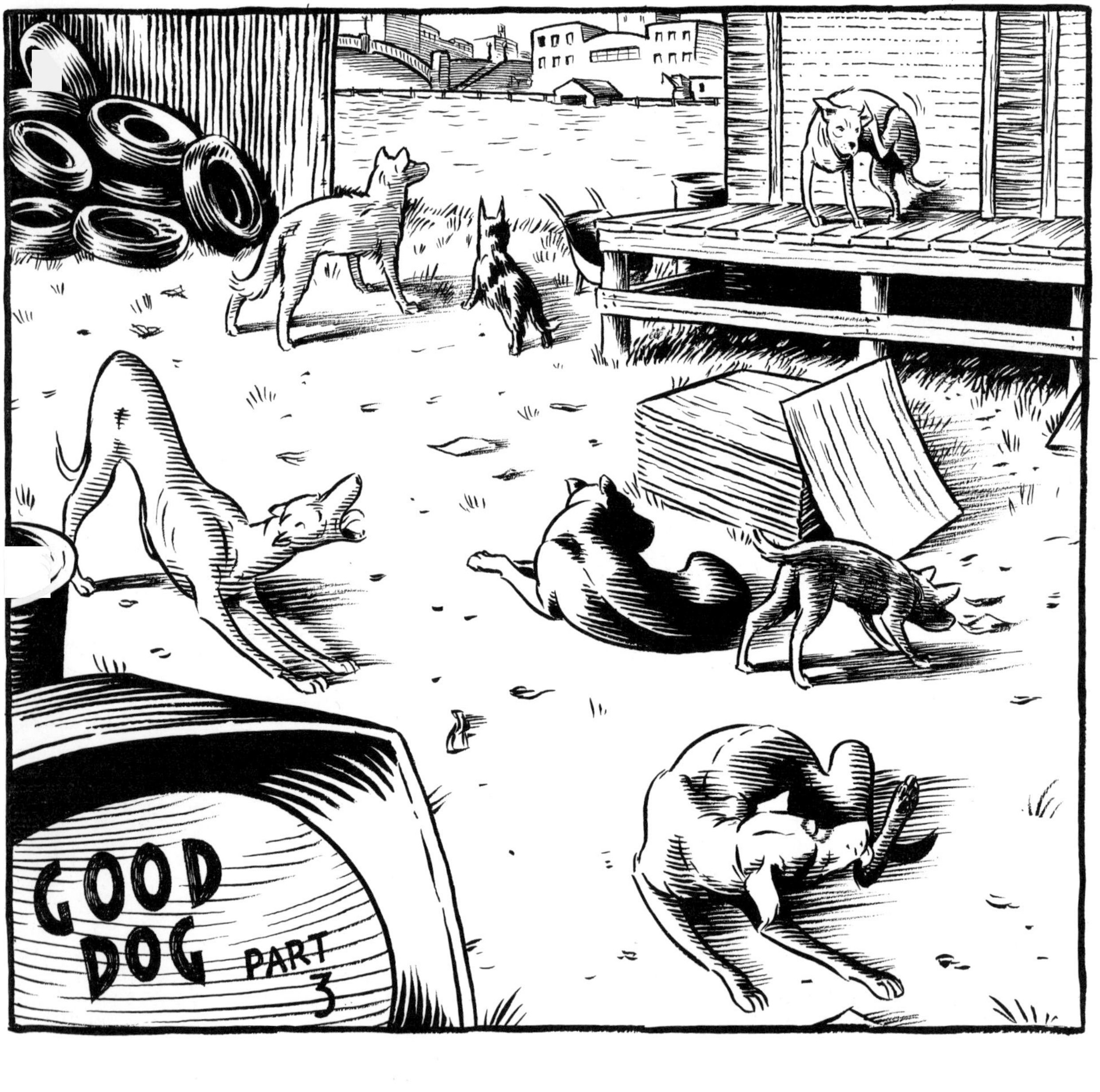
GOOD DOG PART 3

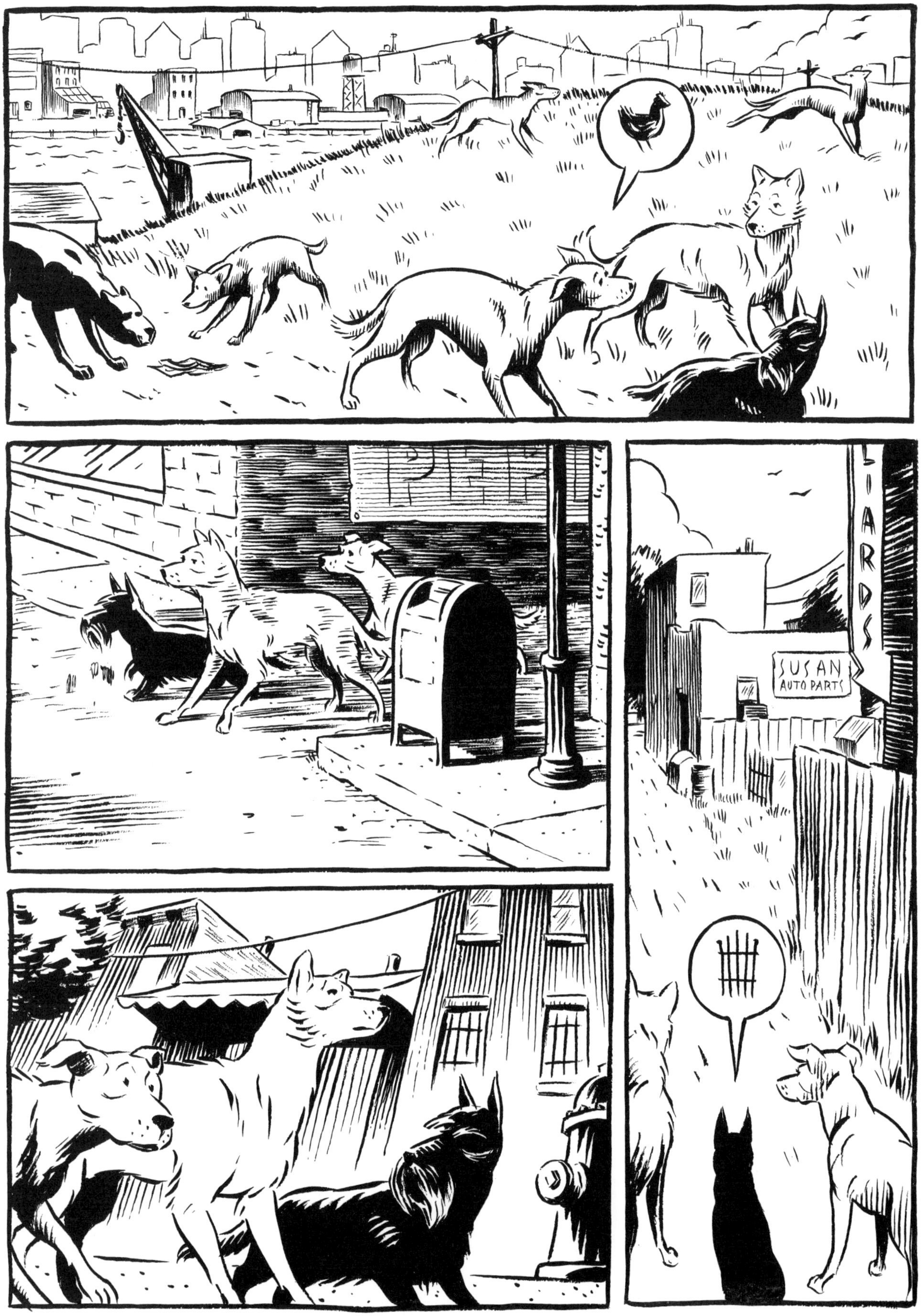
LIARDS
SUSAN
AUTO PARTS

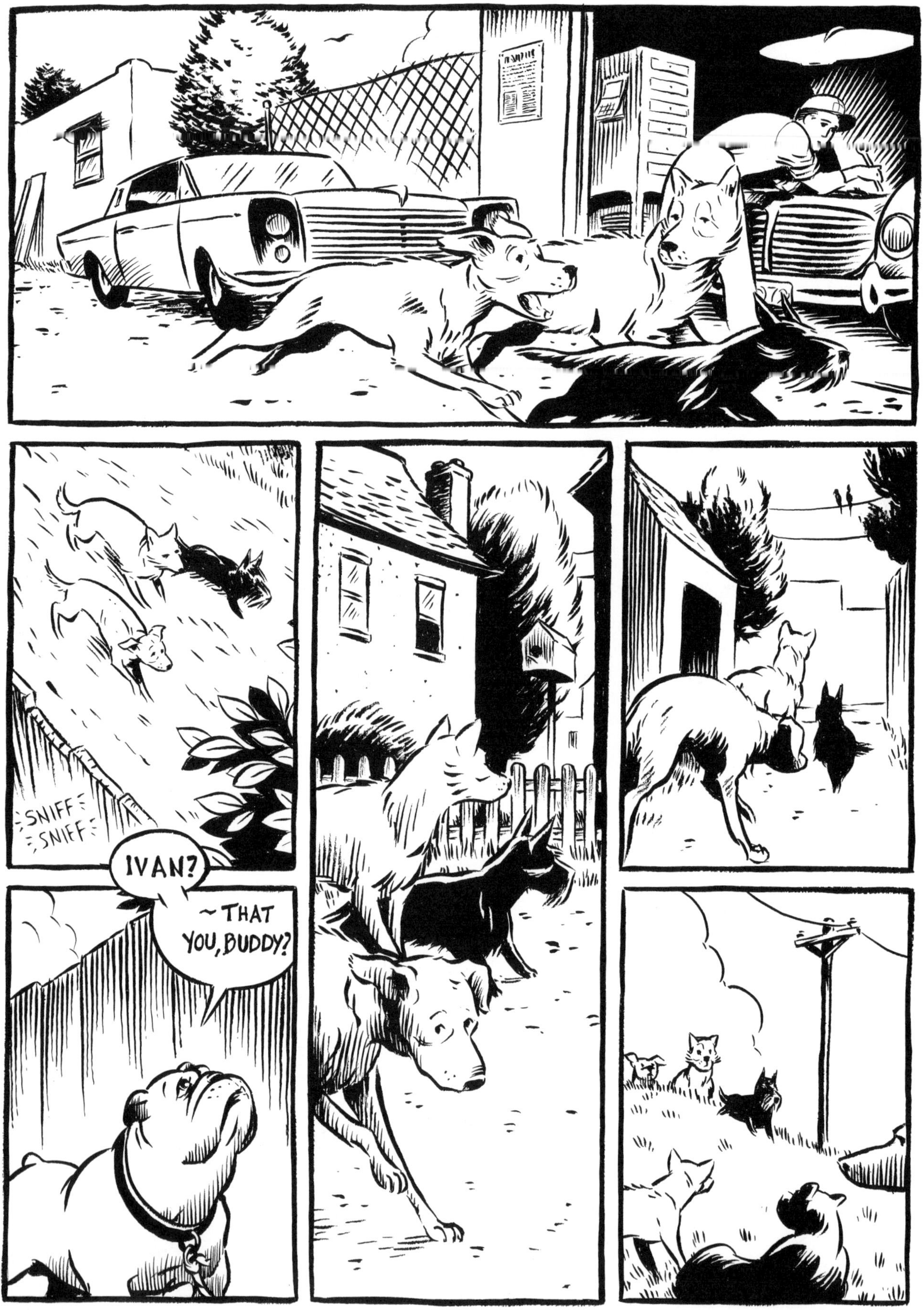
SNIFF SNIFF
IVAN?
~THAT YOU, BUDDY?

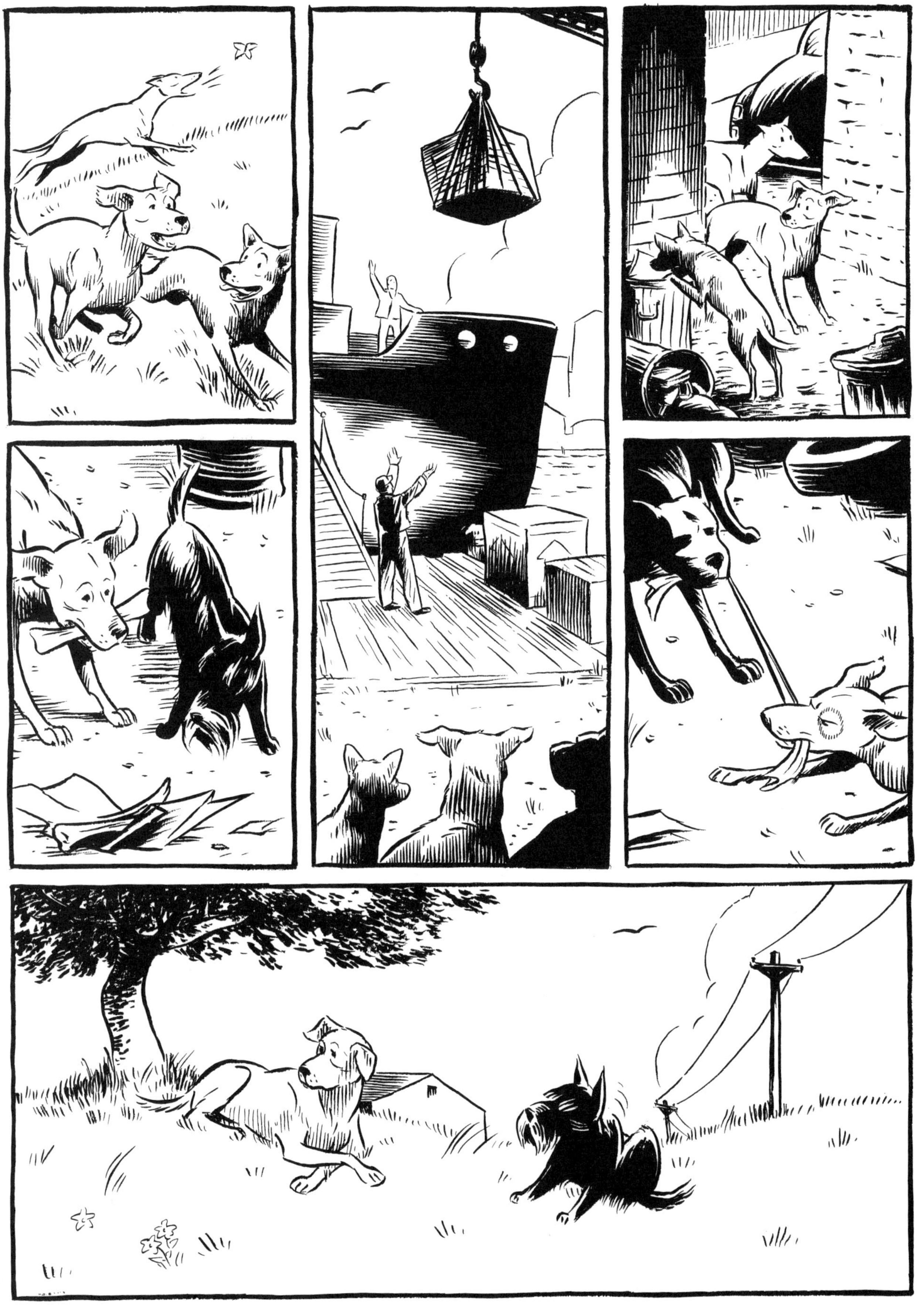

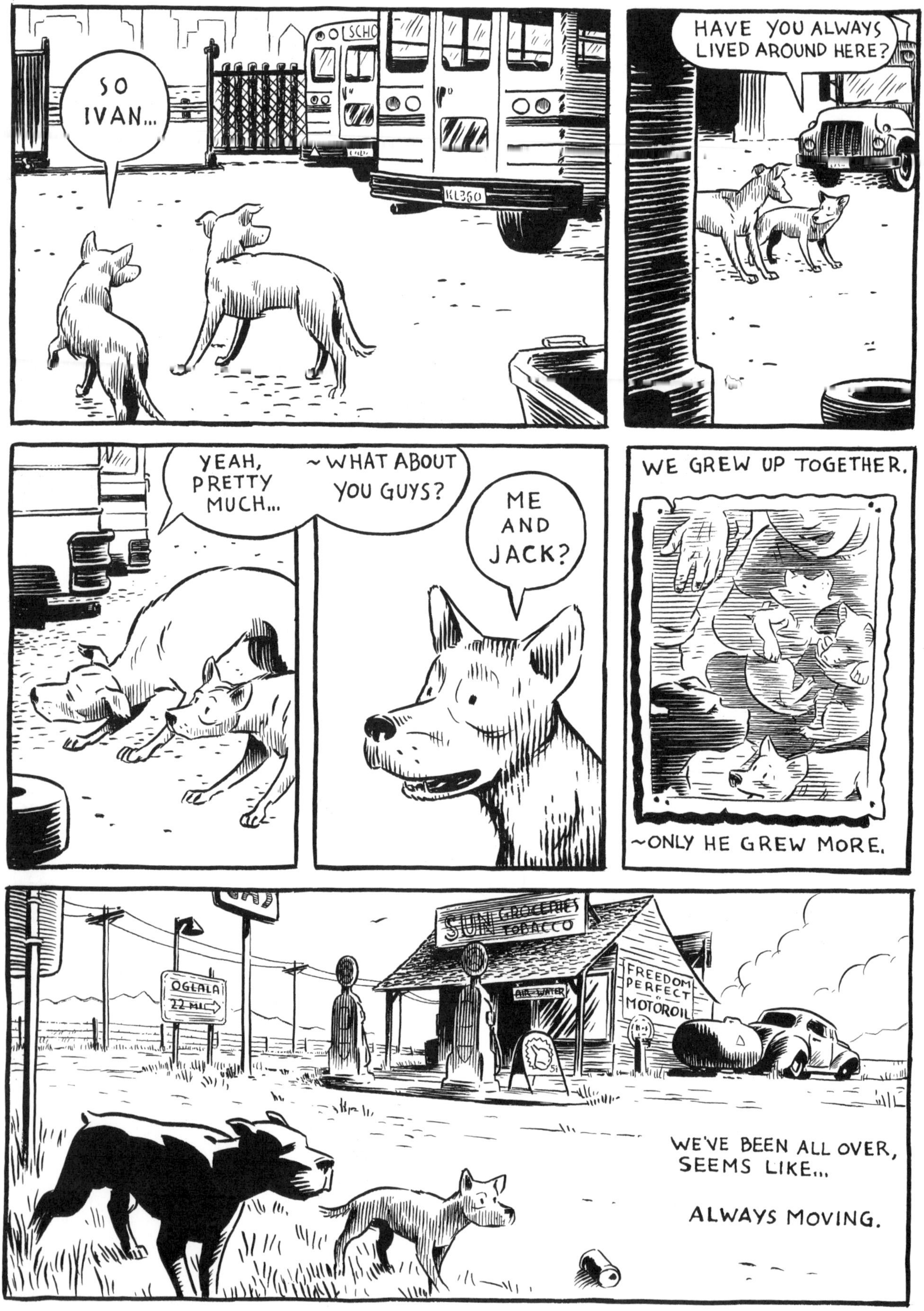
SO IVAN...
HAVE YOU ALWAYS LIVED AROUND HERE?
YEAH, PRETTY MUCH...
~WHAT ABOUT YOU GUYS?
ME AND JACK?
WE GREW UP TOGETHER.
~ONLY HE GREW MORE.
SUN GROCERIES TOBACCO
OGLALA 22 MI
AIR WATER
FREEDOM PERFECT MOTOROIL
WE'VE BEEN ALL OVER, SEEMS LIKE...
ALWAYS MOVING.

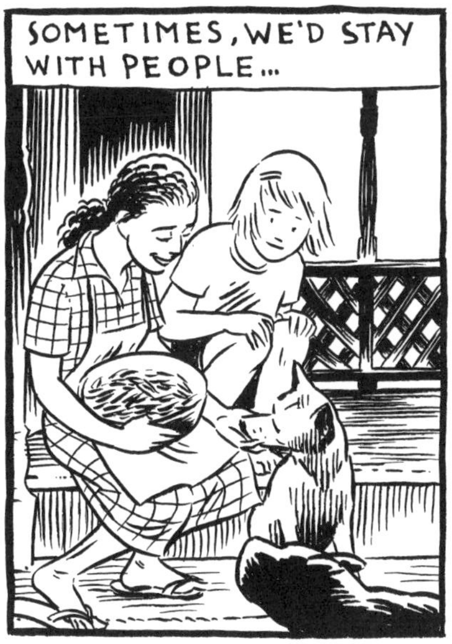
SOMETIMES, WE'D STAY WITH PEOPLE...

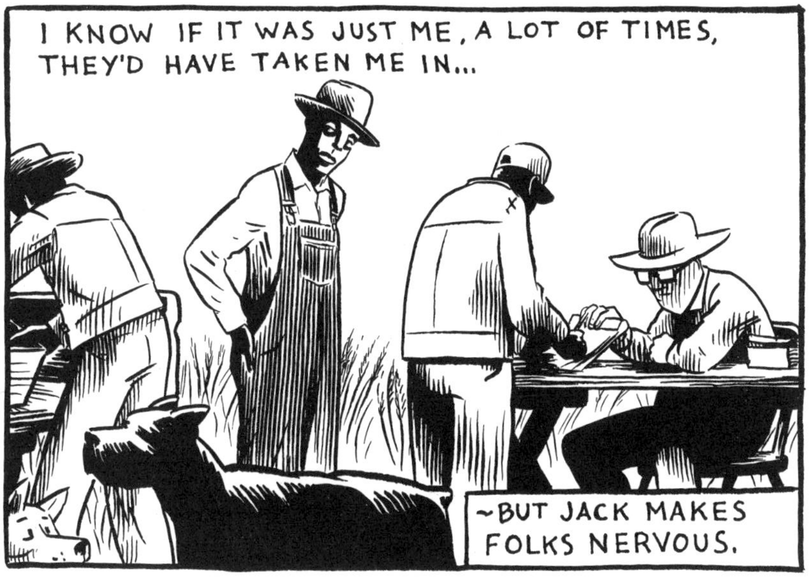
I KNOW IF IT WAS JUST ME, A LOT OF TIMES, THEY'D HAVE TAKEN ME IN...
~BUT JACK MAKES FOLKS NERVOUS.

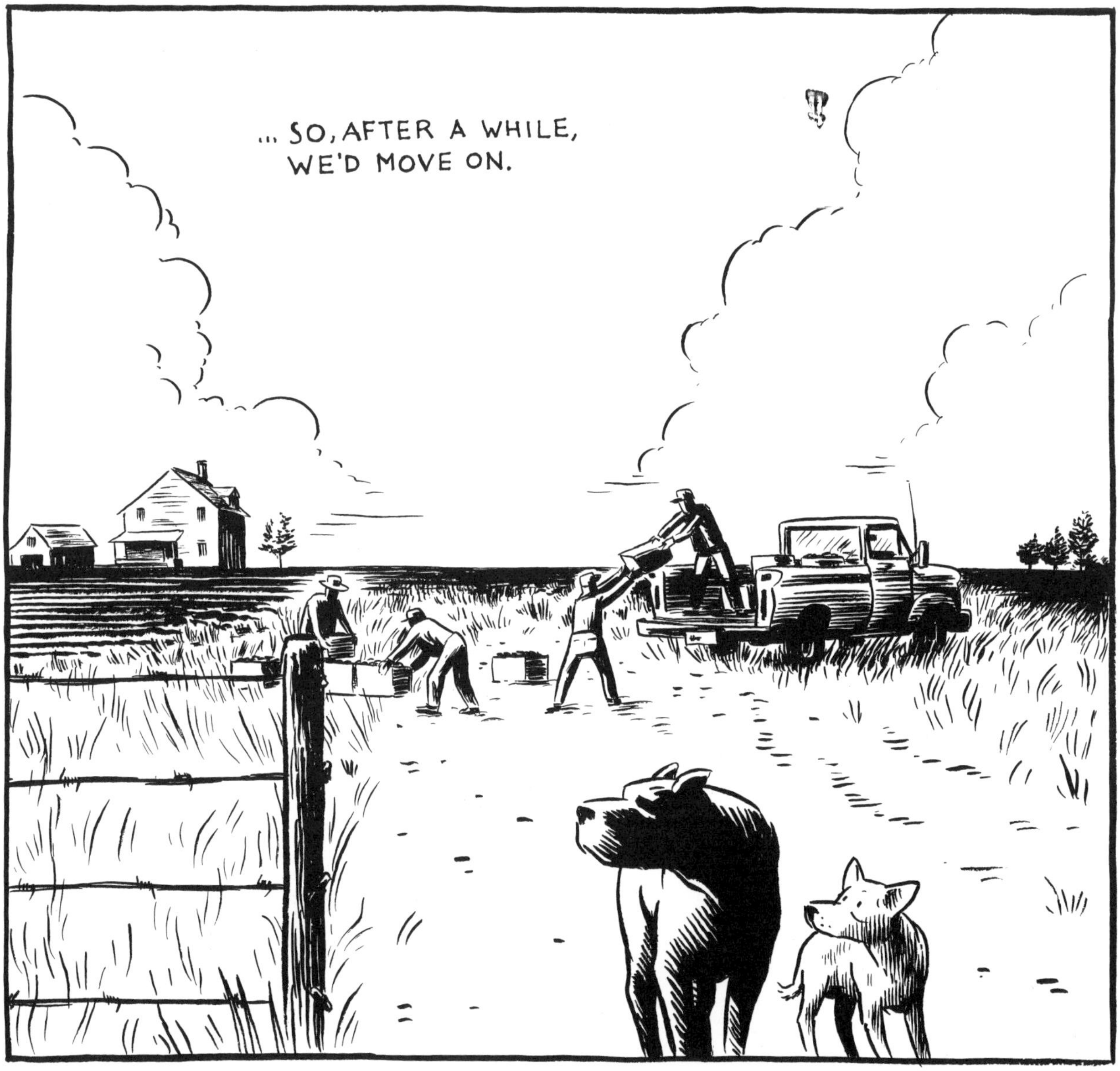
... SO, AFTER A WHILE, WE'D MOVE ON.

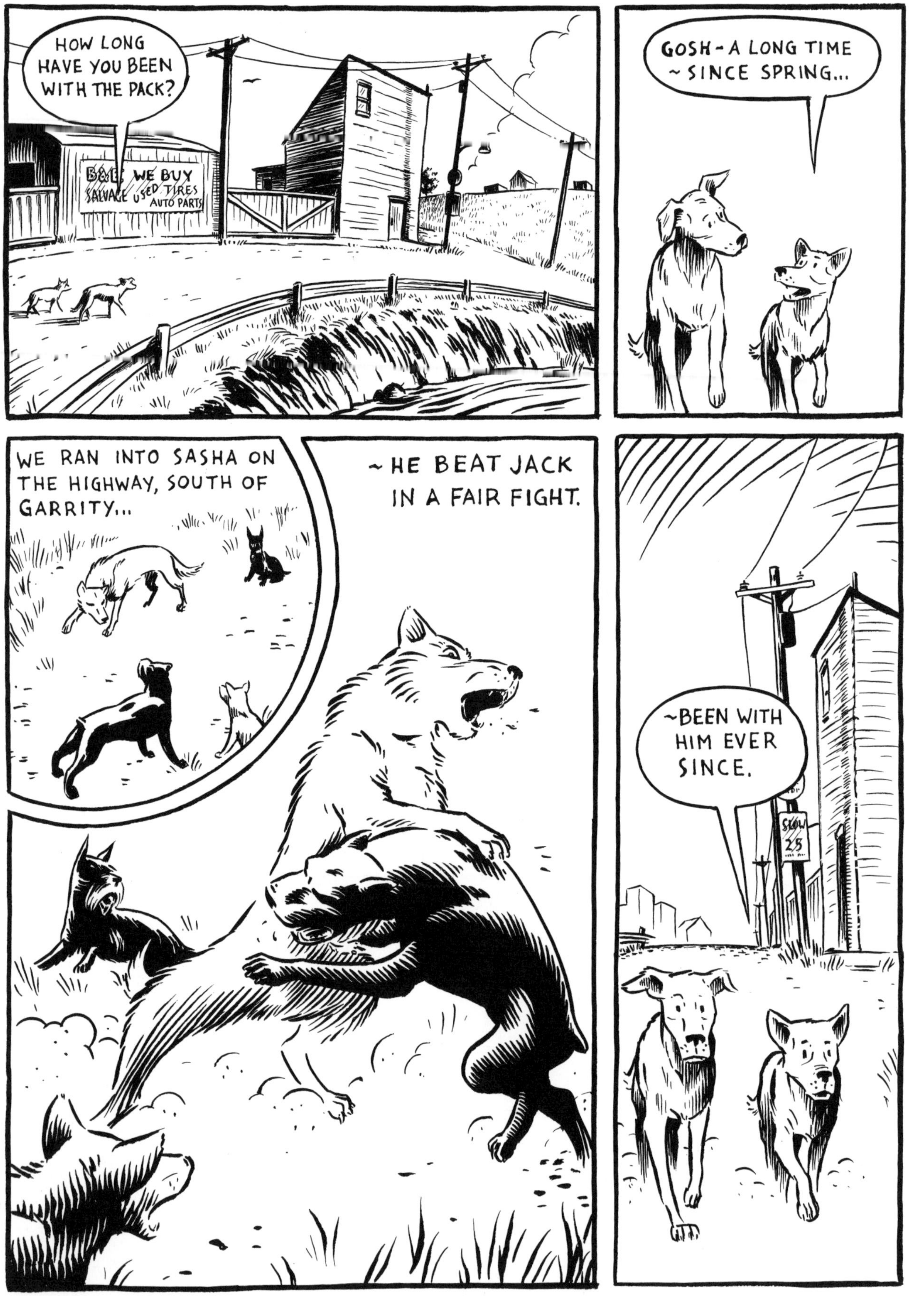
HOW LONG HAVE YOU BEEN WITH THE PACK?
B&E WE BUY SALVAGE USED TIRES AUTO PARTS
GOSH - A LONG TIME ~ SINCE SPRING...
WE RAN INTO SASHA ON THE HIGHWAY, SOUTH OF GARRITY...
~ HE BEAT JACK IN A FAIR FIGHT.
~BEEN WITH HIM EVER SINCE.
SLOW 25

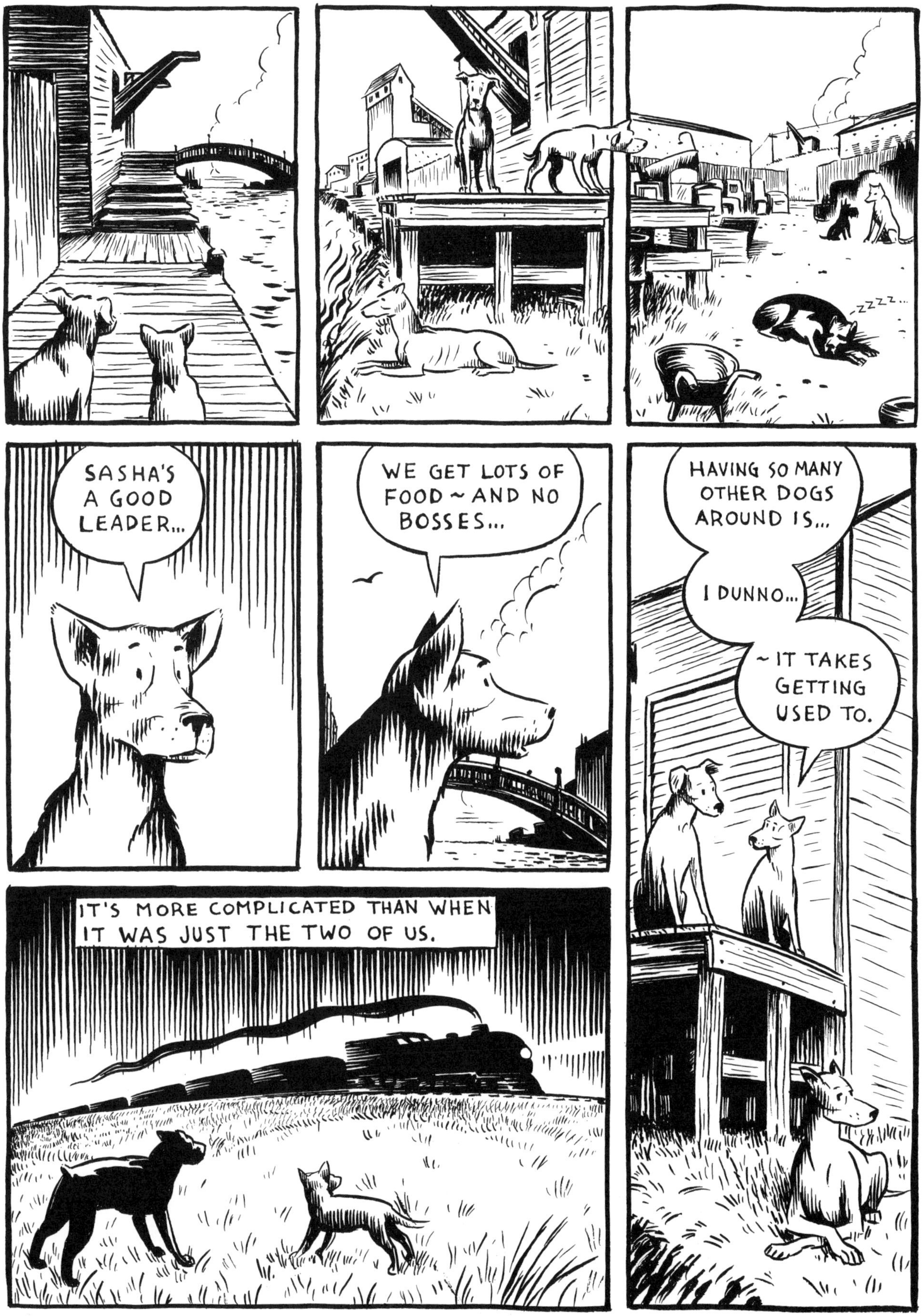
ZZZZ...
SASHA'S A GOOD LEADER...
WE GET LOTS OF FOOD ~ AND NO BOSSES...
HAVING SO MANY OTHER DOGS AROUND IS...
I DUNNO...
~ IT TAKES GETTING USED TO.
IT'S MORE COMPLICATED THAN WHEN IT WAS JUST THE TWO OF US.

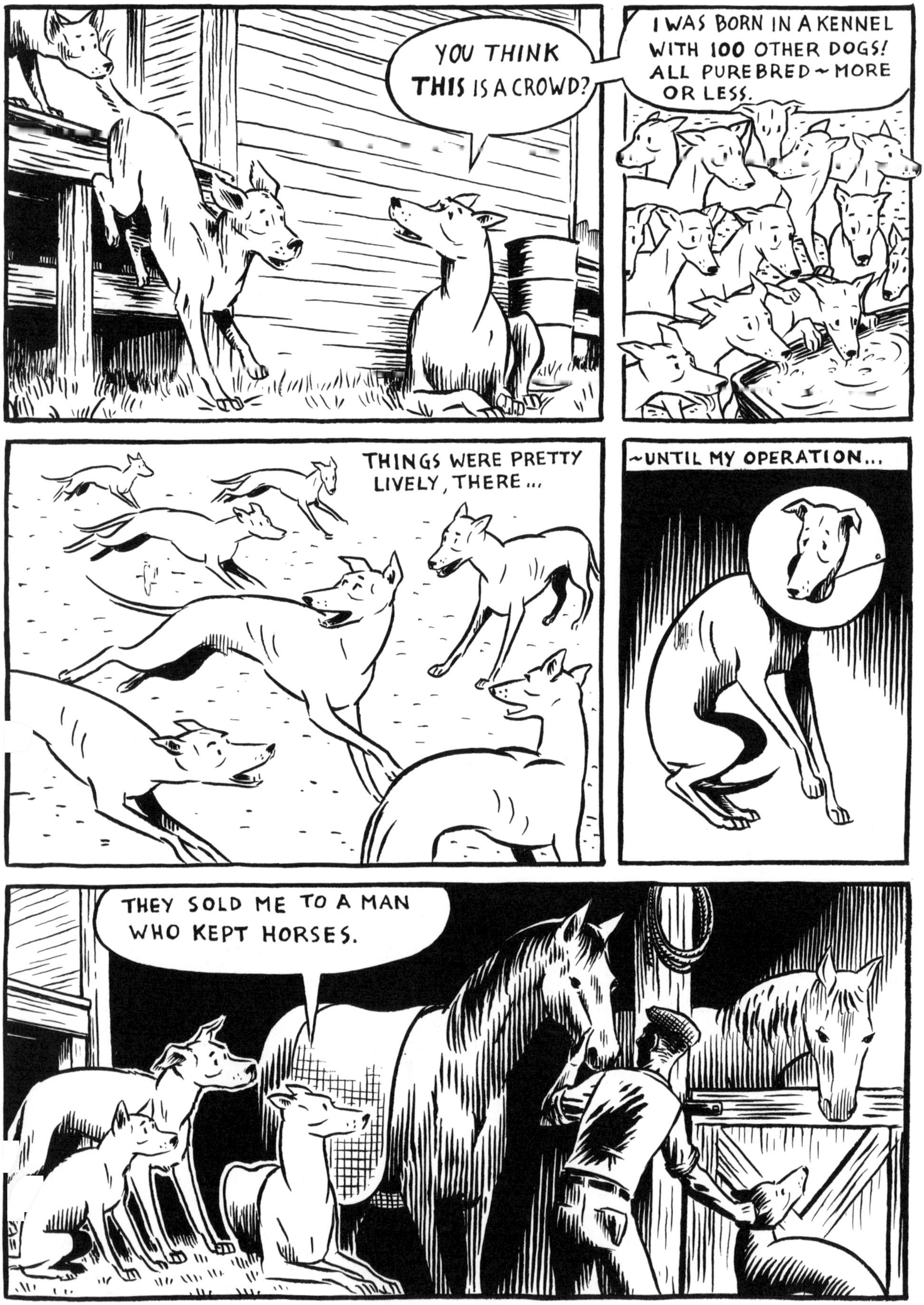
YOU THINK THIS IS A CROWD?
I WAS BORN IN A KENNEL WITH 100 OTHER DOGS! ALL PUREBRED ~ MORE OR LESS.
THINGS WERE PRETTY LIVELY, THERE...
~UNTIL MY OPERATION...
THEY SOLD ME TO A MAN WHO KEPT HORSES.

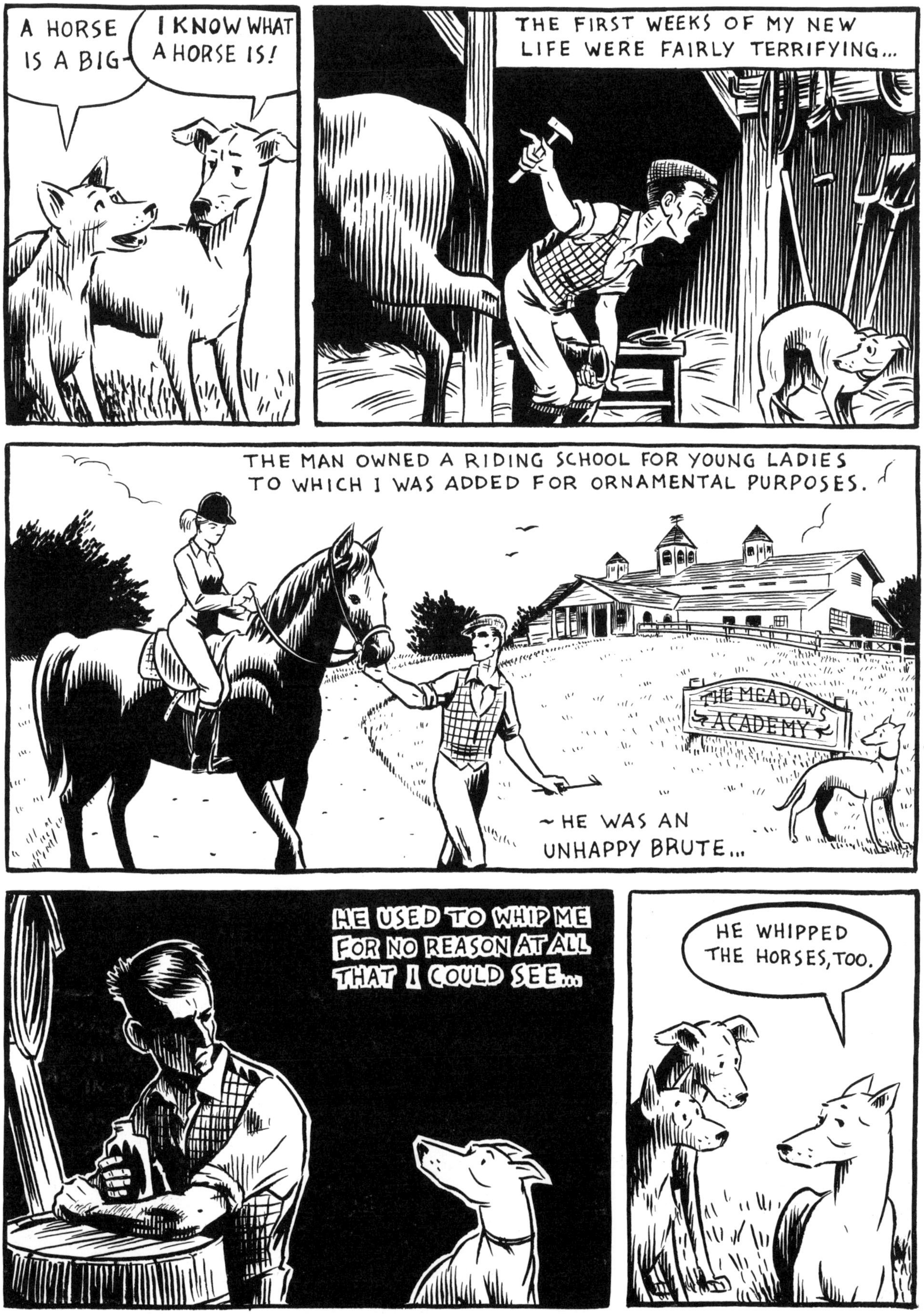
A HORSE IS A BIG-
I KNOW WHAT A HORSE IS!
THE FIRST WEEKS OF MY NEW LIFE WERE FAIRLY TERRIFYING...
THE MAN OWNED A RIDING SCHOOL FOR YOUNG LADIES TO WHICH I WAS ADDED FOR ORNAMENTAL PURPOSES.
THE MEADOWS ACADEMY
~HE WAS AN UNHAPPY BRUTE...
HE USED TO WHIP ME FOR NO REASON AT ALL THAT I COULD SEE...
HE WHIPPED THE HORSES, TOO.

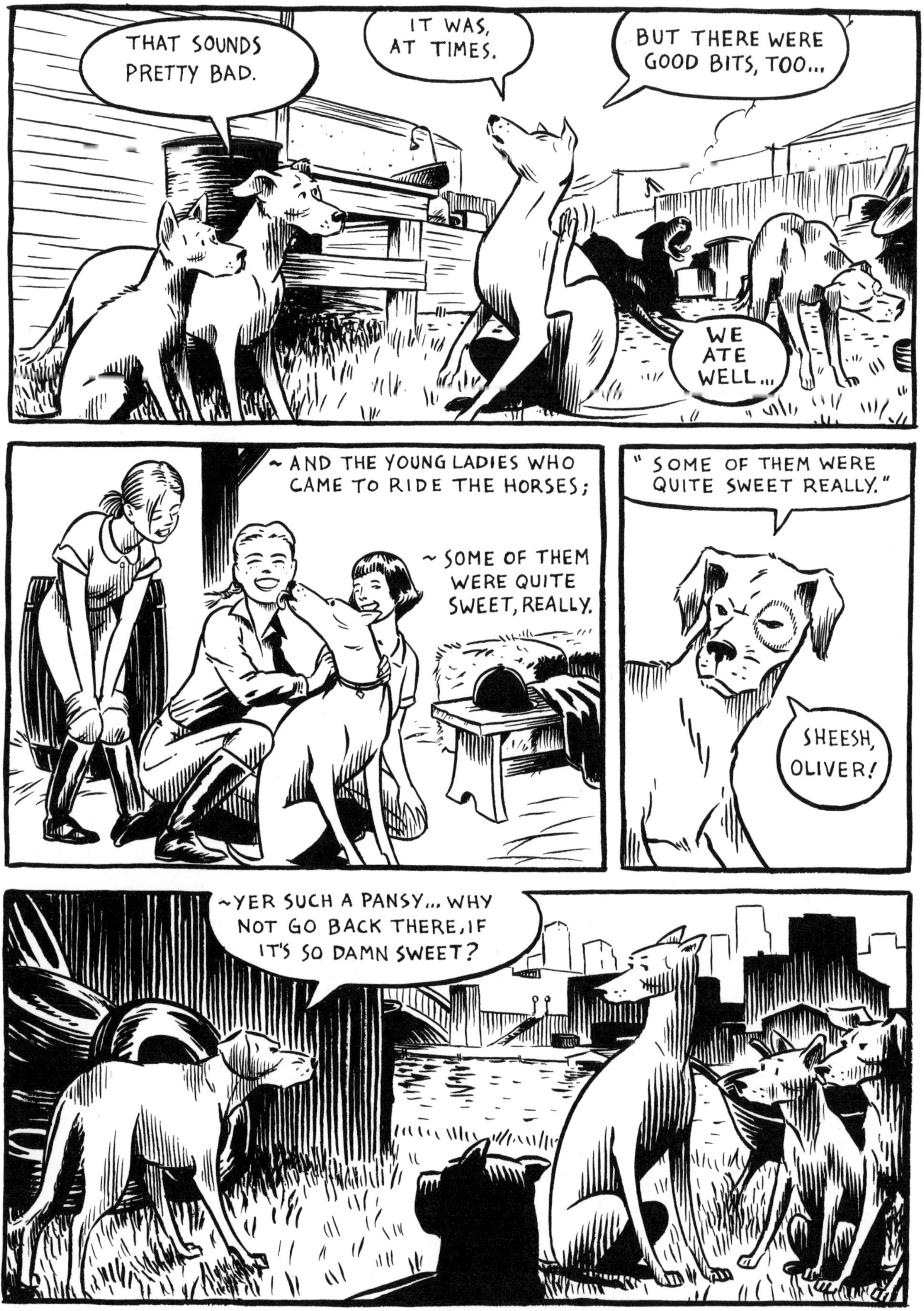
THAT SOUNDS PRETTY BAD.
IT WAS, AT TIMES.
BUT THERE WERE GOOD BITS, TOO...
WE ATE WELL...
~AND THE YOUNG LADIES WHO CAME TO RIDE THE HORSES;
~SOME OF THEM WERE QUITE SWEET, REALLY.
" SOME OF THEM WERE QUITE SWEET REALLY."
SHEESH, OLIVER!
~YER SUCH A PANSY... WHY NOT GO BACK THERE, IF IT'S SO DAMN SWEET?

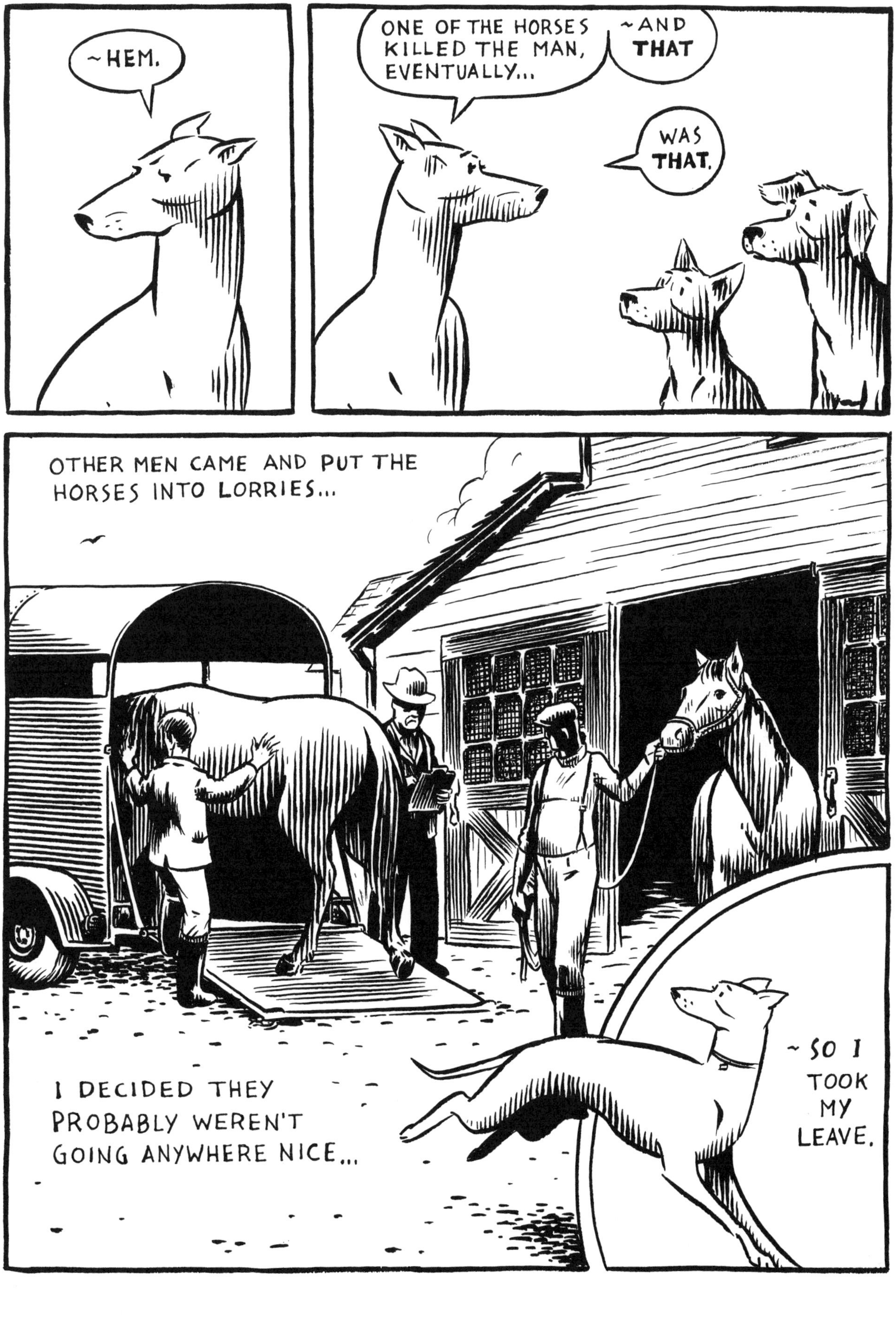
~HEM.
ONE OF THE HORSES KILLED THE MAN, EVENTUALLY...
~AND **THAT**
WAS **THAT**.
OTHER MEN CAME AND PUT THE HORSES INTO LORRIES...
I DECIDED THEY PROBABLY WEREN'T GOING ANYWHERE NICE...
~SO I TOOK MY LEAVE.

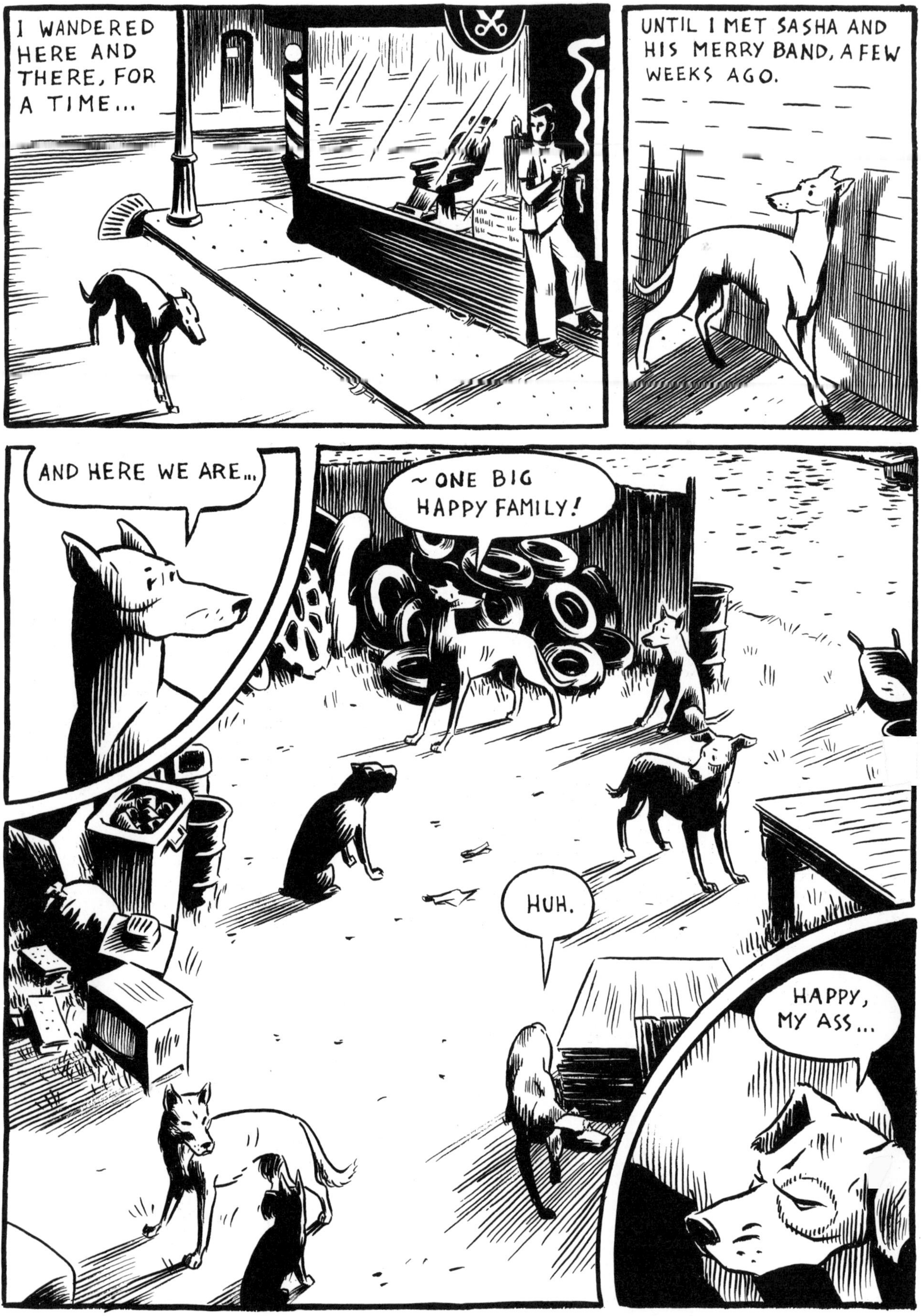
I WANDERED HERE AND THERE, FOR A TIME...
UNTIL I MET SASHA AND HIS MERRY BAND, A FEW WEEKS AGO.
AND HERE WE ARE...
~ONE BIG HAPPY FAMILY!
HUH.
HAPPY, MY ASS...

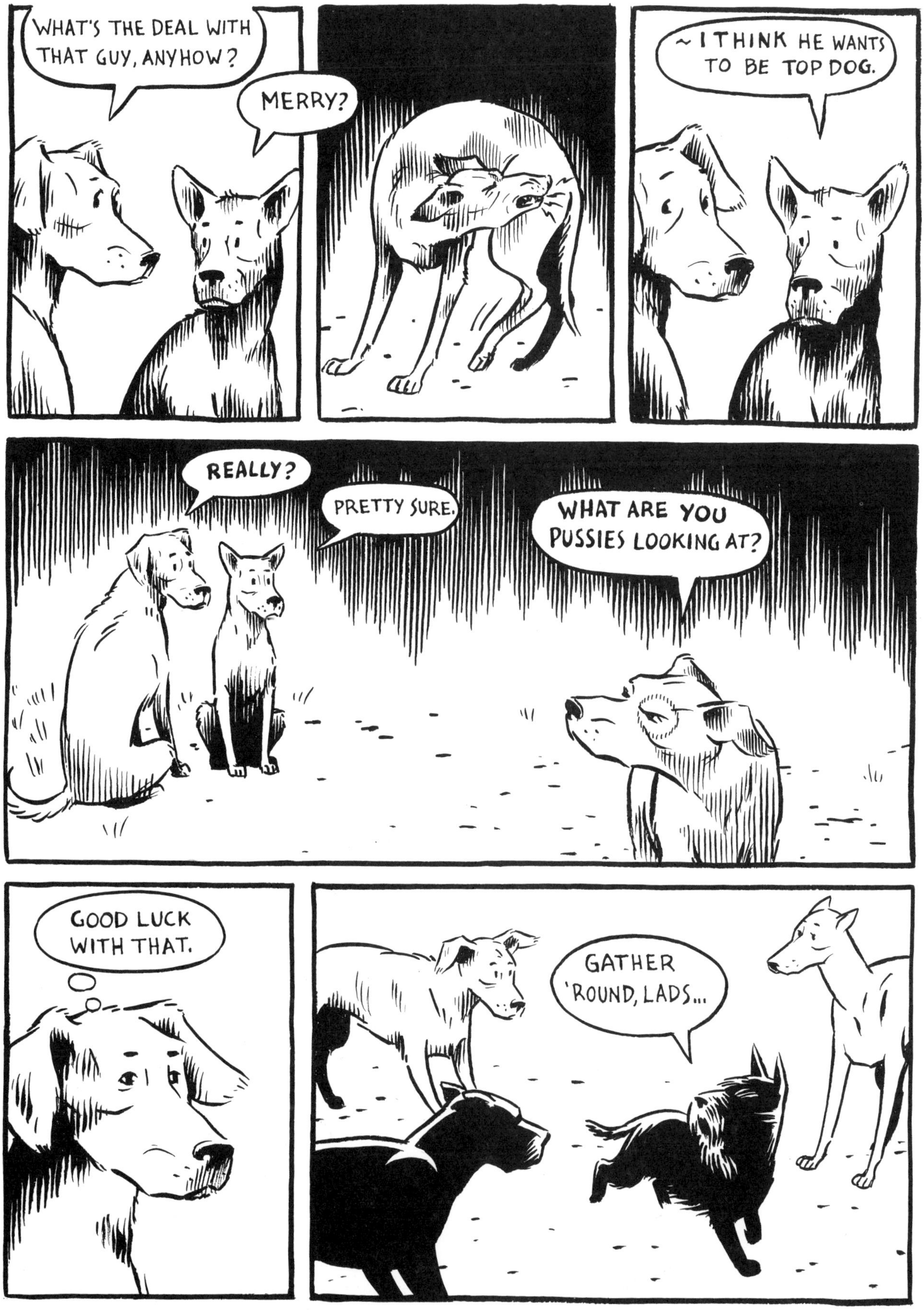
WHAT'S THE DEAL WITH THAT GUY, ANYHOW?
MERRY?
~I THINK HE WANTS TO BE TOP DOG.
REALLY?
PRETTY SURE.
WHAT ARE YOU PUSSIES LOOKING AT?
GOOD LUCK WITH THAT.
GATHER 'ROUND, LADS...

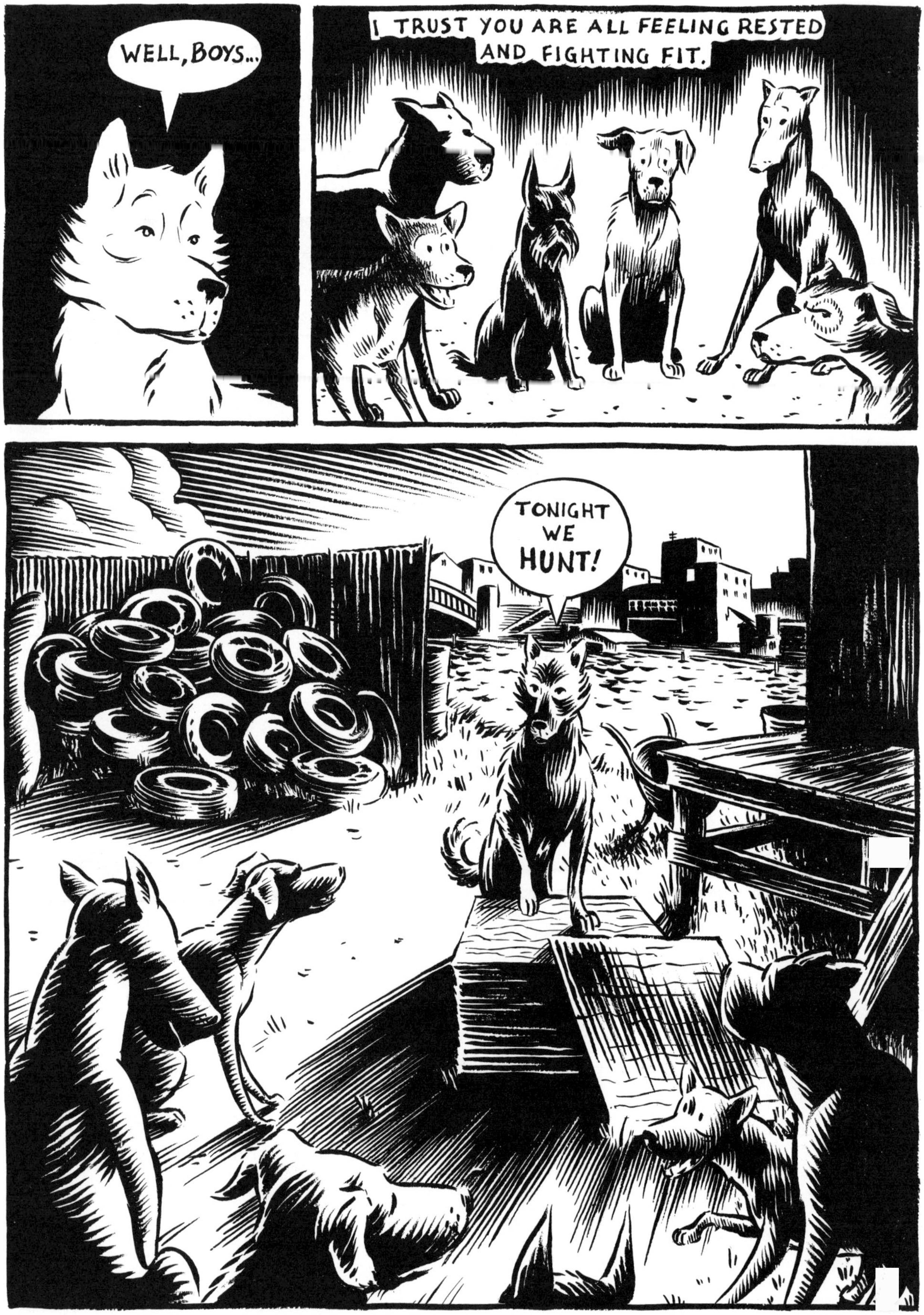
WELL, BOYS...
I TRUST YOU ARE ALL FEELING RESTED AND FIGHTING FIT.
TONIGHT WE HUNT!

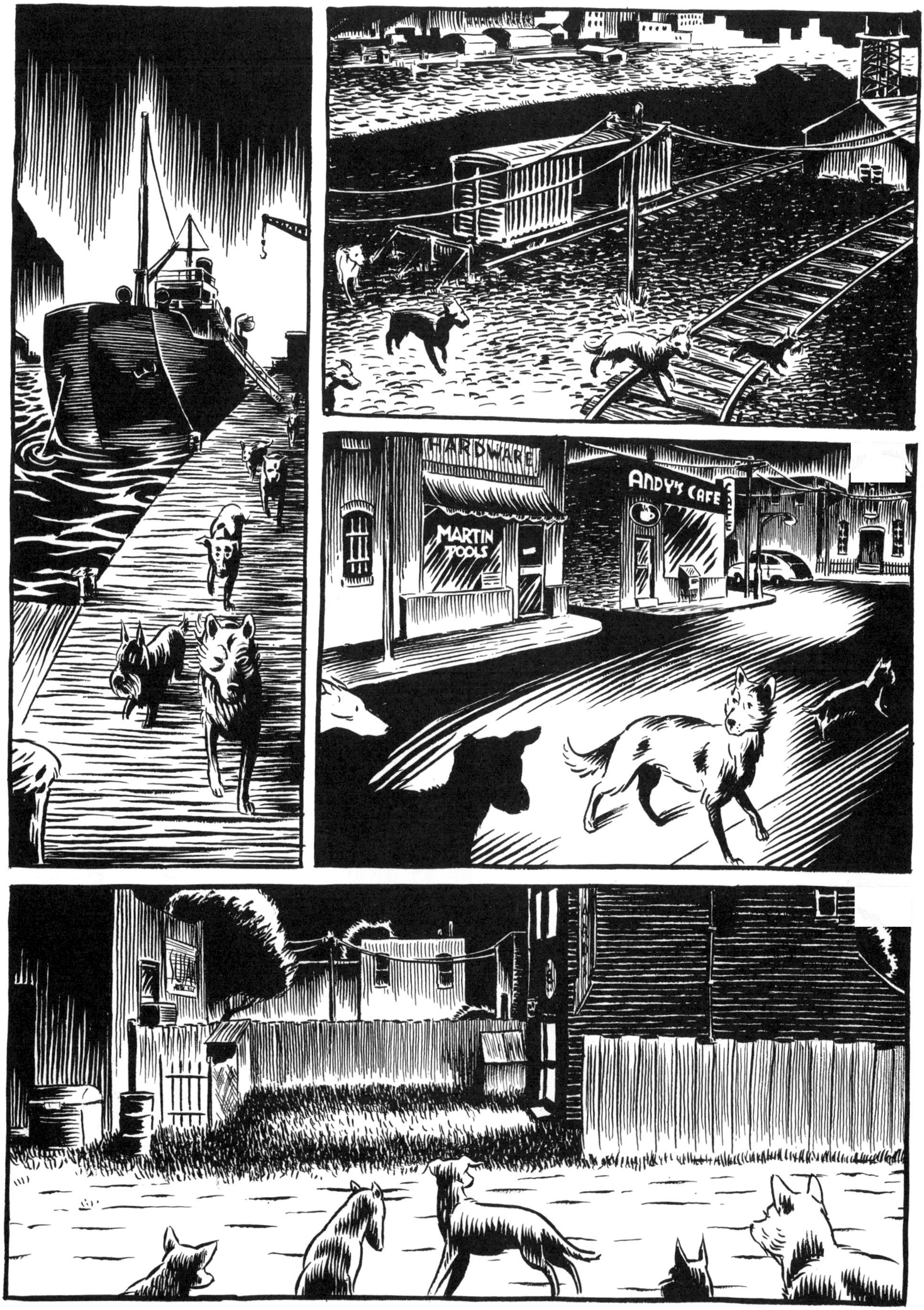
HARDWARE
MARTIN TOOLS
ANDY'S CAFE

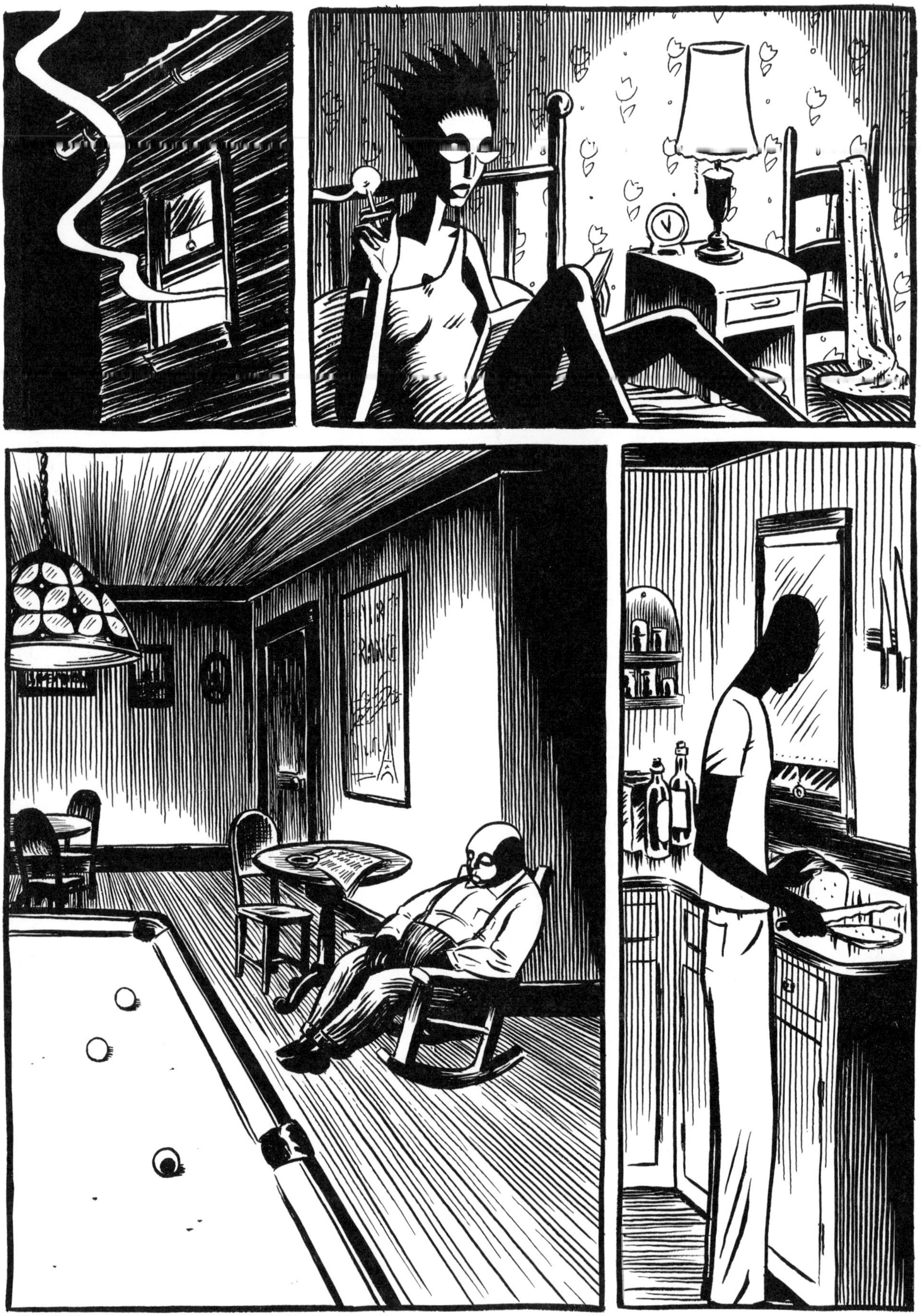

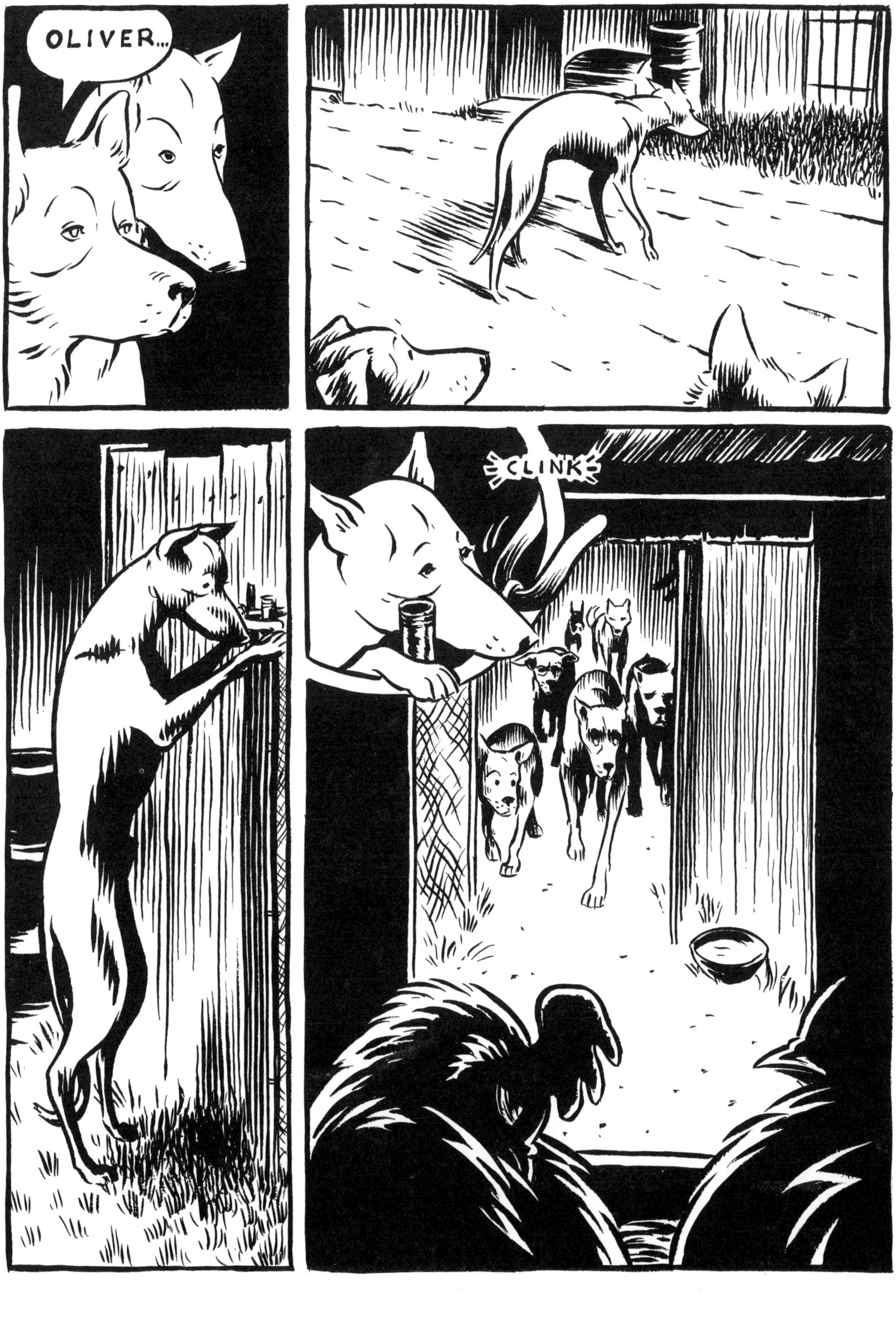
OLIVER...
CLINK

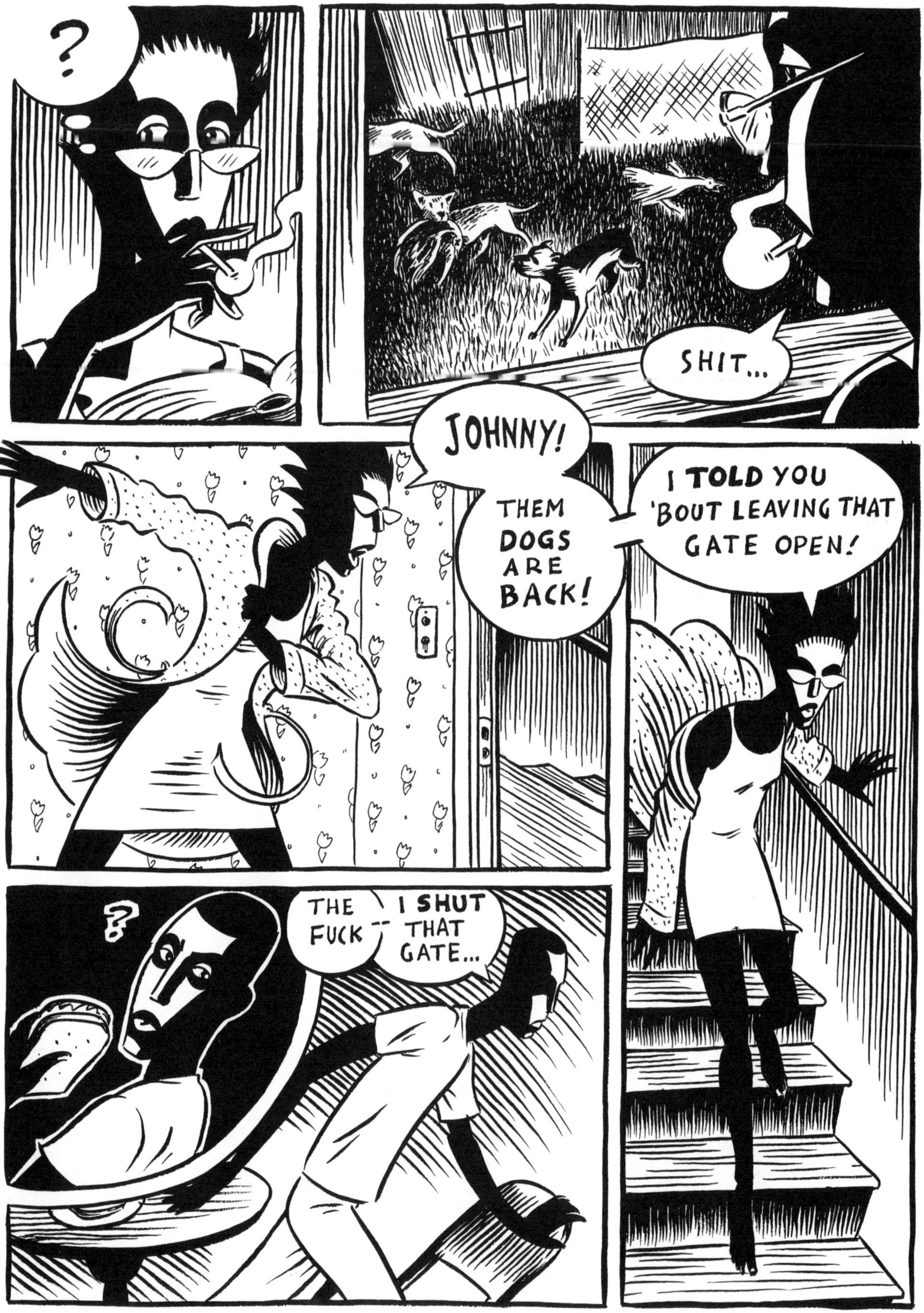
?
SHIT...
JOHNNY!
THEM DOGS ARE BACK!
I TOLD YOU 'BOUT LEAVING THAT GATE OPEN!
?
THE FUCK --
I SHUT THAT GATE...

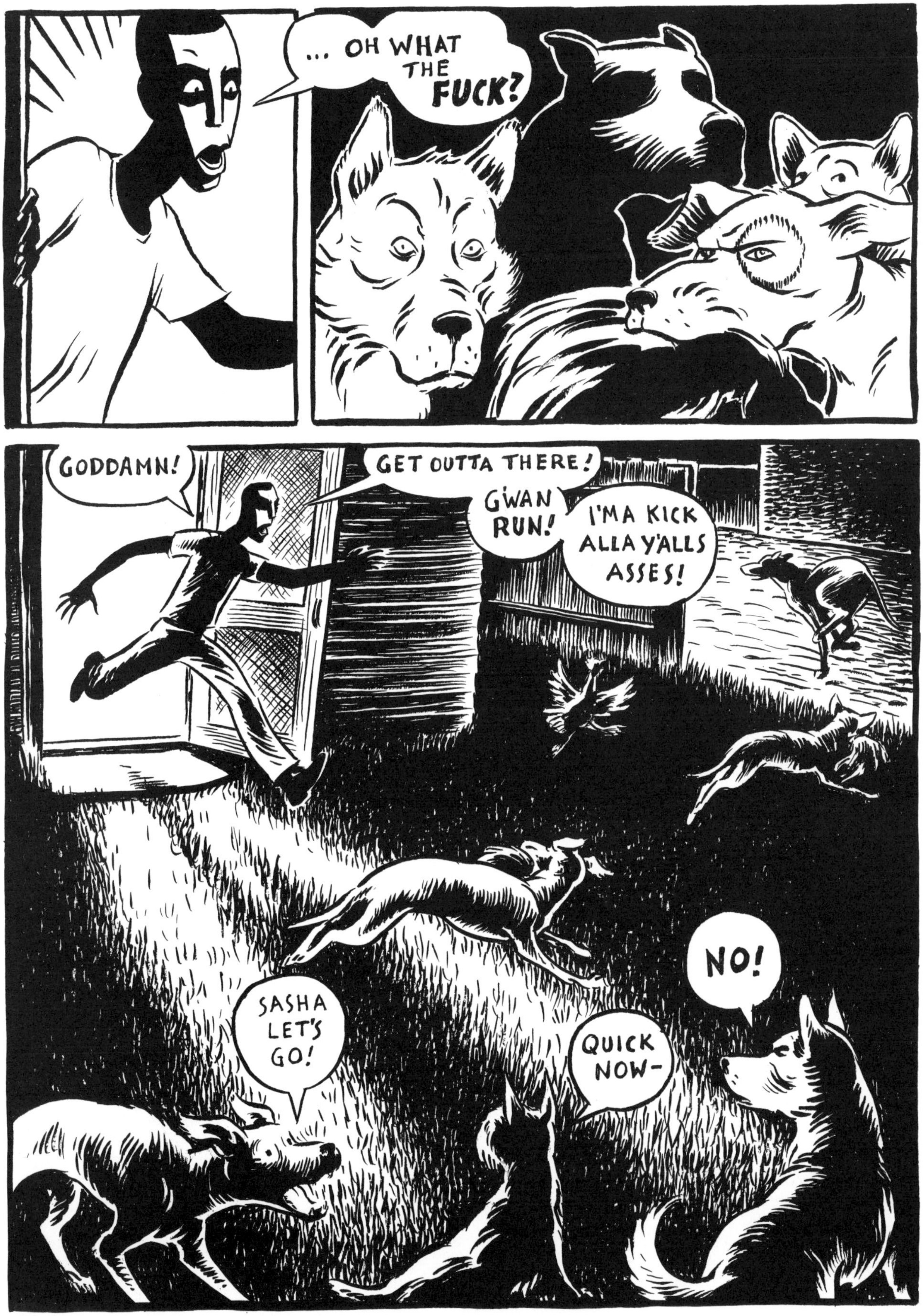
... OH WHAT THE FUCK?
GODDAMN!
GET OUTTA THERE!
GWAN RUN!
I'MA KICK ALLA Y'ALLS ASSES!
SASHA LET'S GO!
QUICK NOW-
NO!

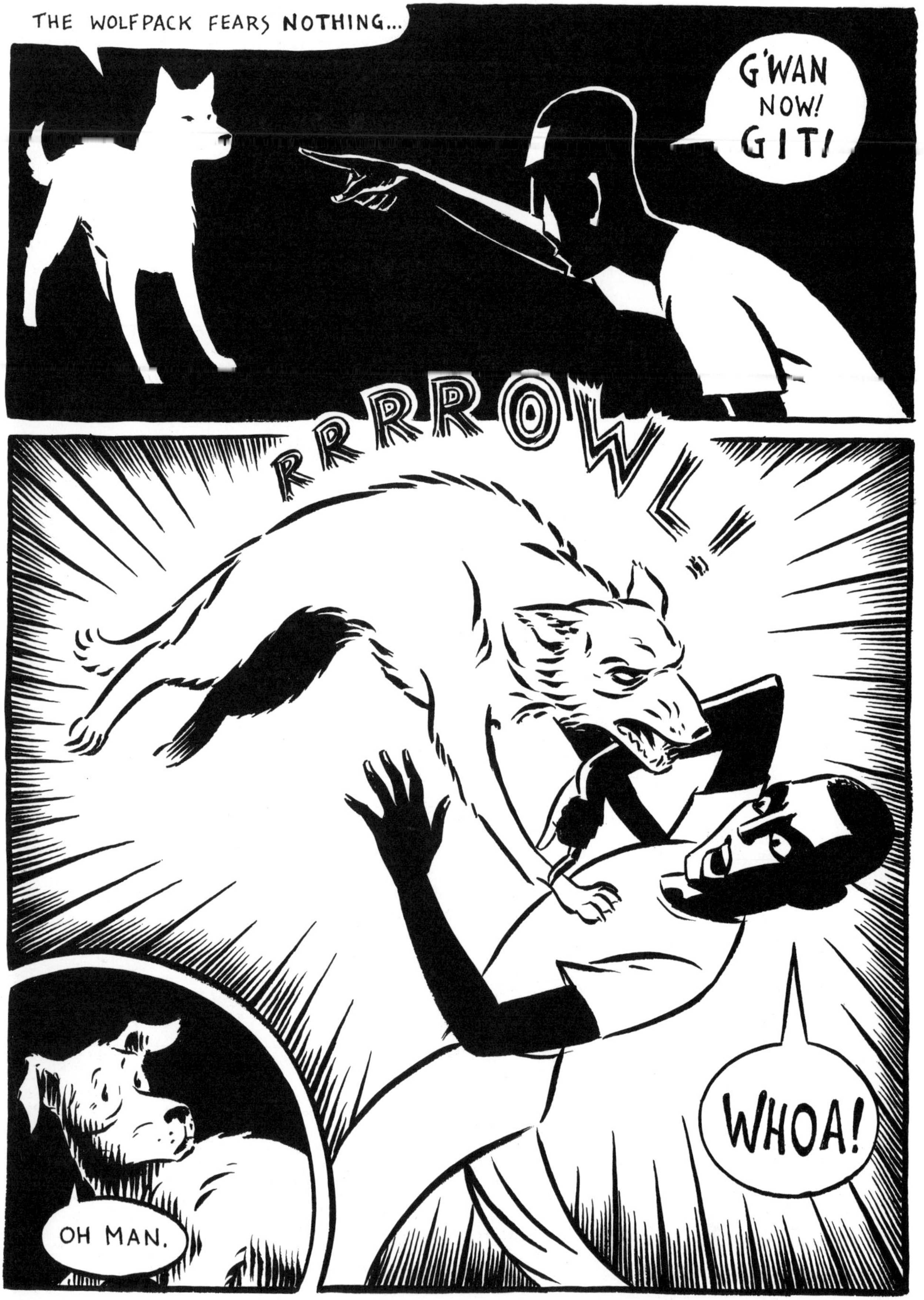
THE WOLFPACK FEARS NOTHING...
G'WAN NOW! GIT!
RRRROWL!!
WHOA!
OH MAN.

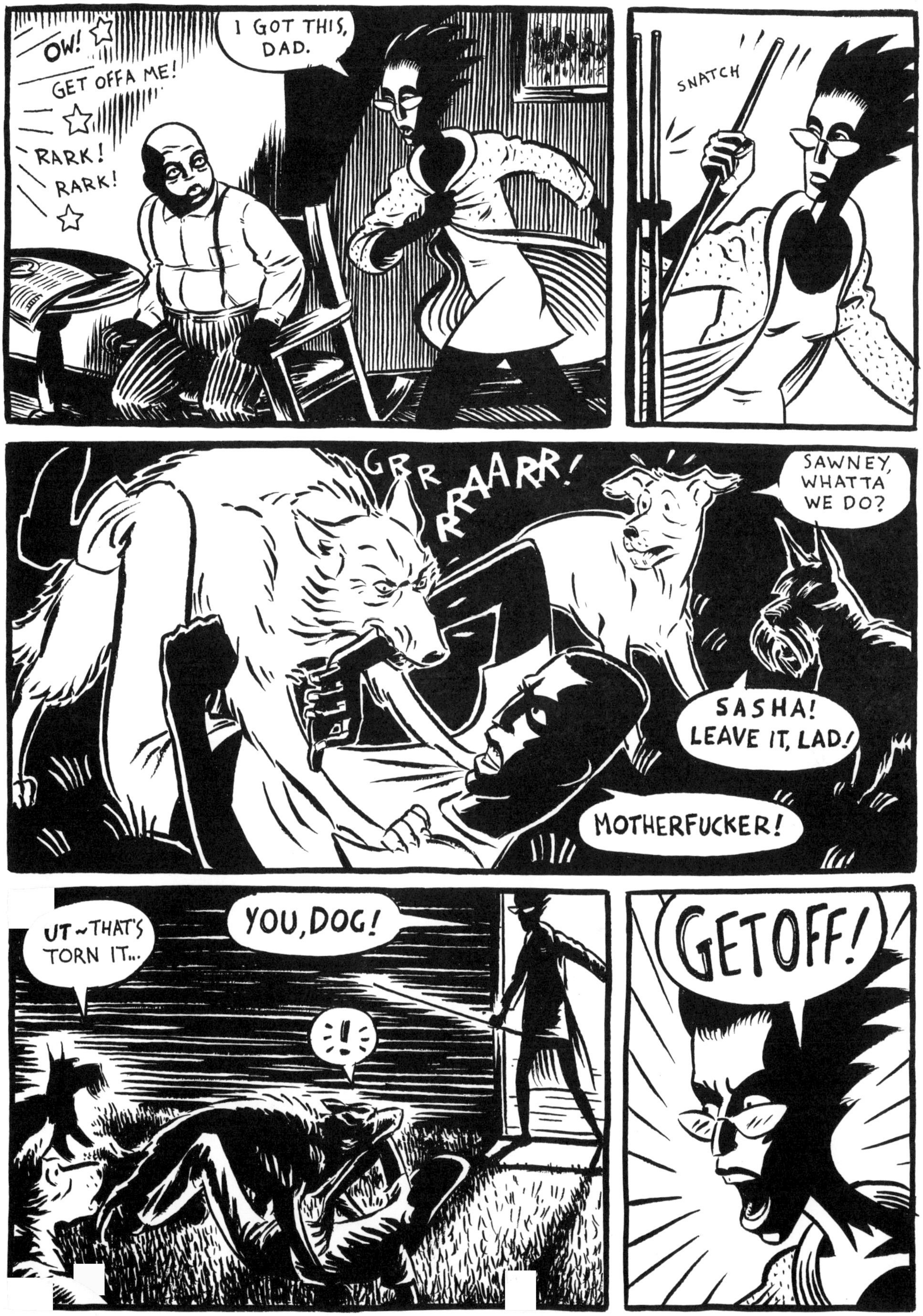
OW!
GET OFFA ME!
RARK!
RARK!
I GOT THIS, DAD.
SNATCH
GRRR
RRAARR!
SAWNEY, WHATTA WE DO?
SASHA! LEAVE IT, LAD!
MOTHERFUCKER!
UT~THAT'S TORN IT...
YOU, DOG!
!
GETOFF!

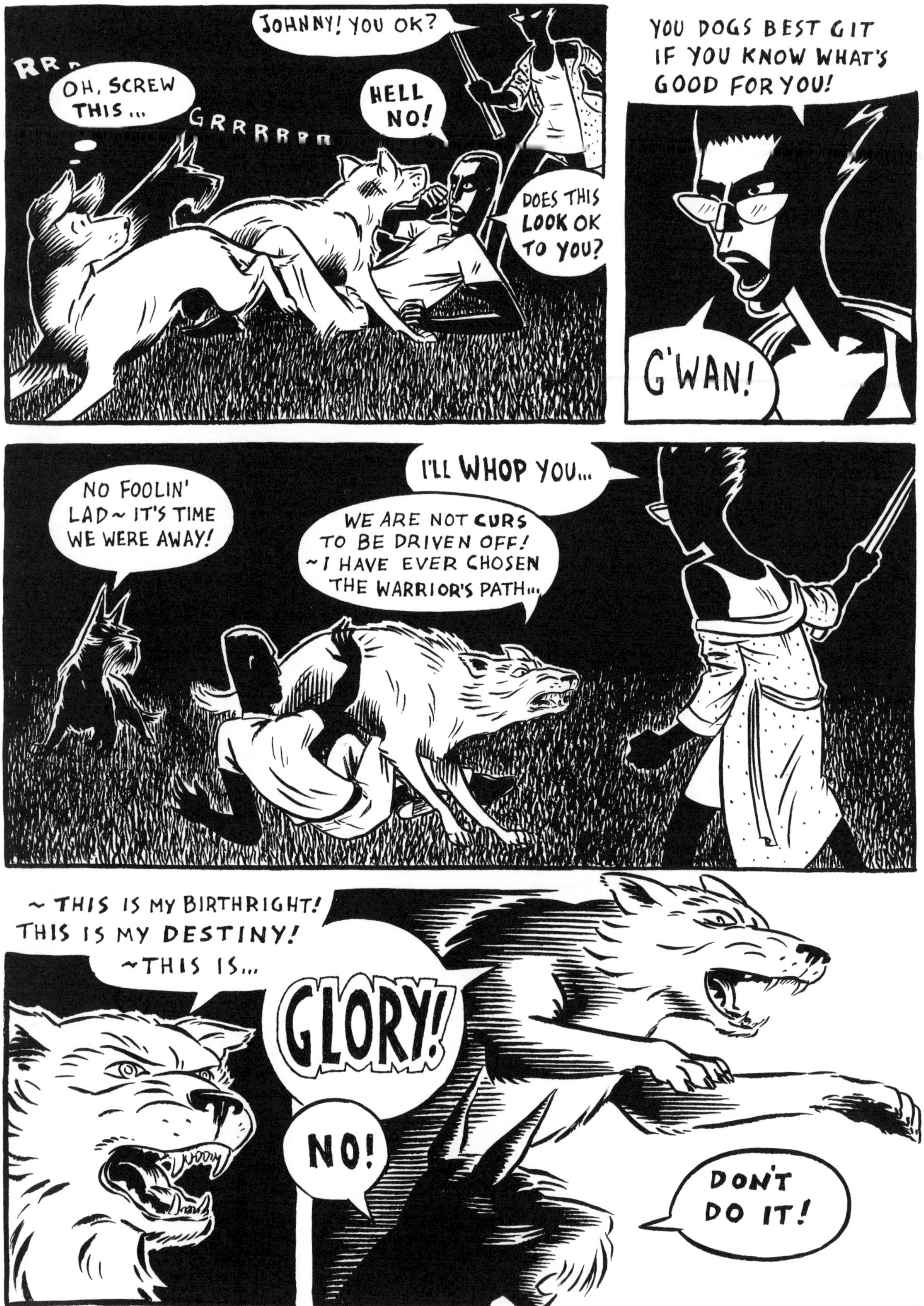
RRR
OH, SCREW THIS...
GRRRRRRR
JOHNNY! YOU OK?
HELL NO!
DOES THIS LOOK OK TO YOU?
YOU DOGS BEST GIT IF YOU KNOW WHAT'S GOOD FOR YOU!
G'WAN!
NO FOOLIN' LAD ~ IT'S TIME WE WERE AWAY!
I'LL WHOP YOU...
WE ARE NOT CURS TO BE DRIVEN OFF! ~I HAVE EVER CHOSEN THE WARRIOR'S PATH...
~ THIS IS MY BIRTHRIGHT! THIS IS MY DESTINY! ~THIS IS...
GLORY!
NO!
DON'T DO IT!

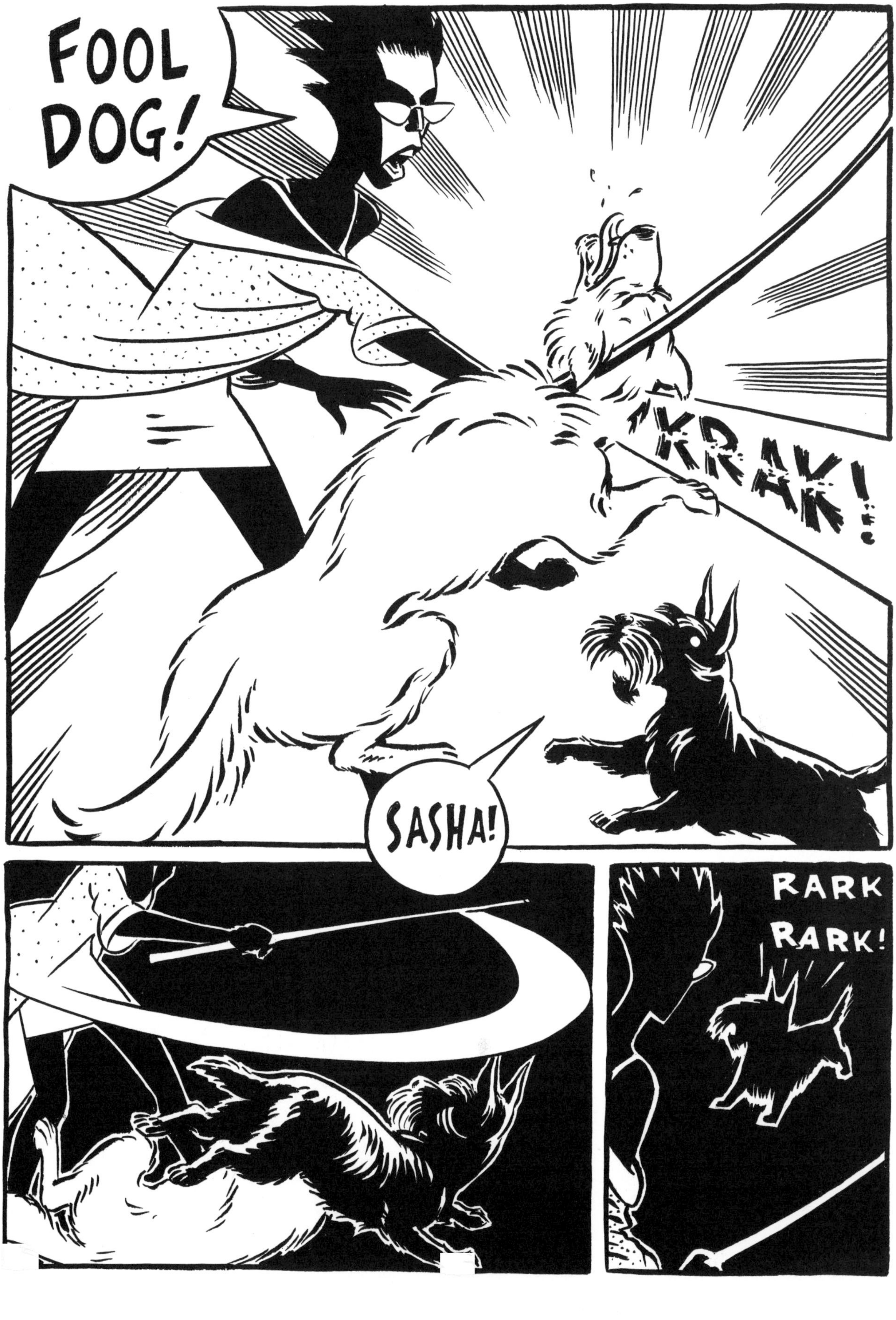
FOOL DOG!
KRAK!
SASHA!
RARK RARK!

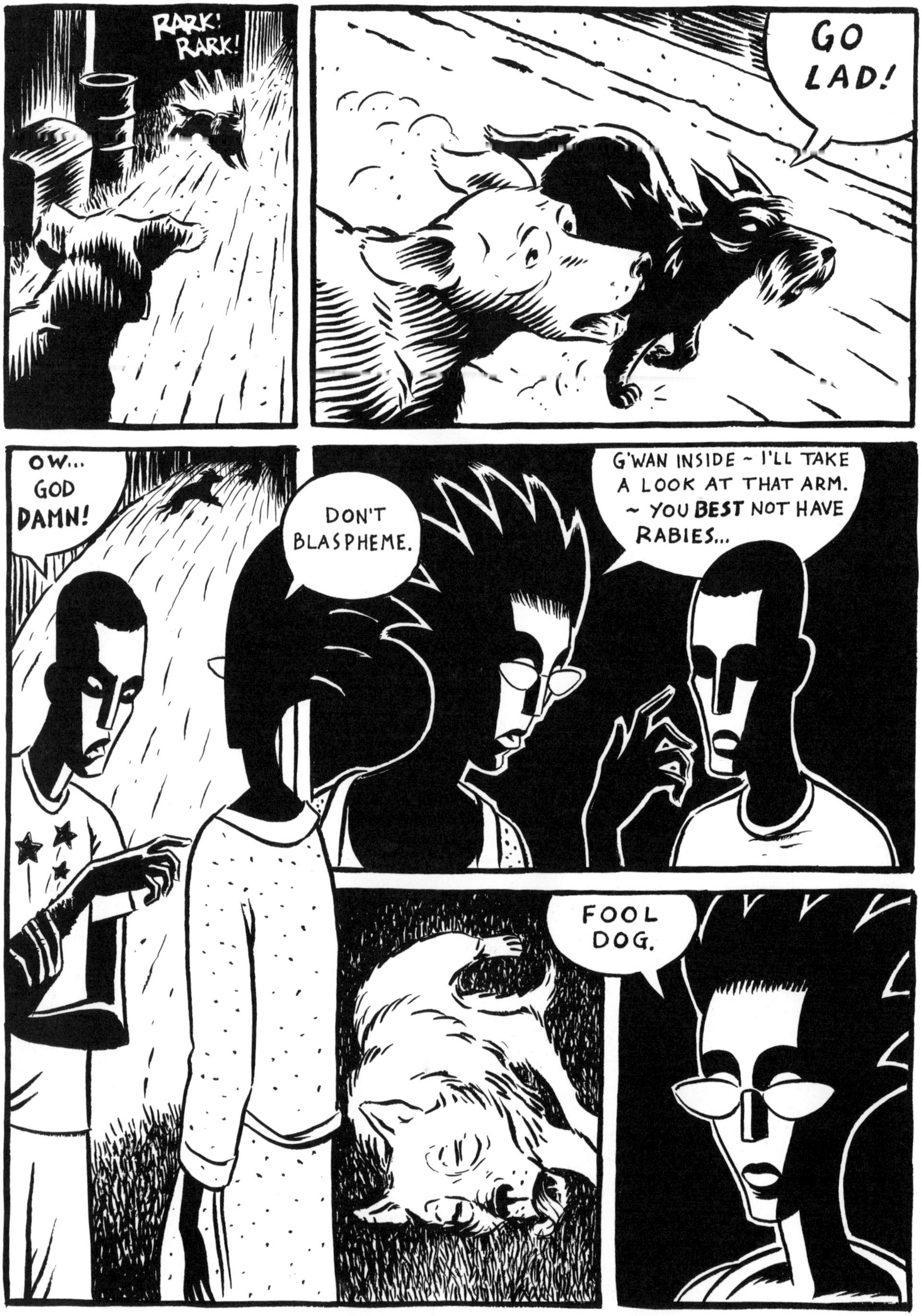
RARK! RARK!
GO LAD!
OW... GOD DAMN!
DON'T BLASPHEME.
G'WAN INSIDE ~ I'LL TAKE A LOOK AT THAT ARM. ~ YOU BEST NOT HAVE RABIES...
FOOL DOG.

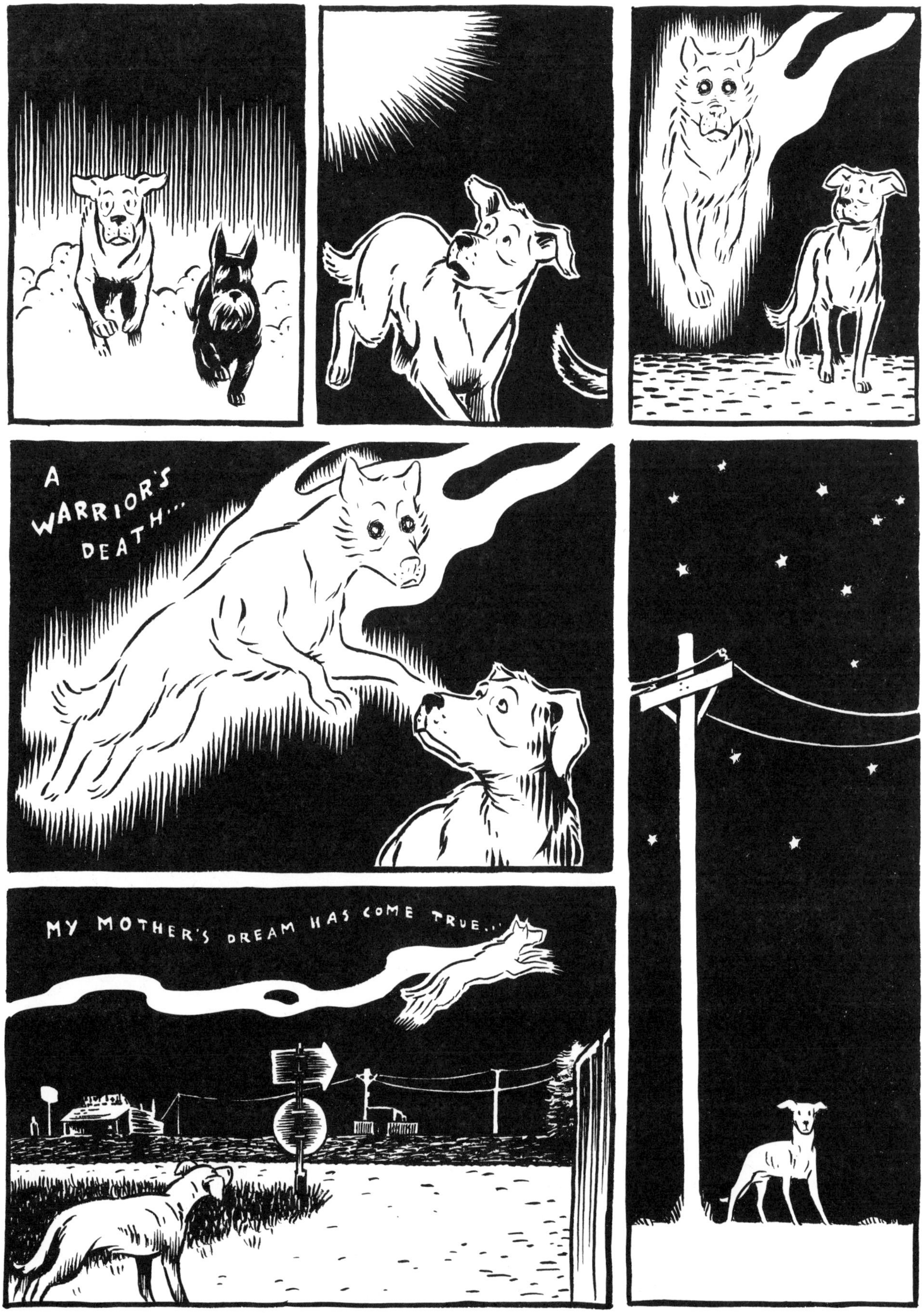
A WARRIOR'S DEATH...
MY MOTHER'S DREAM HAS COME TRUE...

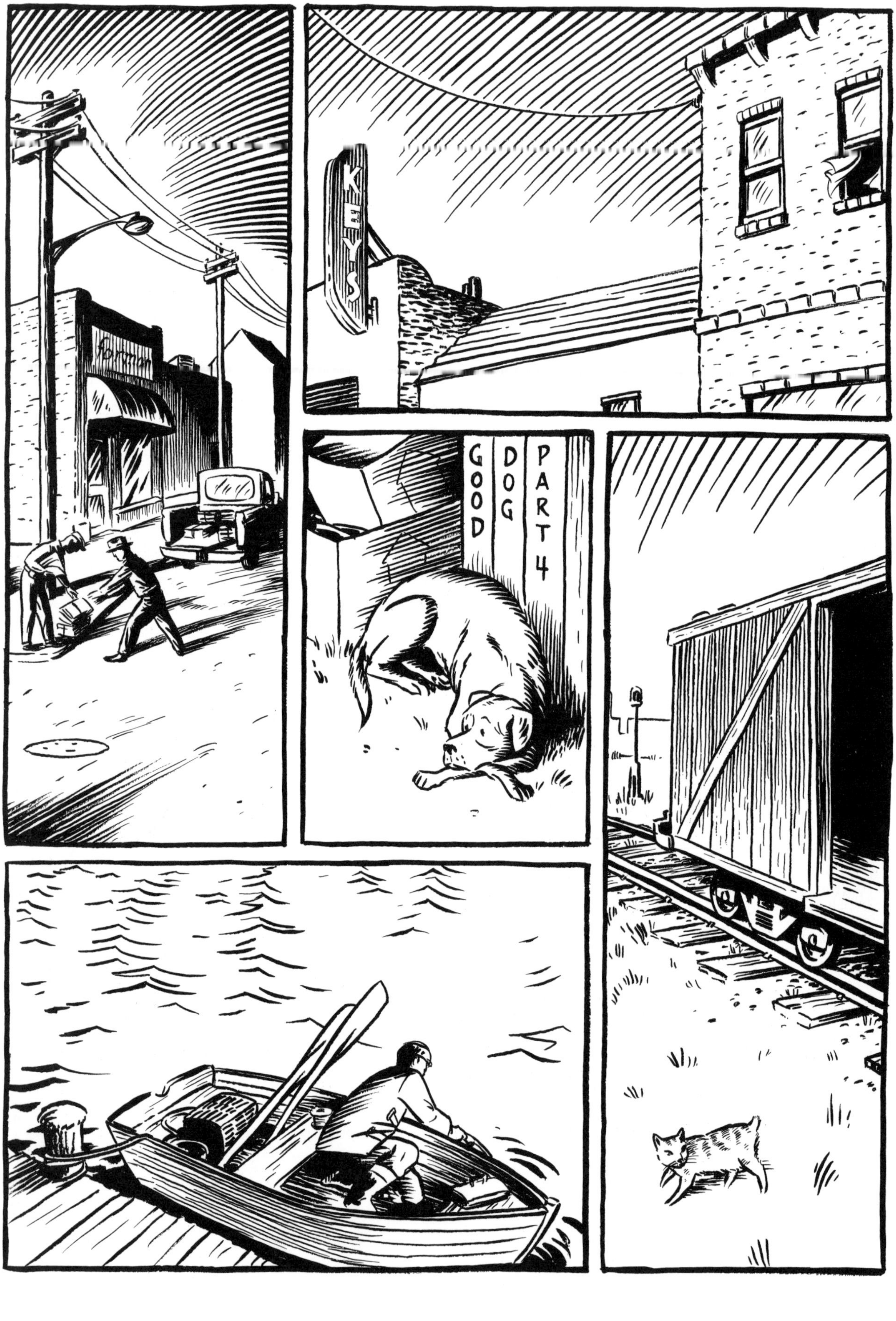
Forman
KEYS
GOOD DOG PART 4

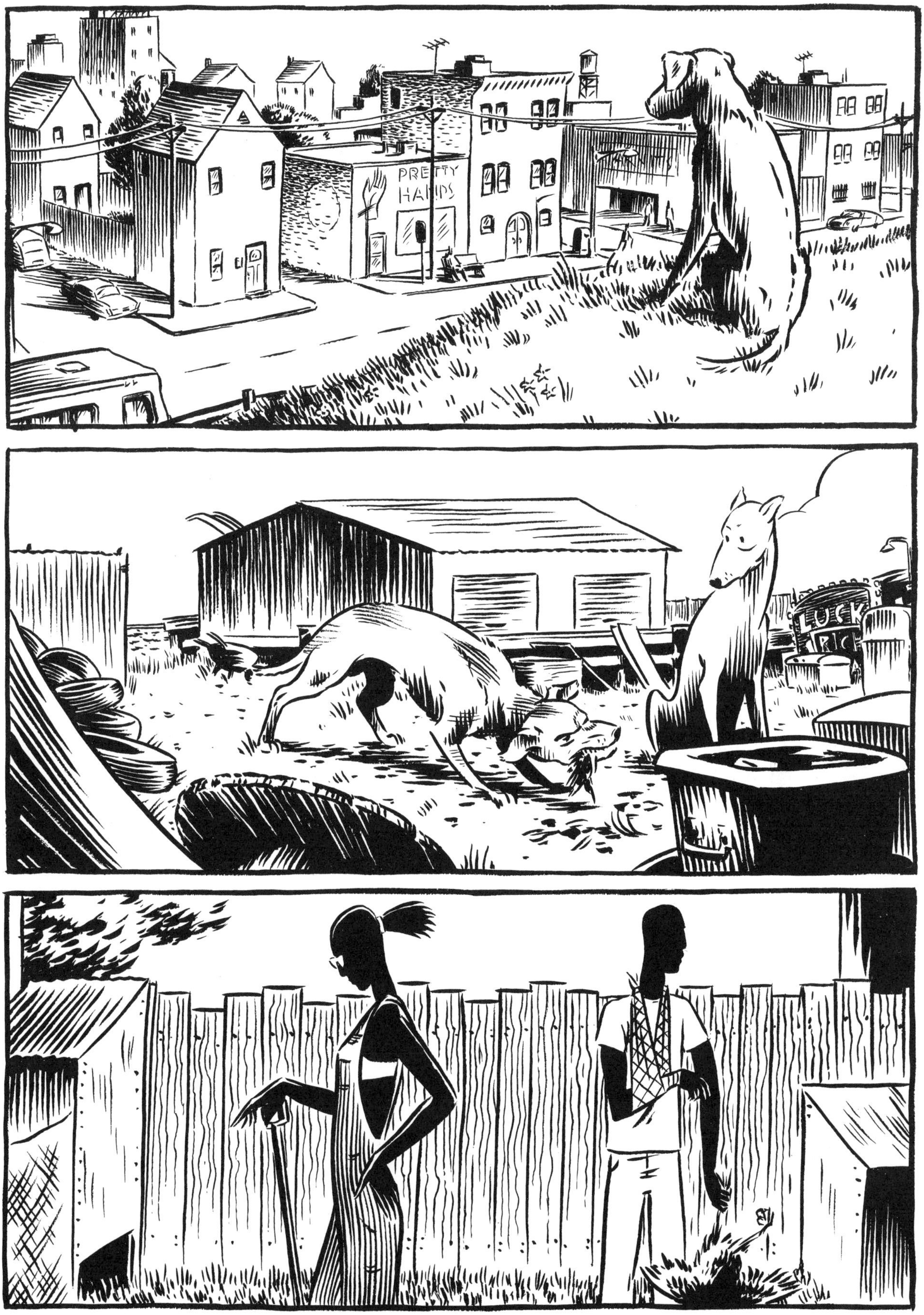
PRETTY HANDS

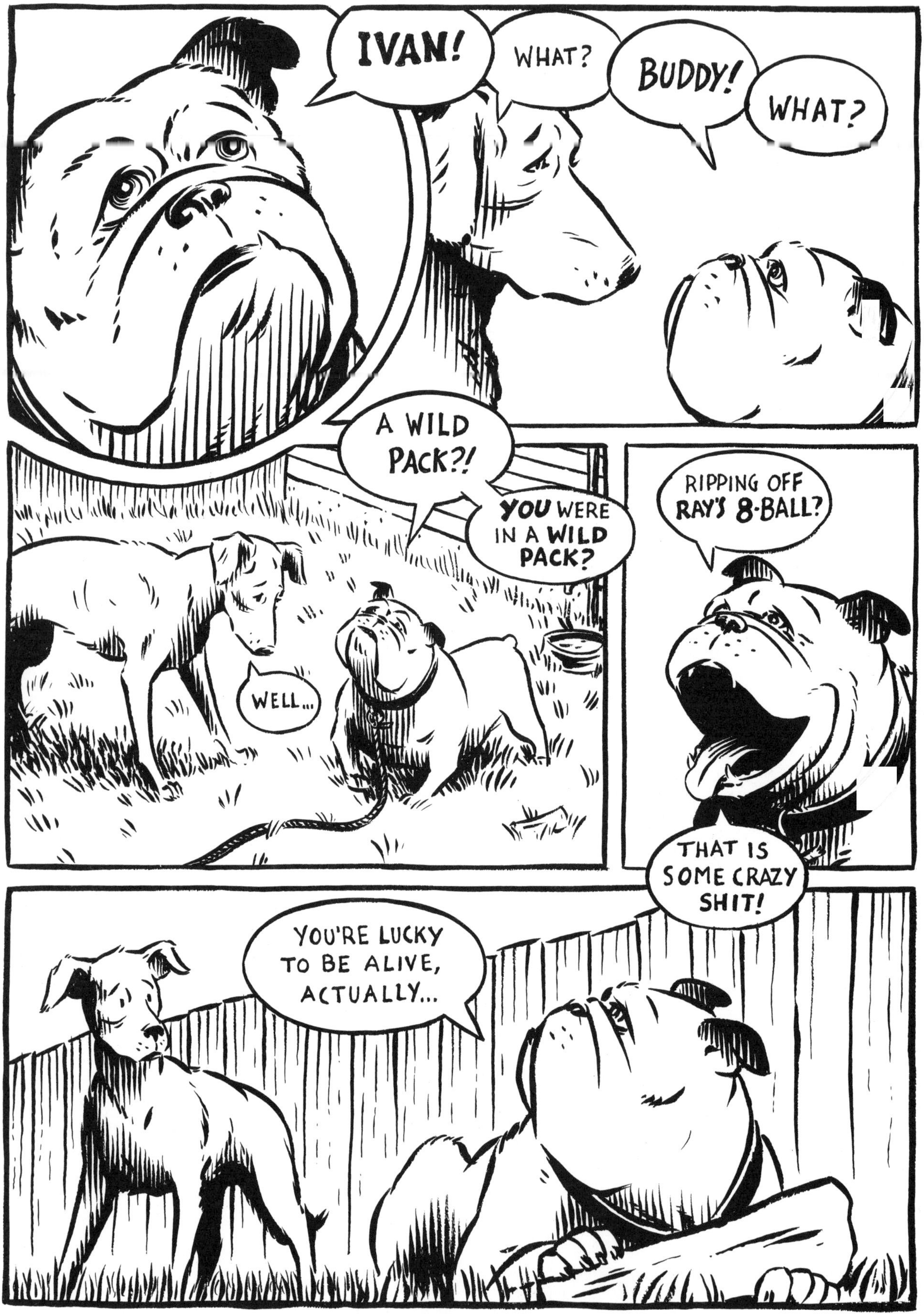
IVAN!
WHAT?
BUDDY!
WHAT?
A WILD PACK?!
YOU WERE IN A WILD PACK?
WELL...
RIPPING OFF RAY'S 8-BALL?
THAT IS SOME CRAZY SHIT!
YOU'RE LUCKY TO BE ALIVE, ACTUALLY...

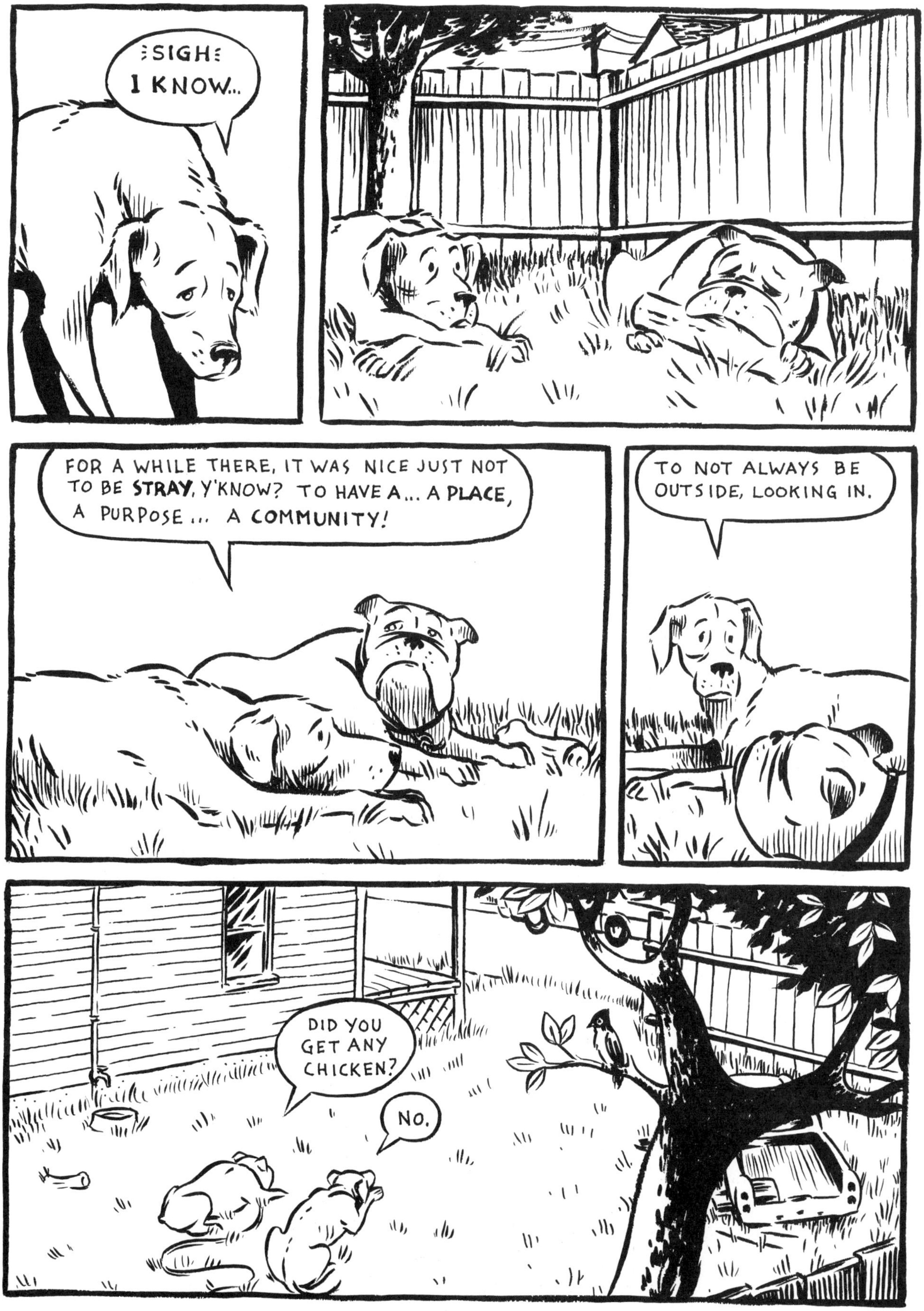
SIGH
I KNOW...
FOR A WHILE THERE, IT WAS NICE JUST NOT TO BE STRAY, Y'KNOW? TO HAVE A... A PLACE, A PURPOSE... A COMMUNITY!
TO NOT ALWAYS BE OUTSIDE, LOOKING IN.
DID YOU GET ANY CHICKEN?
NO.

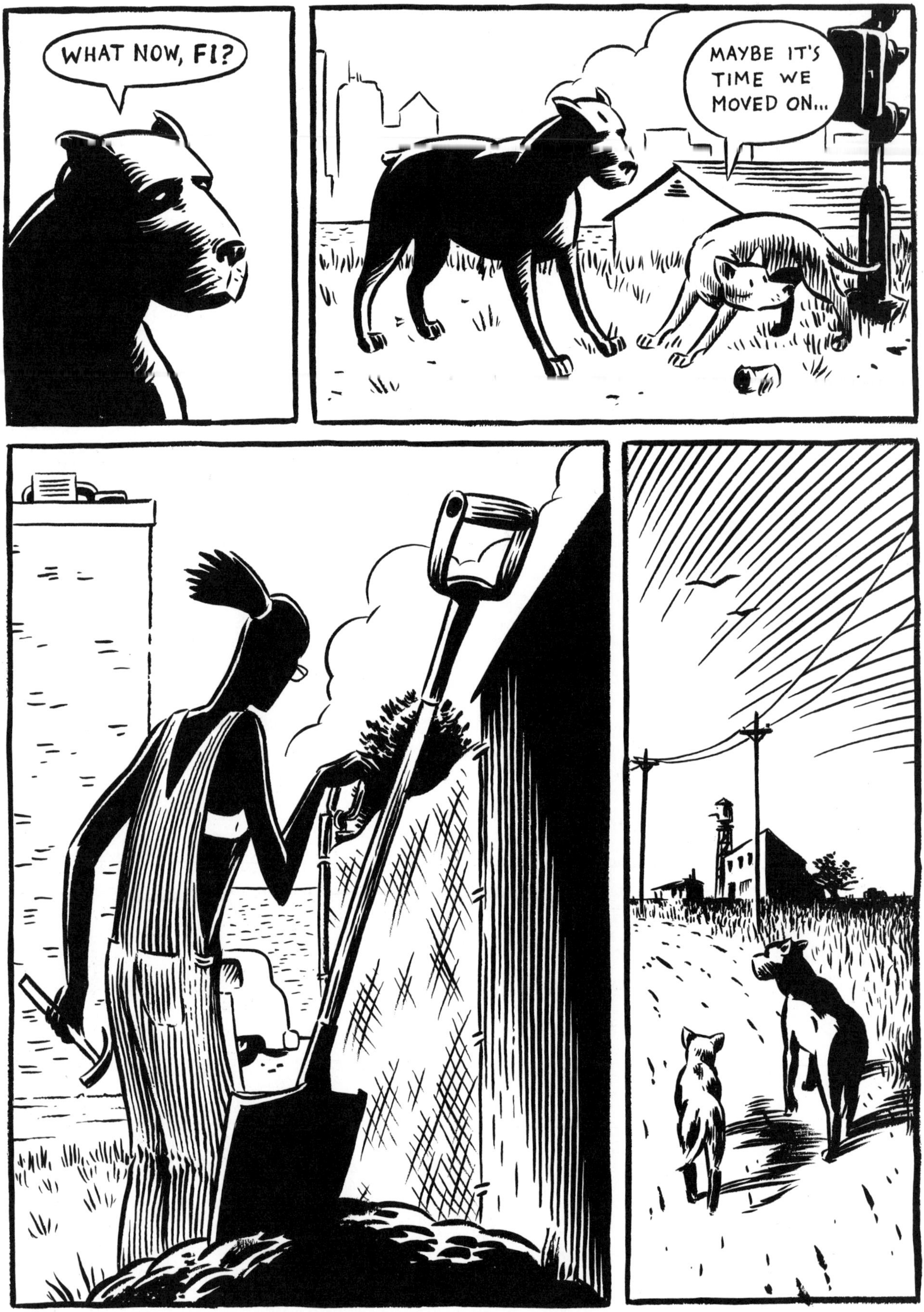
WHAT NOW, FI?
MAYBE IT'S TIME WE MOVED ON...

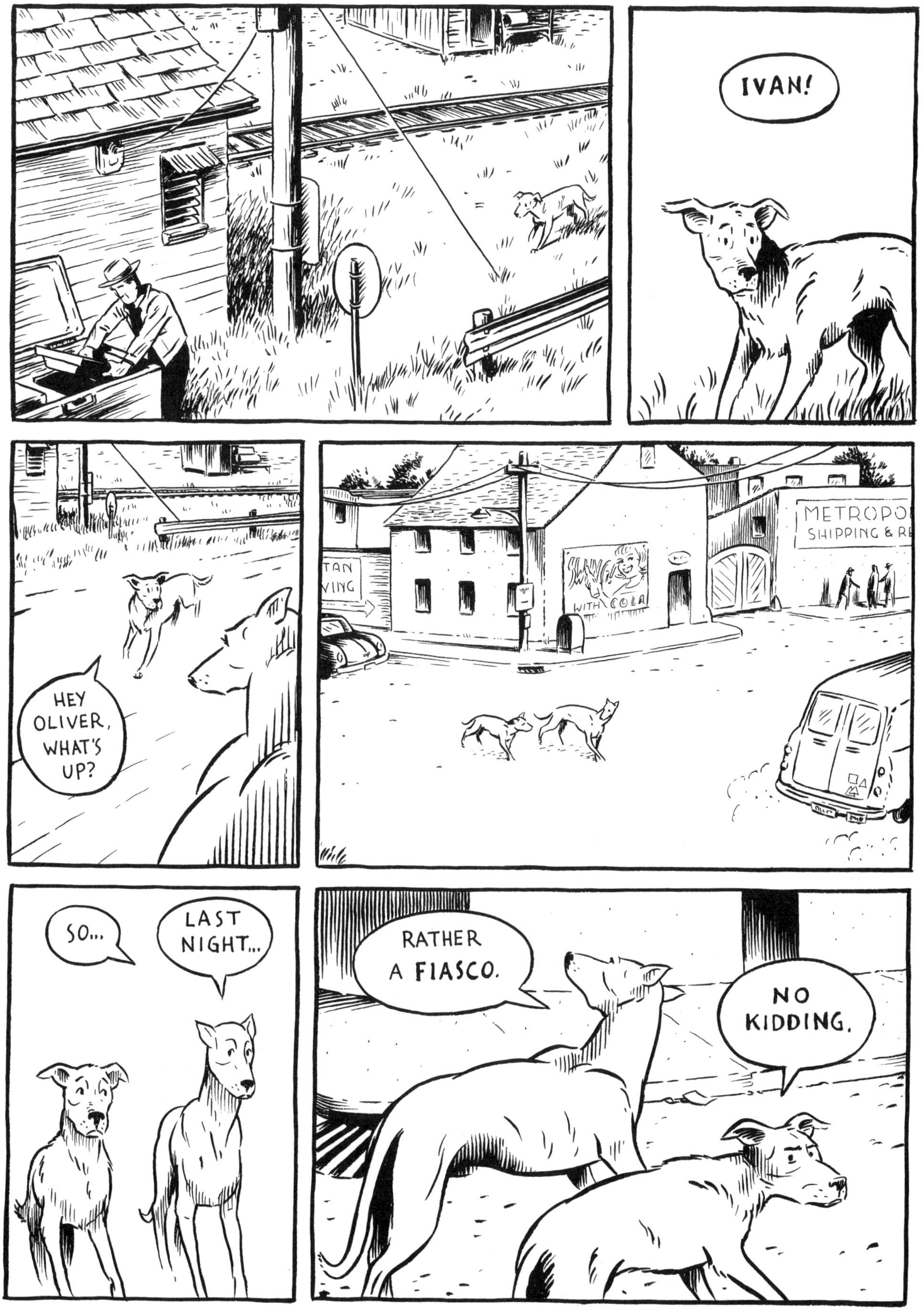
IVAN!
HEY OLIVER, WHAT'S UP?
WITH COLA
SO...
LAST NIGHT...
RATHER A **FIASCO.**
NO KIDDING.

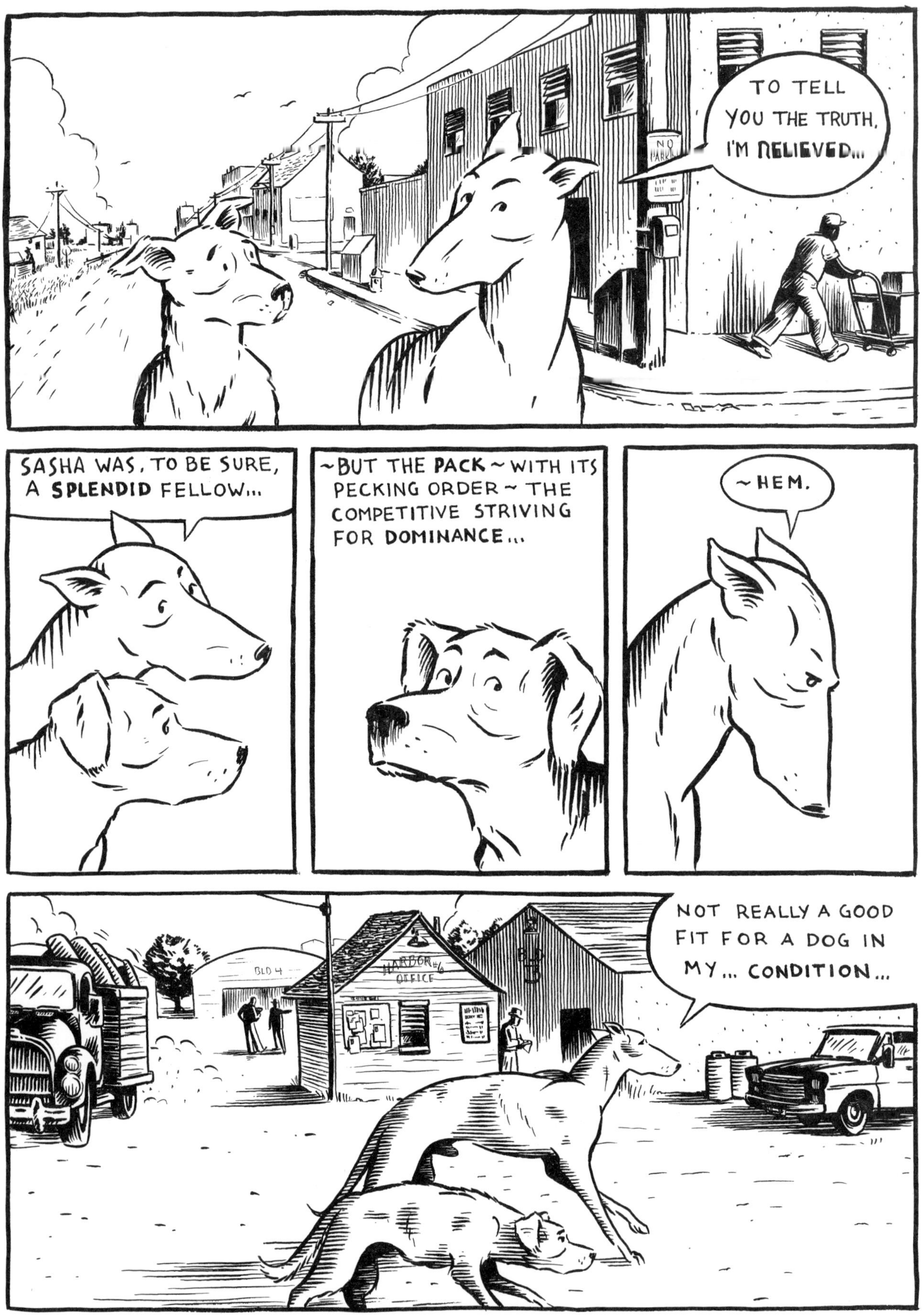
TO TELL YOU THE TRUTH, I'M RELIEVED...
NO PARKING
SASHA WAS, TO BE SURE, A SPLENDID FELLOW...
~BUT THE PACK~ WITH ITS PECKING ORDER~ THE COMPETITIVE STRIVING FOR DOMINANCE...
~HEM.
BLD 4
HARBOR #6 OFFICE
NOT REALLY A GOOD FIT FOR A DOG IN MY... CONDITION...

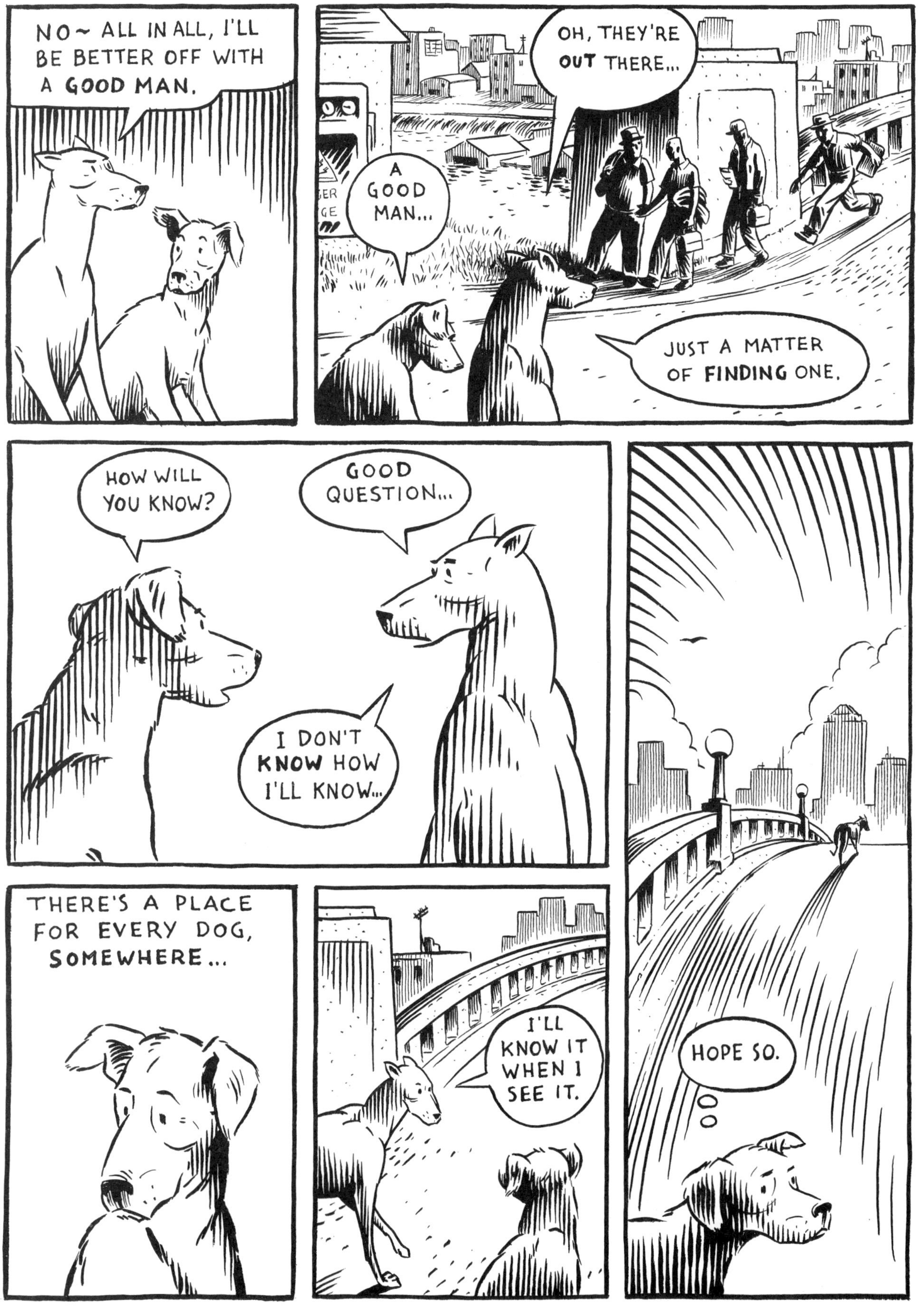
NO~ ALL IN ALL, I'LL BE BETTER OFF WITH A **GOOD MAN**.
OH, THEY'RE **OUT** THERE...
A GOOD MAN...
JUST A MATTER OF **FINDING** ONE.
HOW WILL YOU KNOW?
GOOD QUESTION...
I DON'T **KNOW** HOW I'LL KNOW...
HOPE SO.
THERE'S A PLACE FOR EVERY DOG, **SOMEWHERE**...
I'LL KNOW IT WHEN I SEE IT.

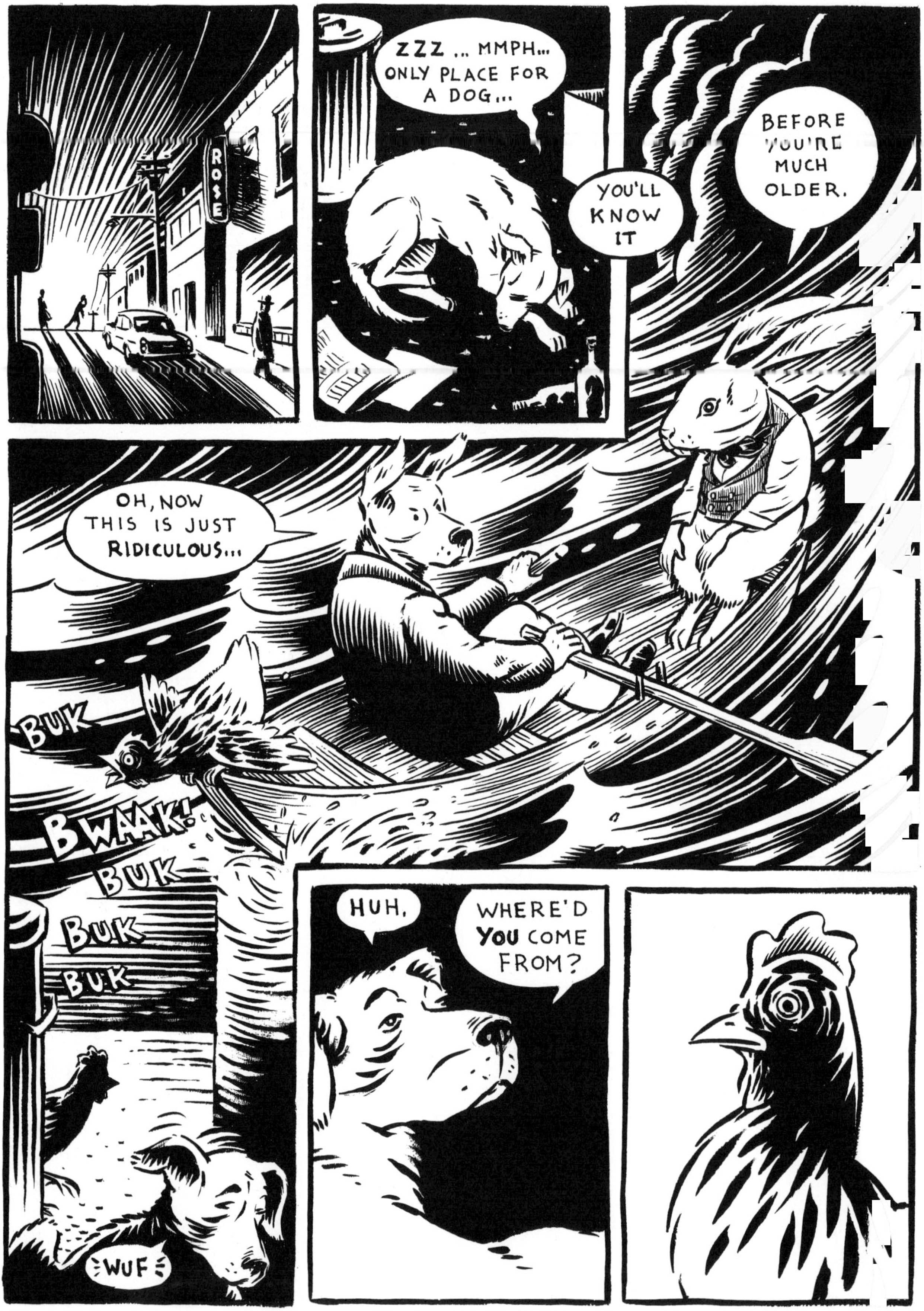
ZZZ ... MMPH... ONLY PLACE FOR A DOG...
YOU'LL KNOW IT
BEFORE YOU'RE MUCH OLDER.
OH, NOW THIS IS JUST RIDICULOUS...
BUK
BWAAK!
BUK
BUK
BUK
WUF
HUH.
WHERE'D YOU COME FROM?

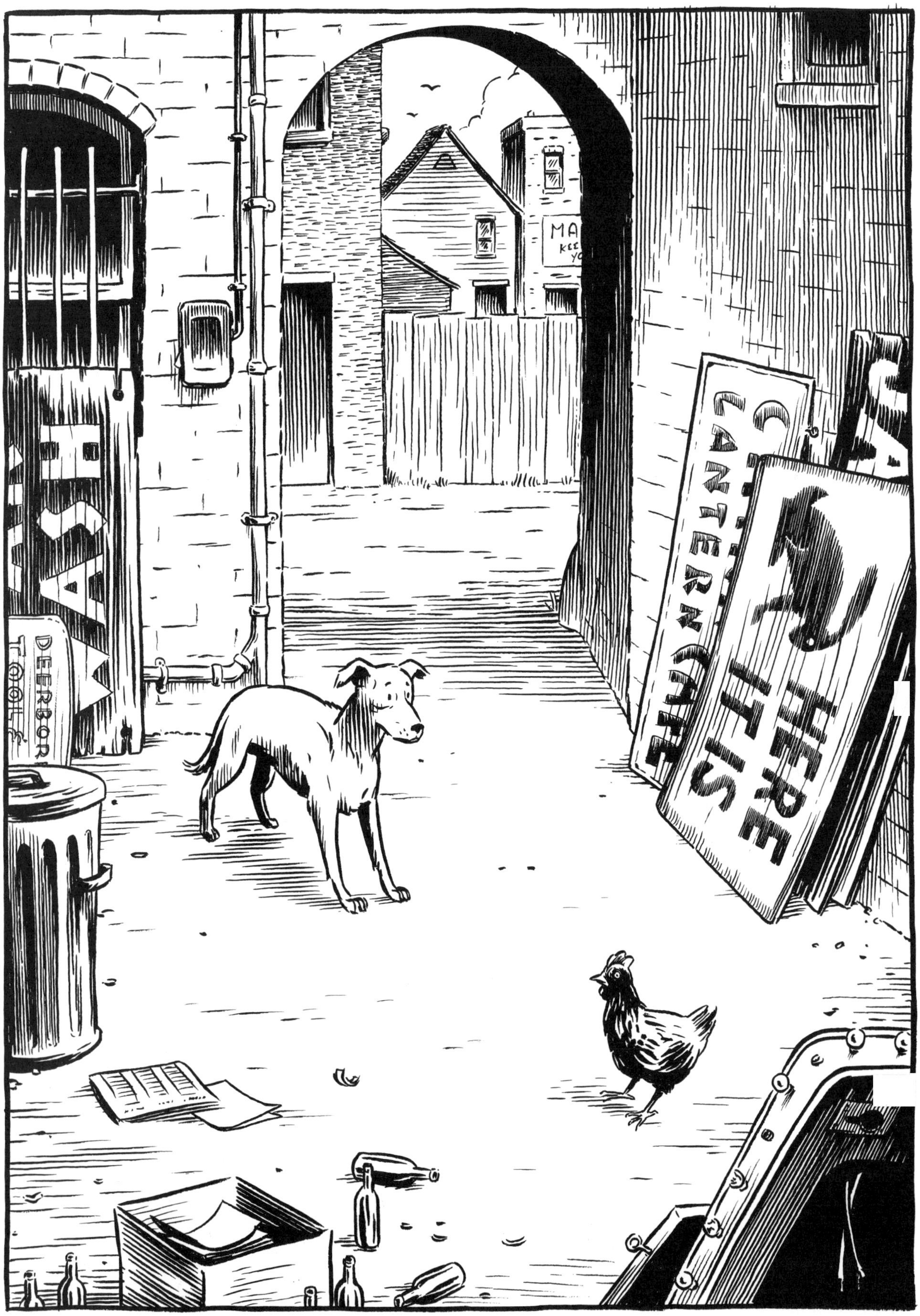
LANTERN CAFE
HERE IT IS

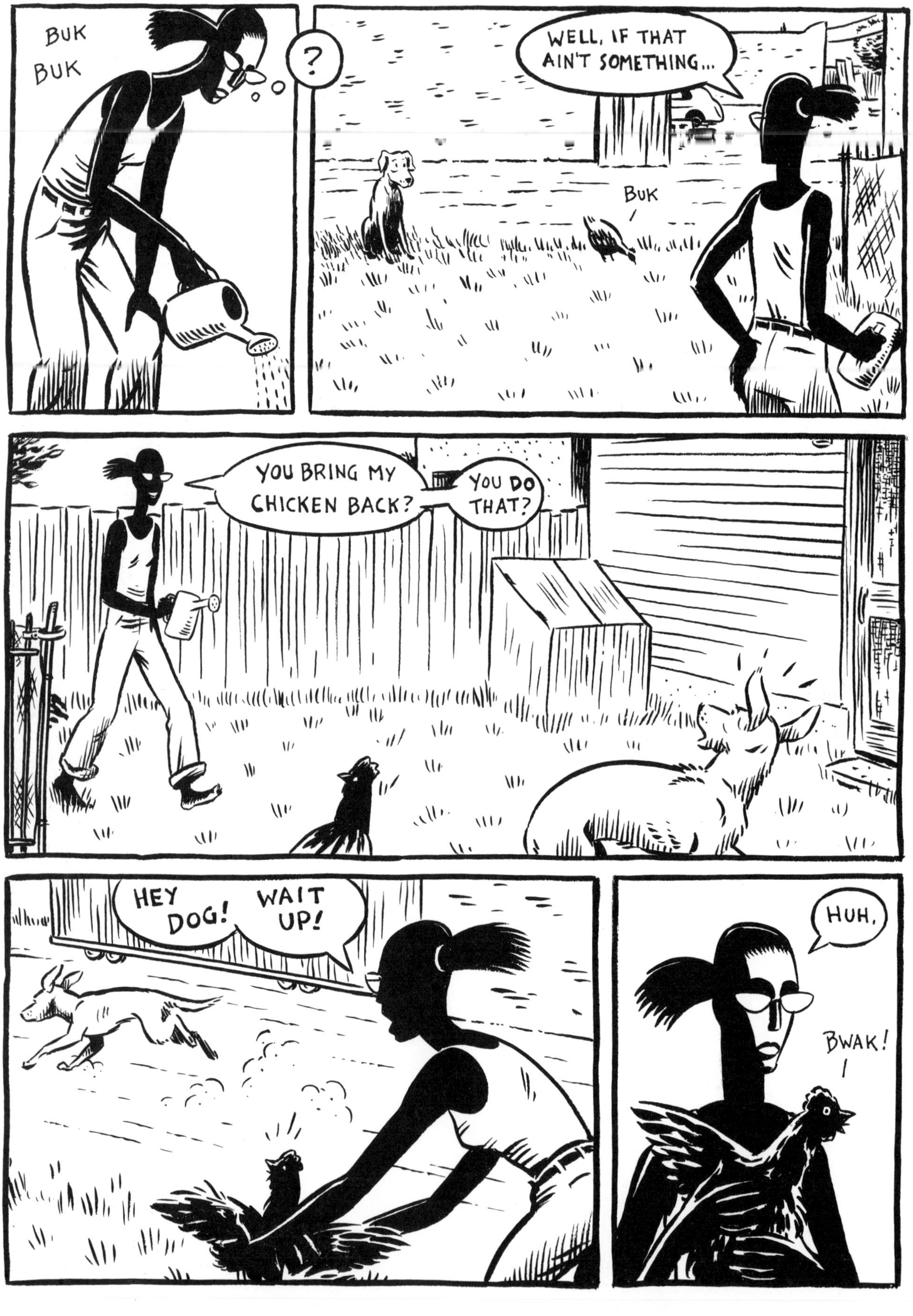
BUK
BUK
?
WELL, IF THAT AIN'T SOMETHING...
BUK
YOU BRING MY CHICKEN BACK?
YOU DO THAT?
HEY DOG!
WAIT UP!
HUH.
BWAK!

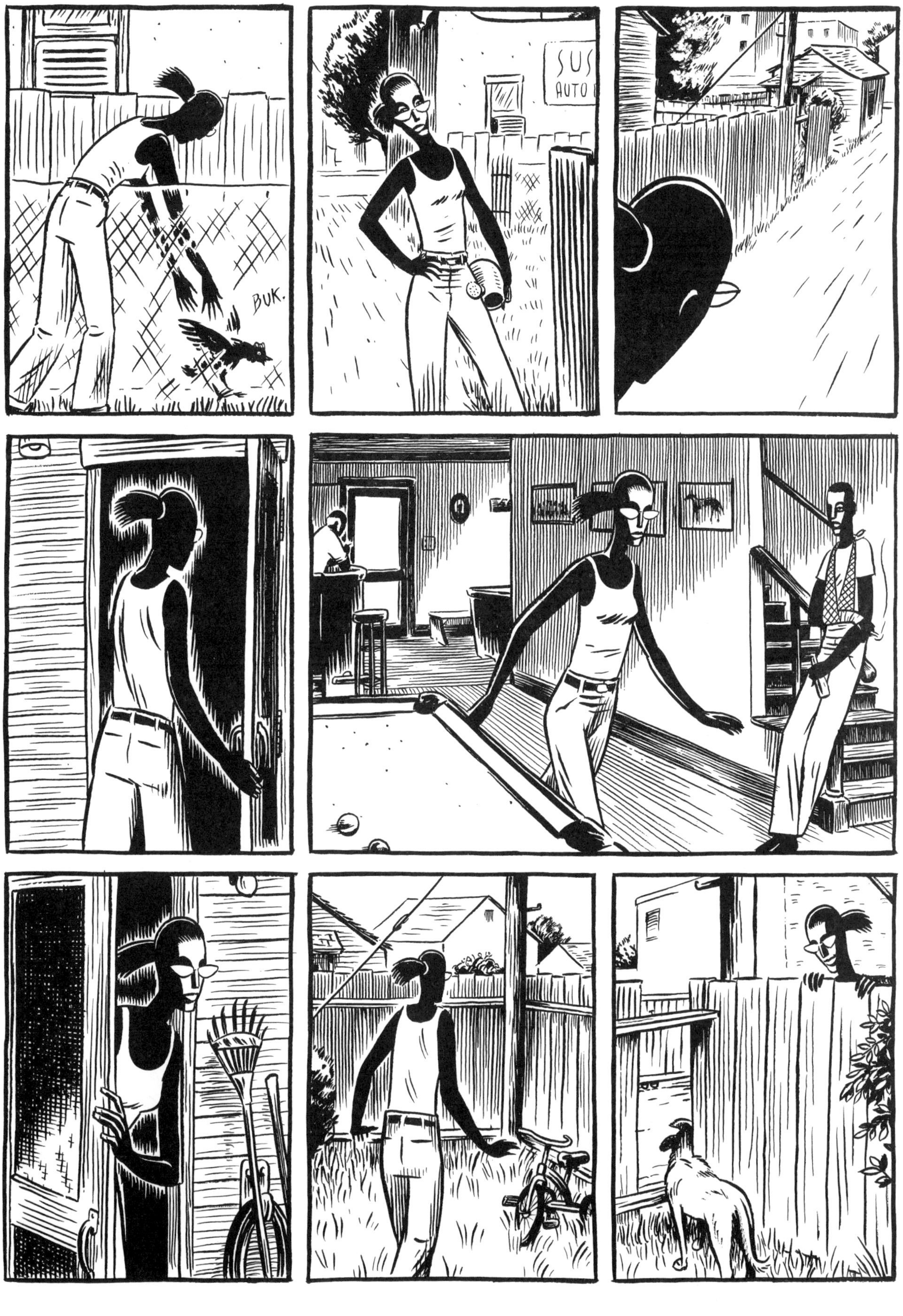
BUK.
SUS
AUTO

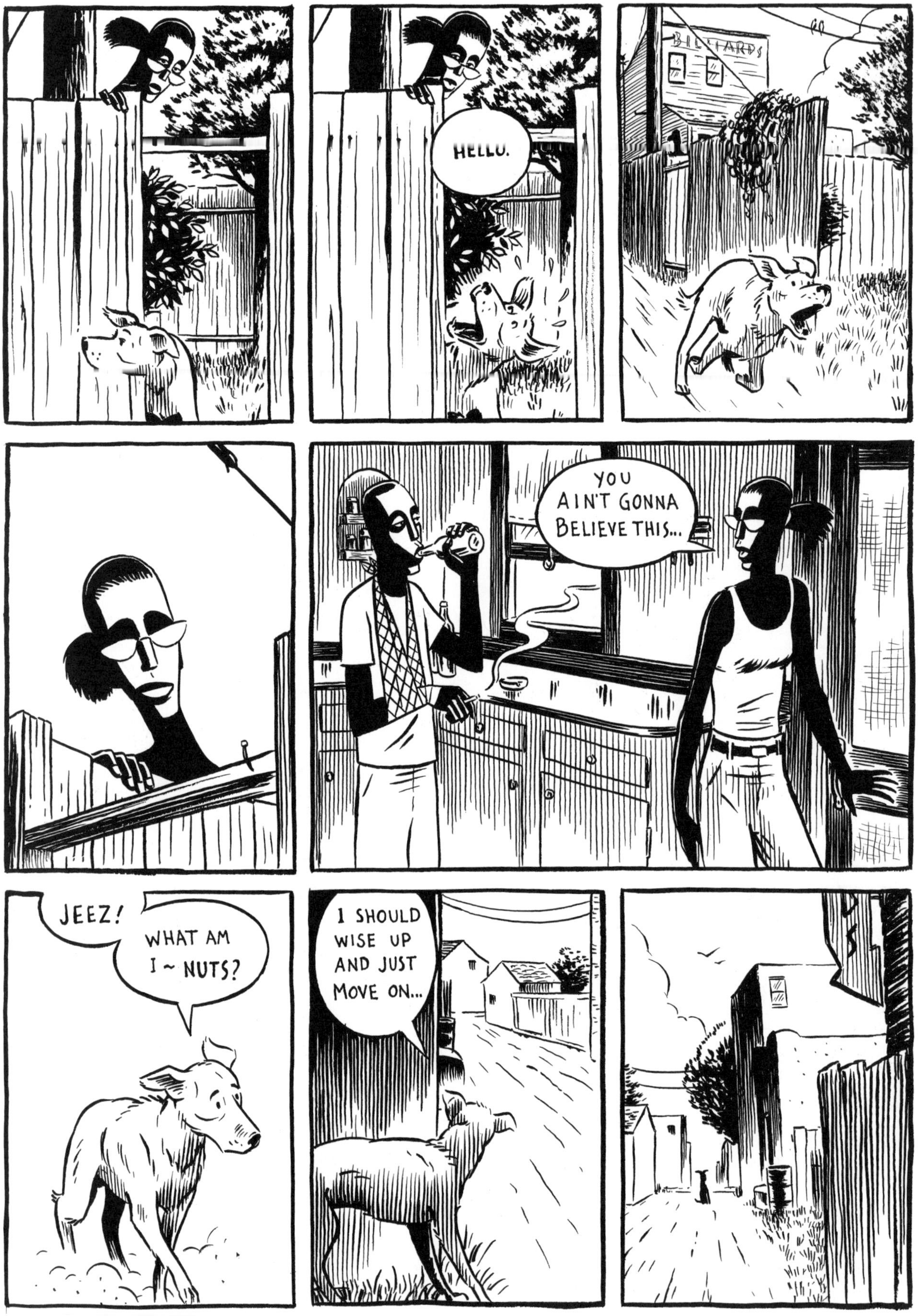
HELLO.
BILLIARDS
YOU AIN'T GONNA BELIEVE THIS...
JEEZ!
WHAT AM I ~ NUTS?
I SHOULD WISE UP AND JUST MOVE ON...

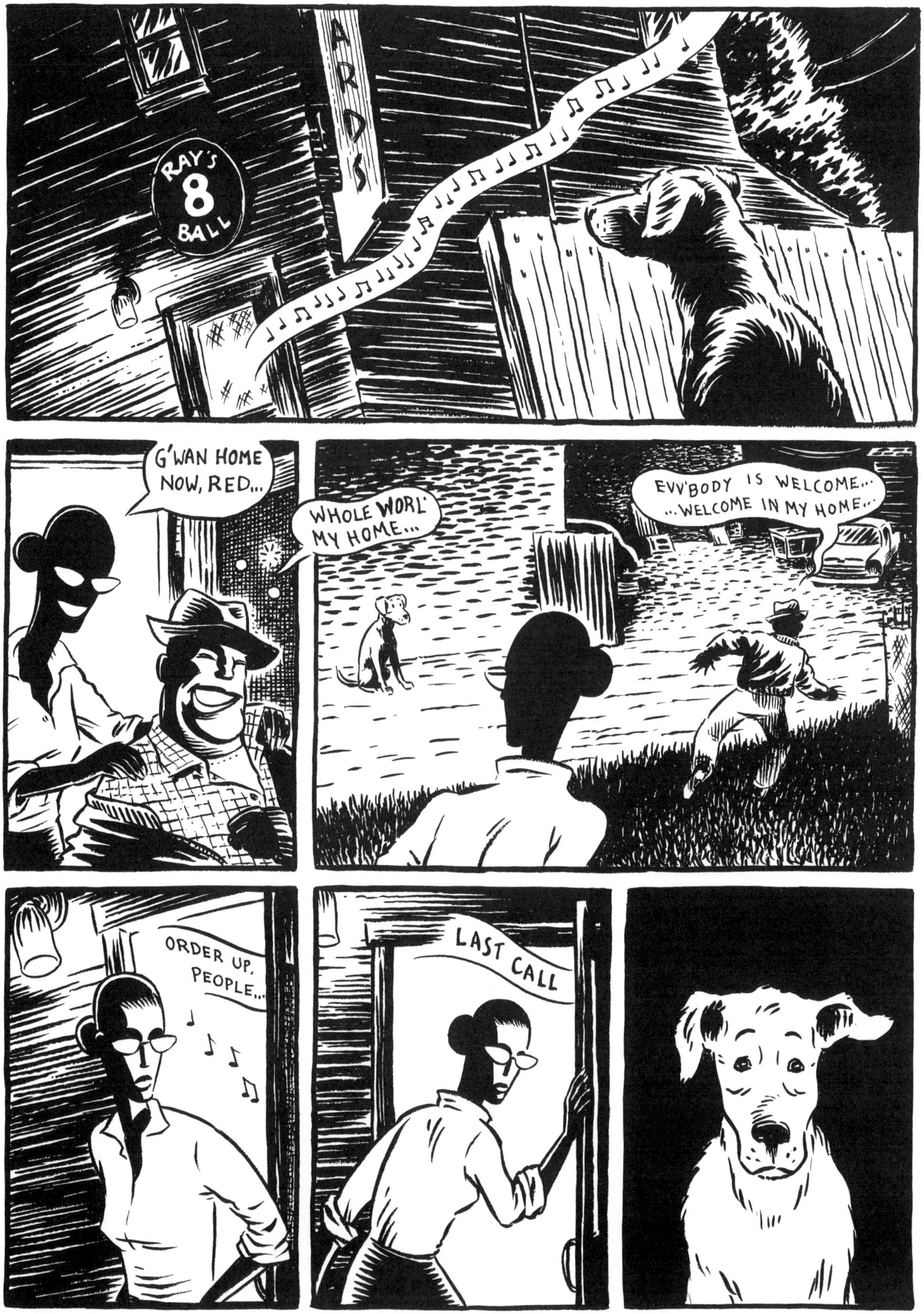
RAY'S 8 BALL
ARDS
G'WAN HOME NOW, RED...
WHOLE WORL' MY HOME...
EVV'BODY IS WELCOME... ...WELCOME IN MY HOME...
ORDER UP, PEOPLE...
LAST CALL

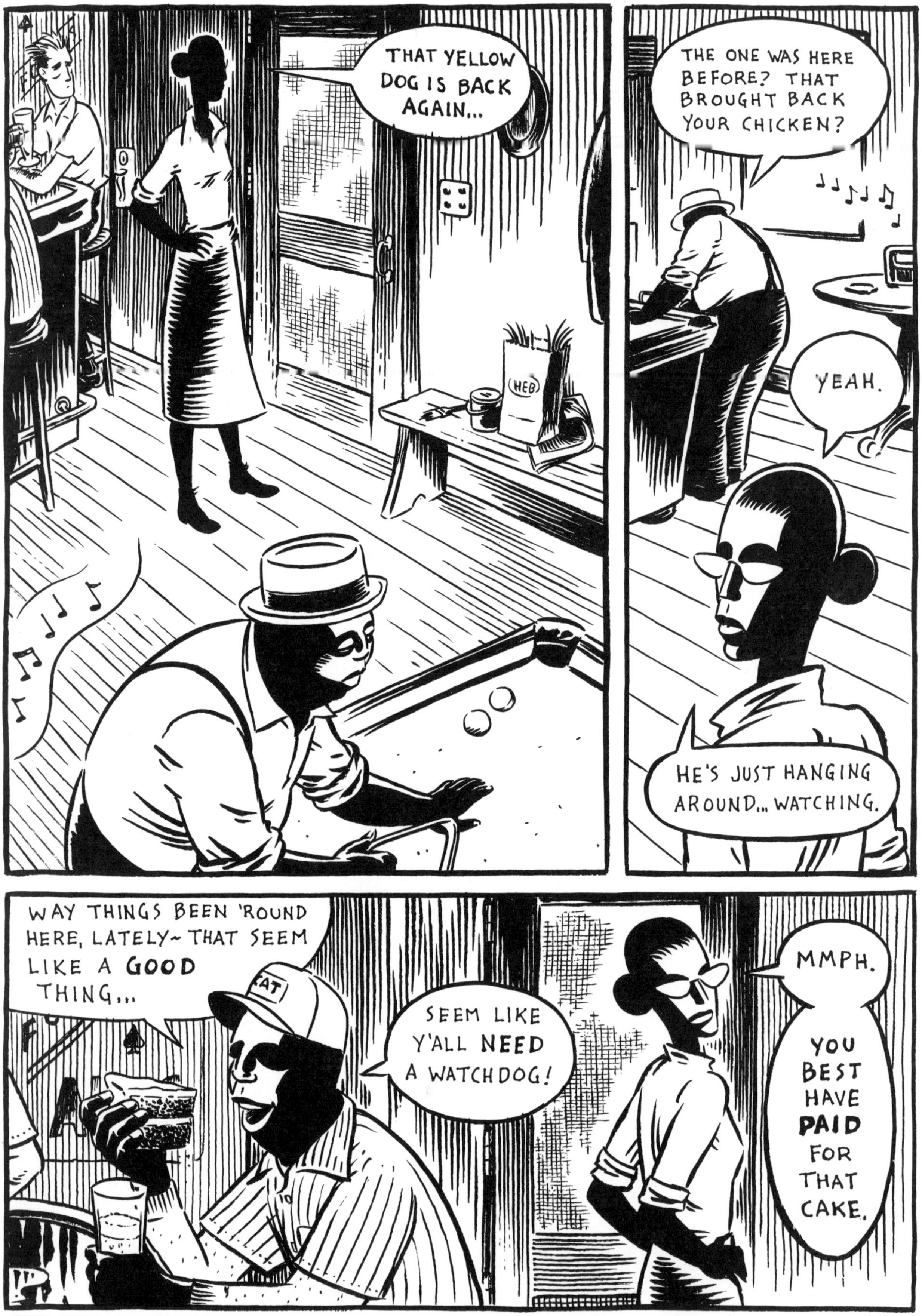
THAT YELLOW DOG IS BACK AGAIN...
THE ONE WAS HERE BEFORE? THAT BROUGHT BACK YOUR CHICKEN?
YEAH.
HE'S JUST HANGING AROUND... WATCHING.
WAY THINGS BEEN 'ROUND HERE, LATELY~ THAT SEEM LIKE A **GOOD** THING...
SEEM LIKE Y'ALL **NEED** A WATCHDOG!
MMPH.
YOU BEST HAVE **PAID** FOR THAT CAKE.

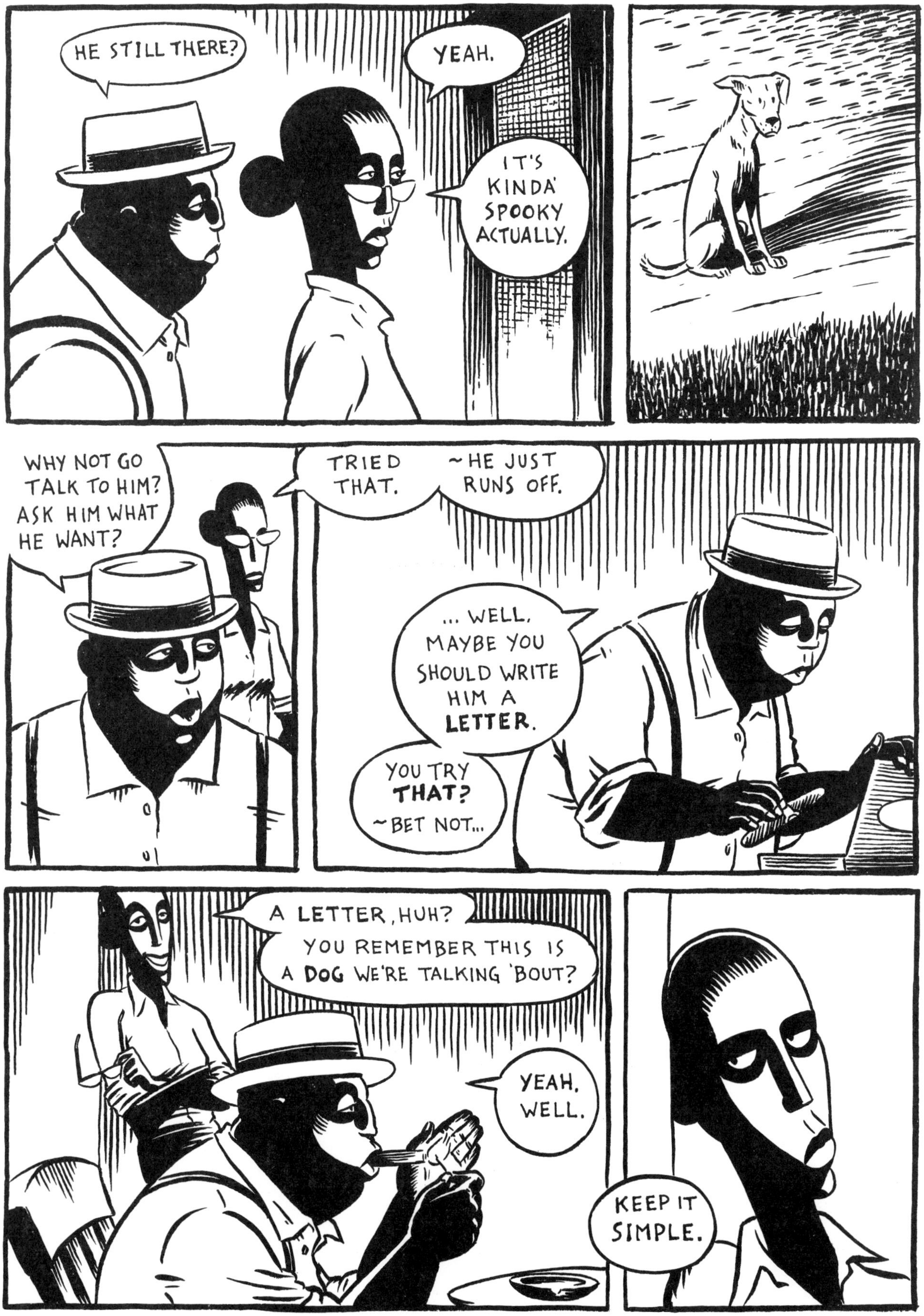
HE STILL THERE?
YEAH.
IT'S KINDA' SPOOKY ACTUALLY.
WHY NOT GO TALK TO HIM? ASK HIM WHAT HE WANT?
TRIED THAT.
~HE JUST RUNS OFF.
... WELL, MAYBE YOU SHOULD WRITE HIM A LETTER.
YOU TRY THAT? ~BET NOT...
A LETTER, HUH?
YOU REMEMBER THIS IS A DOG WE'RE TALKING 'BOUT?
YEAH, WELL.
KEEP IT SIMPLE.

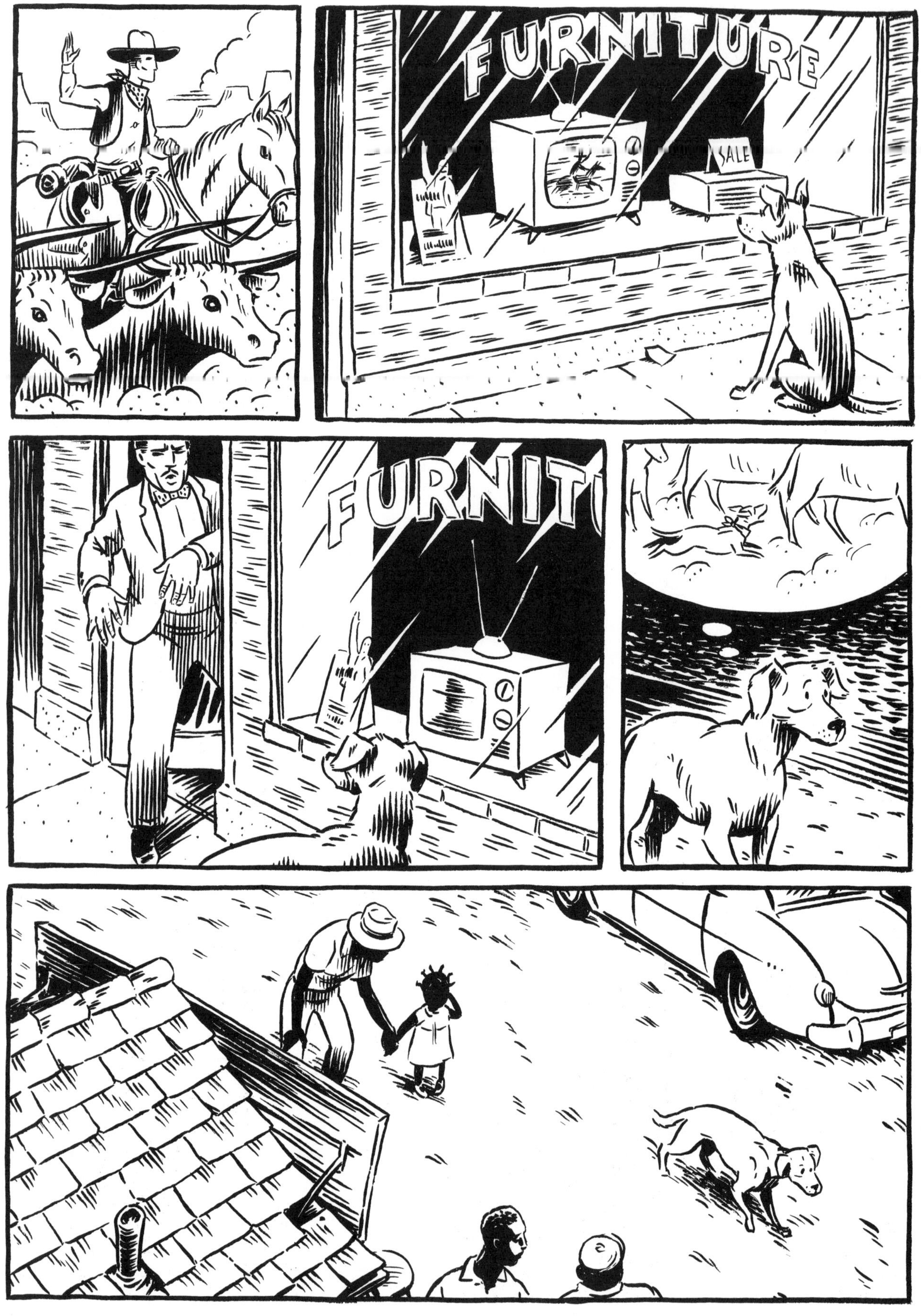
FURNITURE
SALE
FURNIT

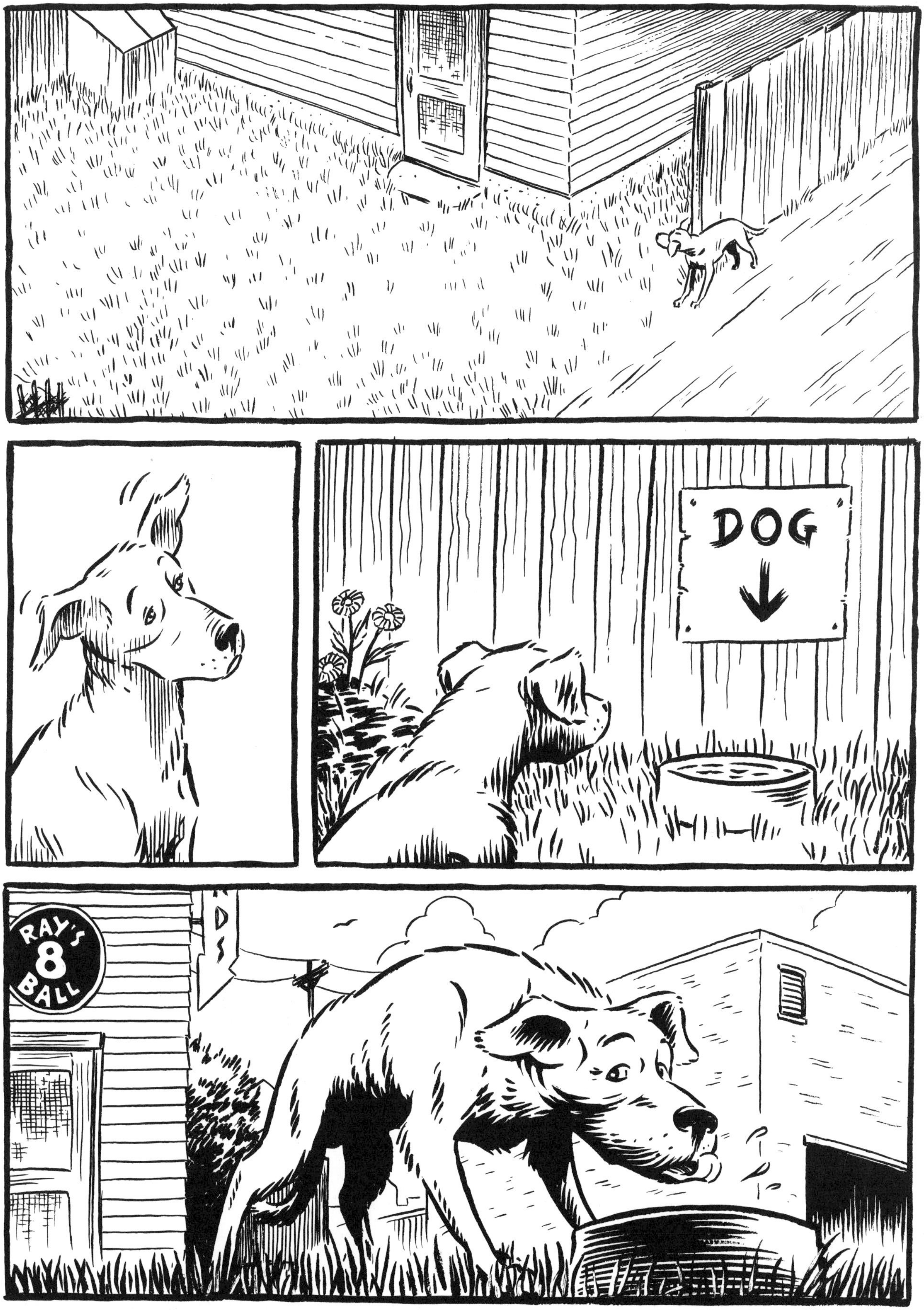
DOG
RAY'S
8
BALL

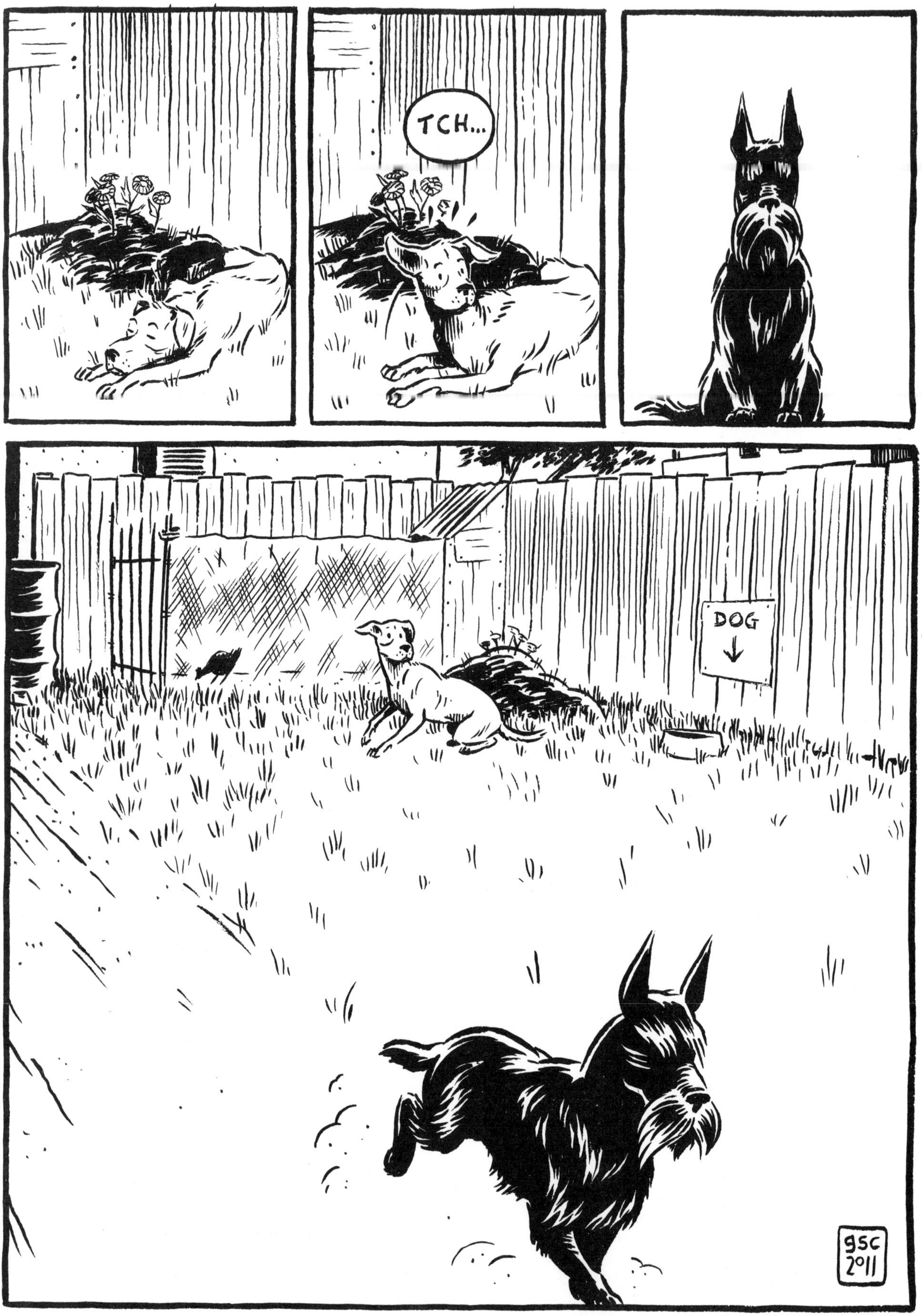
TCH...
DOG ↓
gsc 2011

GRAHAM CHAFFEE IS A PROFESSIONAL TATTOOIST AND COMICS
ARTIST. HIS PREVIOUS BOOKS ARE **THE BIG WHEELS** (1993) AND
THE MOST IMPORTANT THING & OTHER STORIES (1995).
HE LIVES IN LOS ANGELES AND DOES NOT OWN A DOG.

WWW. GSCHAFFEETATTOOS.COM

D0647070

The *Latin* Music Scene

The Stars ♪ The Fans ♪ The Music

Erika Alexia Tsoukanelis

Enslow Publishers, Inc.
40 Industrial Road
Box 398
Berkeley Heights, NJ 07922
USA

http://www.enslow.com

Library of Congress Cataloging-in-Publication Data
Tsoukanelis, Erika Alexia.
  The Latin music scene : the stars, the fans, the music / Erika Alexia Tsoukanelis.
     p. cm. — (The music scene)
  Includes bibliographical references and index.
  Summary: "Read about the music, stars, clothes, contracts, and world of Latin
music"—Provided by publisher.
  ISBN-13: 978-0-7660-3399-3
  ISBN-10: 0-7660-3399-6
  1. Popular music—Latin America—History and criticism—Juvenile literature.
I. Title.
  ML3475.T76 2009
  782.42164—dc22

                           2008048013

Printed in the United States of America

10 9 8 7 6 5 4 3 2 1

To Our Readers:
This text has not been authorized by the musicians or bands mentioned
throughout this book.

   We have done our best to make sure all Internet addresses in this
book were active and appropriate when we went to press. However, the
author and the publisher have no control over and assume no liability for
the material available on those Internet sites or on other Web sites they
may link to. Any comments or suggestions can be sent by e-mail to
comments@enslow.com or to the address on the back cover.

♻ Enslow Publishers, Inc., is committed to printing our books
on recycled paper. The paper in every book contains 10% to
30% post-consumer waste (PCW). The cover board on the
outside of each book contains 100% PCW. Our goal is to do
our part to help young people and the environment too!

Cover Photo Credit: AP Photo/Mitchell Zachs
Interior Photo Credits: Alamy/Photos 12, p. 23; AP Photo/
Keystone/Regina Kuehne, p. 6; AP Photo/Jeff Christensen, p. 11;
AP Photo/George Gongora-Corpus Christi Caller-Times, p. 22; AP
Photo/Mike Albans, p. 25; AP Photo/Matt Sayles, p. 26; AP Photo/
Jason DeCrow, p.27; Chris Cufarro, courtesy of Upground, p. 29;
Corbis/Bob Sacha, p. 34; Getty Images/Vladimir Rys/Bongarts, p. 2; Getty
Images/Frank Micelotta, p. 5; Getty Images/Getty Images, p. 10; Getty
Images/Thomas Coex/AFP, p. 14; Getty Images/Albert L. Ortega/WireImage,
p. 33; Getty Images/John Shearer/WireImage, p. 35; Getty Images/Chris
Jackson, p. 36; The Image Works/PA/Topham, p. 20; The Image Works/Skip
O'Rourke, p. 28; Landov/Ana Martinez/Reuters, p. 1; Landov/UPI Photo/
Michael Bush, p. 9; Landov/Tomas Bravo/Reuters, p. 16; Landov/Enrique
Marcarian/Reuters, p.17; Landov/Carlos Barria/Reuters, p. 37; Landov/
Jose Miguel Gomez/Reuters, p. 39; MPTV, p. 8; PhotoEdit/Sky Bonillo,
p. 41; Rapport Press/Robert Caplin, p. 31; Retna Ltd./Camera Press/
Nigel Norrington, p. 12; Retna Ltd./Marissa Roth, p. 19; Retna Ltd./
Sara De Boer, p. 21; SuperStock/Arlene Sandler, p. 38.

Cover: Juanes performs in Miami, Florida, in 2005.
Title page: Husband and wife Latin megastars Jennifer Lopez
and Marc Anthony sing together in San Juan, Puerto Rico.
Right: Ricky Martin performs at the closing ceremony of the
2006 Winter Olympics in Turin, Italy.

Contents

① Hot Stuff

¡Hola! Do you love to dance salsa or merengue? Are you a fan of **Shakira** or **Wyclef Jean**? You're not alone!

Latin music is written, recorded, and performed all over the world. People listen and dance to it on every continent. Latin music is hot!

HOT *Latin Female Singers*

Lopez talks about her art: "Being an artist is about baring your soul. If you're not doing that, you're not creating anything that's worth anything. I always see myself as a performer first, so I will always want to make music, act in movies, even onstage."[1]

Jennifer Lopez is a world-famous actress and singer. She also has her own line of clothing and perfume. In 2007, Lopez won the American Music Award for Favorite Latin Artist.

Artist **Paulina Rubio** began acting, singing, and dancing in Mexico City when she was five years old. Rubio's album *Ananda (Happiness)* won a 2007 Latin Billboard Award for best Latin pop album. It was also nominated for a Latin Grammy that year.

HOT Latin Male Singers

Marc Anthony has sold more albums than any other salsa performer in history.[2] He is also an actor and movie producer. Anthony married Jennifer Lopez in 2004.

David Bisbal was born in Almería, Spain. He was discovered at the age of twenty-two on a Spanish reality television show called *Operación Triunfo*. The show is a lot like *American Idol*.

Bisbal's third studio album, *Premonición (Premonition)*, was released in 2006. The album went platinum in Spain. This means it sold more than a million copies. Bisbal remixed and recorded the song "Torre de Babel" with Latin artists ***Wisin y Yandel*** and ***Vincente Amigo***.

Anthony once said, "Every one of my accomplishments is an accomplishment for Latino people. When you break down doors, when you break barriers, it means something to your people. Because it's not just me, I'm one of them, they're all of me."[3]

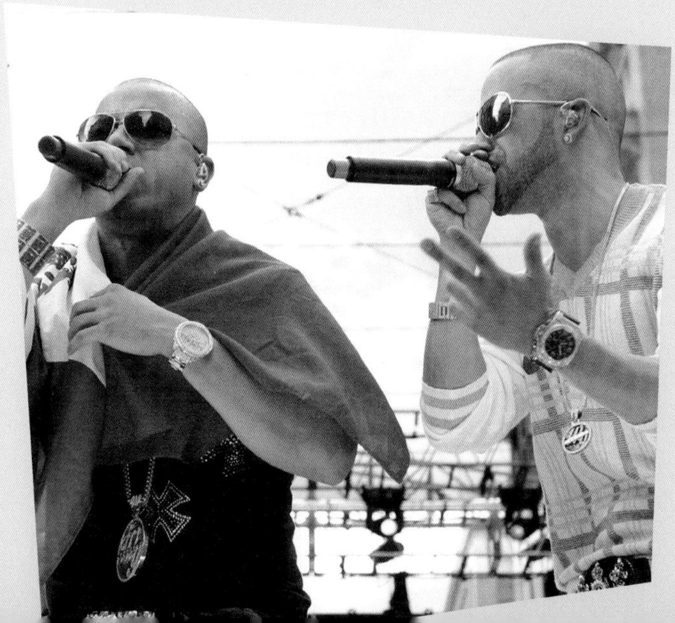

HOT Latin Band

Wisin y Yandel met in their hometown of Cayey, Puerto Rico. They got their first record contract in 1999. In 2009, they won a Grammy Award for their album *Los Extraterrestres* (The Extraterrestrials).

Fans cheer at a Manu Chao concert in Switzerland.

2 "I'm Your Biggest Fan!"

Since there are so many types of Latin music, there are many different types of fans. What type of fan are you?

¿No habla español? You don't have to speak Spanish to be a fan of Latin music. The music speaks its own language. Many English-speaking musicians like the sounds of Spanish so much that they record songs in Spanish. *Beyoncé*, an African-American singer, recorded an all-Spanish album called *Irreemplazable (Irreplaceable)*.

Fans of Jennifer Lopez draw pictures of the star and post them on one of her most popular fan Web sites. News about Lopez's life is posted on these sites almost every day.

The Sound on the Street Many Latin music fans live in cities. Reggaeton (reg-ay-TONE) is a favorite type of Latin music in Puerto Rican cities. Reggaeton artists include the hot band ***Calle 13***—two stepbrothers who call themselves Residente ("Resident") and Visitante ("Visitor").

Talk About Pop Latin pop songs appeal to young fans who listen to the newest music they can find. ***La Quinta Estación*** is a famous Spanish band. They play pop and rock songs with lyrics about dancing and love.

Down in Mexico Fans who like a big, joyful sound may really like Mexican music. The Mexican artist ***Mariano Barba*** won four Latin Billboard Awards in 2007.

Spicing It Up with Salsa Salsa music fans learn difficult dance moves to go along with this rhythmic sound. The salsa musician ***India*** has been called the Princess of Salsa. India says, "Singing salsa to me is spiritual, it's powerful."[4] Many salsa fans agree.

3 Outfitted

Performers want to look their best when they go on stage or have their picture taken. Latin stars often hire people to help choose their clothing and makeup. The clothing styles of Latin music stars have changed a lot over the years.

Former Fashions

Celia Cruz was born in Cuba in 1925. She is often called the Queen of Latin Music. When Cruz began her career in the 1950s, she performed in long, glamorous gowns and expensive jewelry.

Desi Arnaz was an Afro-Cuban jazz musician, comedian, television producer, and actor. He is most famous for his role as Ricky Ricardo in the 1950s television show *I Love Lucy.* Arnaz often wore a tuxedo on stage. Other times, he dressed in thin ties and suits with big shoulder pads.

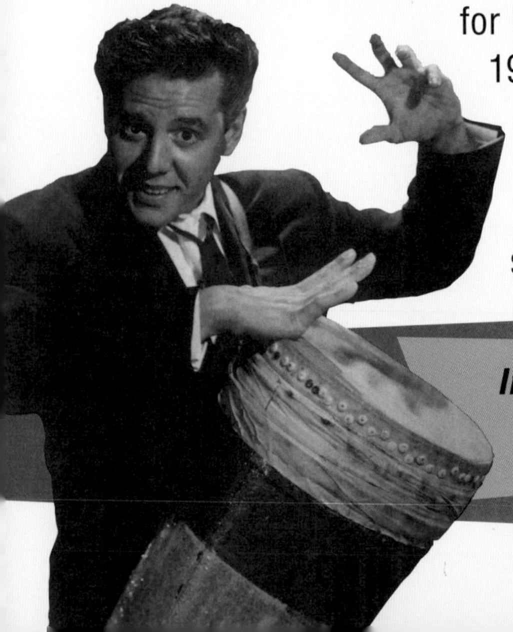

In the 1950s, TV star Desi Arnaz often performed in a suit and tie.

Today's
Latin Runway

Thalia, a Mexican soap opera and pop star, has her own fashion line. She usually wears fancy dresses, like female Latin music performers did years ago. Thalia always wears jewelry and makeup when she's having her picture taken.

Thalia wrote a beauty book in English and Spanish. *It is called* Thalia: ¡Belleza! Lessons in Lipgloss and Happiness.

La Bruja is a female poet and Latin rap artist who wears urban clothing. You can find her in T-shirts, jeans with graffiti painted on them, thick parkas, and wool hats.

Puerto Rican pop singer *Luis Miguel* dresses in elegant jackets and button-down shirts. He usually wears dark colors.

Hector El Father is a reggaeton artist. He prefers to wear casual street clothes, such as oversize blue jeans, baseball caps, and heavy gold jewelry.

Hector El Father celebrates winning an award for young Spanish-speaking artists in 2007.

9

The different styles of Latin music come from Spanish-speaking cultures. Culture is a group's way of life. For example, how do they spend their time? What do they wear, eat, and talk about? Many Latin cultures have two passions in common: baseball and beaches!

Out to the *Ball Field*

Cubans, Puerto Ricans, and people from the Dominican Republic share a love of baseball. In fact, baseball is the Dominican Republic's national sport. In Puerto Rico, professional baseball stars play in the Caribbean League, and athletes from the American mainland often join their teams. Cuba is home to Orlando "El Duque" Hernandez, a well-known player for the New York Mets.

Musician and baseball player Daddy Yankee was about to join the Seattle Mariners when a stray bullet hit him accidentally. The bullet is still lodged in his hip. The injury ended Daddy Yankee's baseball career, but it also encouraged him to take his music more seriously.[5]

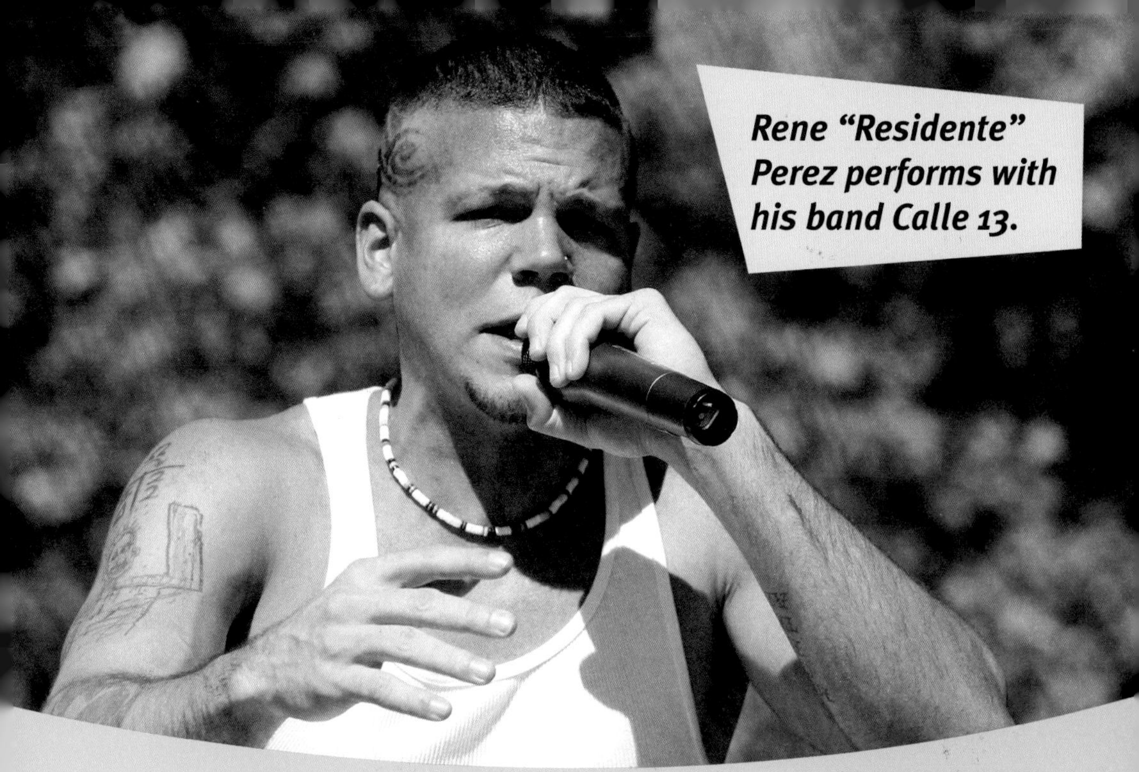

Rene "Residente" Perez performs with his band Calle 13.

Singing in the Sand

Most Latin music comes from warm countries with lots of coastline. Sounds of the beach play a big part in Latin music styles.

Tropical music is a type of Latin sound that includes salsa, merengue, bachata, and other Caribbean styles. Tropical music videos are often filmed on or near the beach.

In June 2007, Batanga.com hosted Batanga Beach Break. More than 3,000 Latinos from around the United States joined together on the New Jersey shore to watch the band **Calle 13** perform. Batanga Beach Break was so popular that it is turning into an annual event.

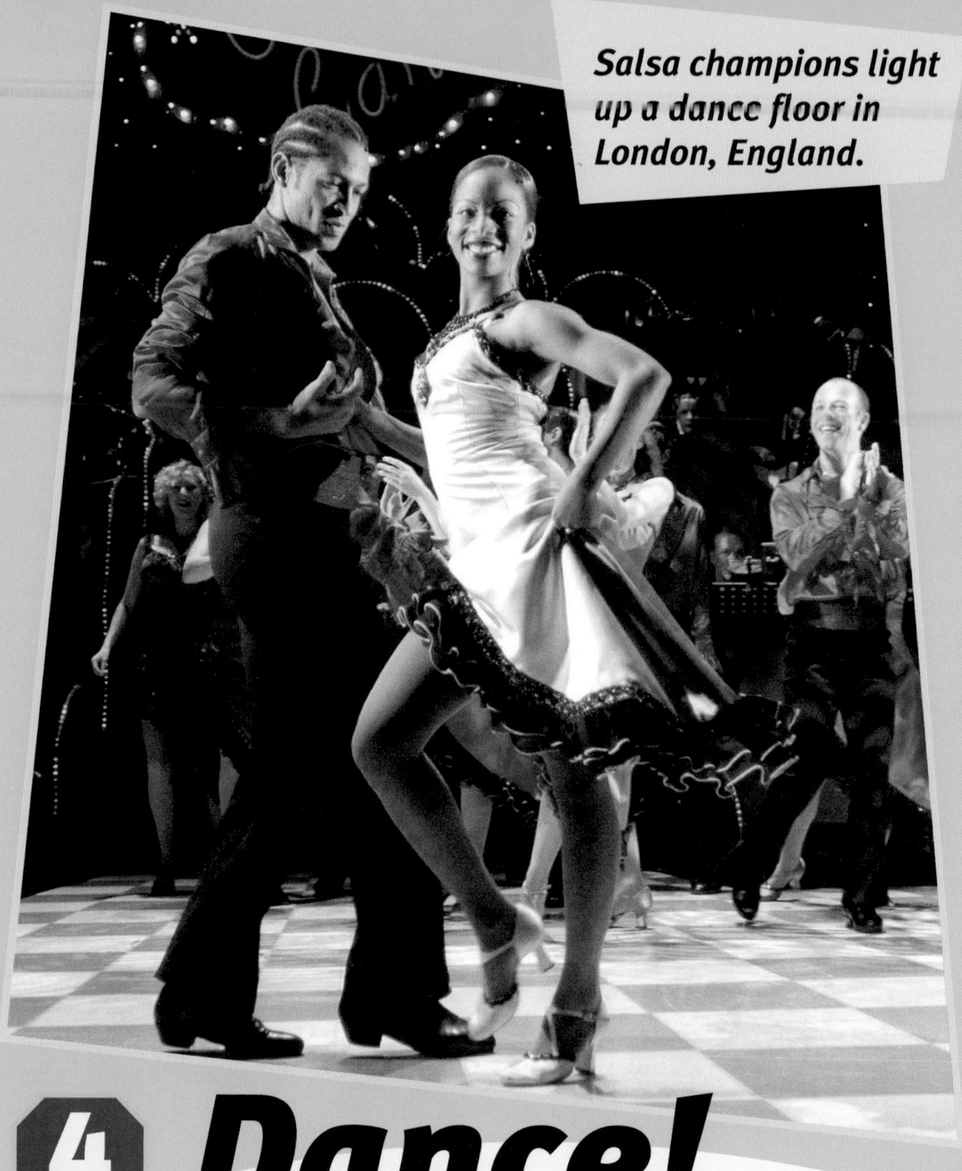

Salsa champions light up a dance floor in London, England.

4 Dance!

Salsa

There are no strict rules about how salsa should be danced, but there are three main styles: Cuban, New York, and Los Angeles.

The main instrument of salsa music is called the clave. Claves are two small sticks of wood. Musicians hit them together to make a special rhythm, which is also called the clave. Salsa dancing is usually done with a partner. Dancers spin around each other, change places, and move their hips to the music.

Merengue

Merengue started in the Dominican Republic and Haiti. Merengue music and dancing are very lively and cheerful. Two people dance together to a two-step beat. They hold their upper bodies still while their knees bend and their hips move left and right. With their hands linked, the dancers twirl and make twisty pretzel shapes with their arms.

Reggaeton

This popular dance music began in Panama. It is a blend of Jamaican, Latin-American, hip-hop, and rap styles. Reggaeton has a catchy beat called the dem bow. Dancers move their hips and even do acrobatics. The singer **Ivy Queen** writes upbeat, happy songs. She is well known for her reggaeton dance grooves.

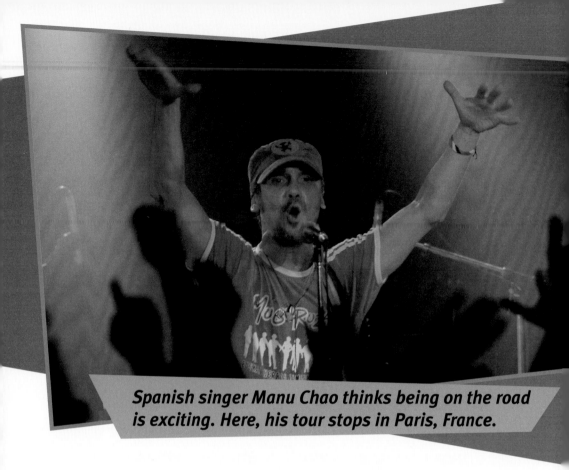

Spanish singer Manu Chao thinks being on the road is exciting. Here, his tour stops in Paris, France.

5 *On the Road*

Highs and Lows Latin music performers spend months and months touring the country and the world. They take planes and tour buses to various clubs and arenas. Life on the road can be both exciting and tiring.

The internationally popular, Spanish-born singer *Manu Chao* finds touring exciting. He says, "I love going to sleep in one city and waking in another. . . . the band is really positive, a great family. I can imagine touring with these guys for years."[6]

Jennifer Lopez jokes, "When I'm on tour, I like to sleep."[7]

Starting Out Live

Like most musicians, Latin music artists need to play long hours in small bands and at small clubs in order to get ahead. If people like what they hear, musicians are invited to play at larger and larger places.

Big Crowd, Small Crowd

Someone once asked Colombian pop star *Juanes* if he liked playing at a small club in London, England. He answered, "You know, sometimes I prefer to play in places like that because you can feel the crowd, and the energy is more concentrated. When you play in arenas or stadiums, of course it's really cool, but the dimensions [sizes] are different—people are further away from you, and it's another kind of feeling. But I would say I prefer to play in small clubs, it's more fun!"[8]

Fans crowd the main square in Mexico City for a huge live concert in 2008.

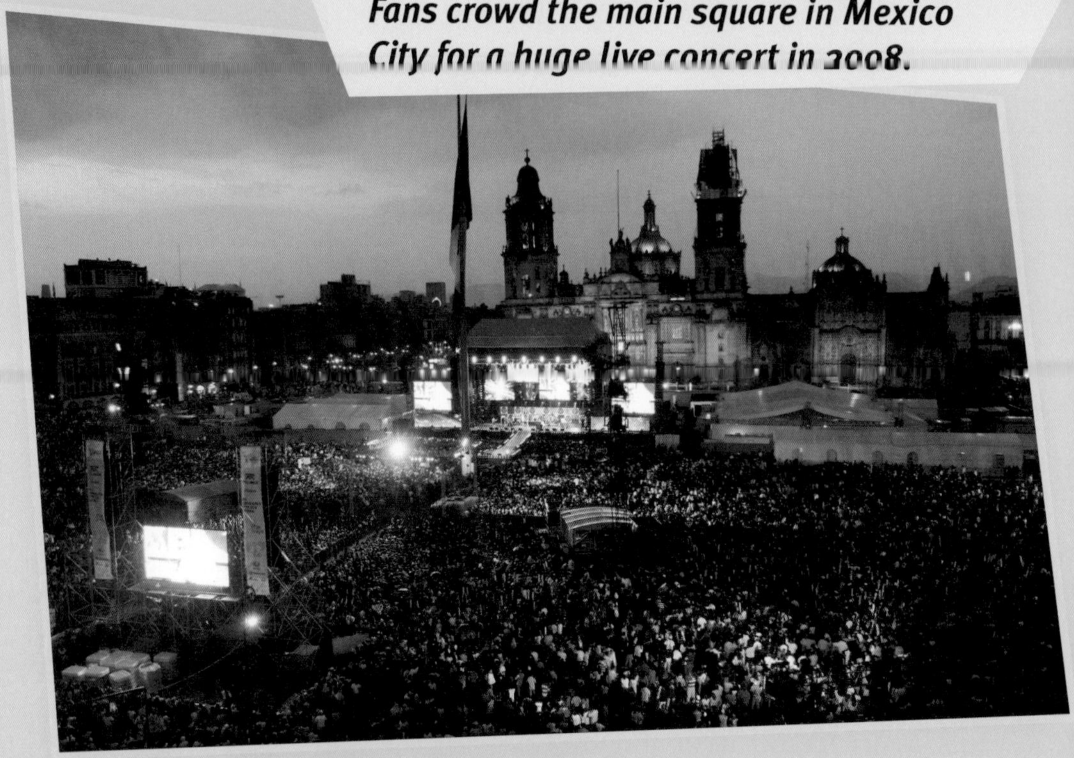

6 Live!

Many Latin music fans dress up when they go to concerts. Once the music starts, there isn't much sitting around. If you're not dancing, you probably won't stay still for long. Friends and strangers will pull you onto the dance floor. Puerto Rican pop star ***Ricky Martin*** even invited former U.S. president George W. Bush to dance when he played at the president's 2001 inauguration!

Latin music fans love the strong rhythms of a live performance. When salsa star **Albert Torres** was asked what has kept him dancing since the age of five, he answered, "It is the smiles and joy I see in the eyes of so many worldwide when they experience the joy that salsa brings into their lives."[9]

Fans of **Sidestepper**, a Colombia-based electronica band, pack so tightly into clubs that it's hard for anyone to get out the door! Fans squeeze together and yell out silly Spanish lyrics like *"bacalao sala'o!"* ("salty codfish") because everyone is packed in like fish![10]

The beautiful Latin pop superstar **Shakira** says of her concerts, "My main goal is to be able to not only entertain (fans), but make sure they leave the [arenas] fulfilled and happy, and make sure they have had an unforgettable night. I'll do everything possible to make sure that happens."[11]

⑦ *Ear Candy*

Listen up! You can hear Latin music in all sorts of places. The radio and the Internet are great places to find new local artists or to download MP3s. Better-known artists have CDs for sale.

Radio Waves

Most major American cities have Latin music radio stations. To find a station near you, type the phrase "Latin music radio station," plus the name of your town, into an Internet search engine. If there is a station close by, it will pop up on the results page.

XM Satellite Radio has four channels of Latin music. Channel 90, called Fuega, plays reggaeton. Viva, channel 91, plays Latin pop hits. Channel 92, Aguila, is a regional Mexican station. Channel 94, which is called Caliente, plays tropical music.

Surf for Sounds

Latin music fans can listen to some songs for free online. They can also download MP3s for songs or albums on Web sites devoted to Latin music. An MP3 is a computer file that contains music or video.

Downloading songs without getting permission or paying for them is illegal. It cheats artists out of what they should earn for their work. Make sure to follow the rules.

On Disc

Fans can buy CDs online or in music stores. Most major music stores let you listen to short pieces of each song before buying the whole CD.

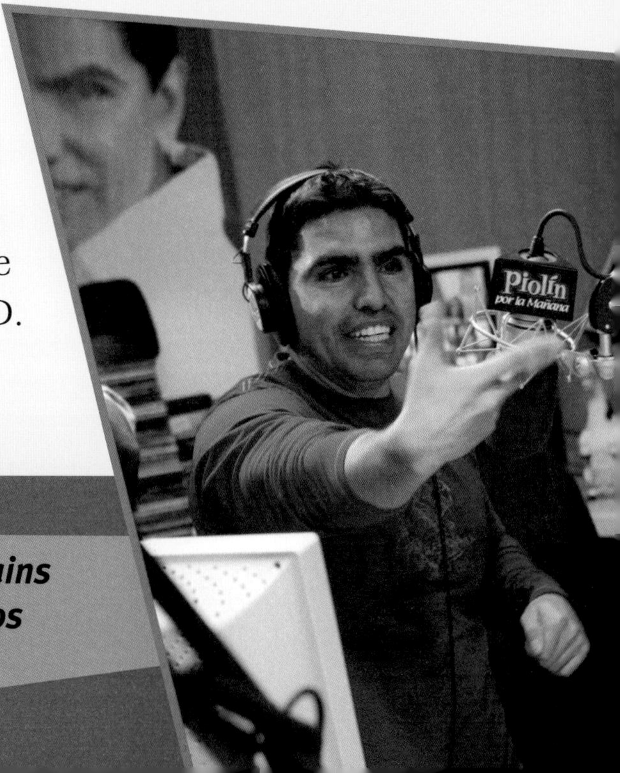
Piolín
por la Mañana

DJ Eddie Sotelo entertains Latin music fans at a Los Angeles radio station.

8 *Hottest Videos*

You can find Latin music videos online or on cable television. Mun2 is a national cable television station for young Latinos. Fans of all ages can appreciate the videos played on Mun2.

Enrique Iglesias, the son of the famous Spanish singer Julio Iglesias, made an artistic video for his song "Tired of Being Sorry." In the video, he wanders a city street at night and argues with his girlfriend.

Shakira's "Hips Don't Lie" is an award-winning music video. She sings the song with Wyclef Jean. Shakira, who began her career as a belly dancer in Colombia, shows off her belly dancing moves in the video.

Enrique Iglesias belts out a song at the MTV Europe Music Awards in 2002.

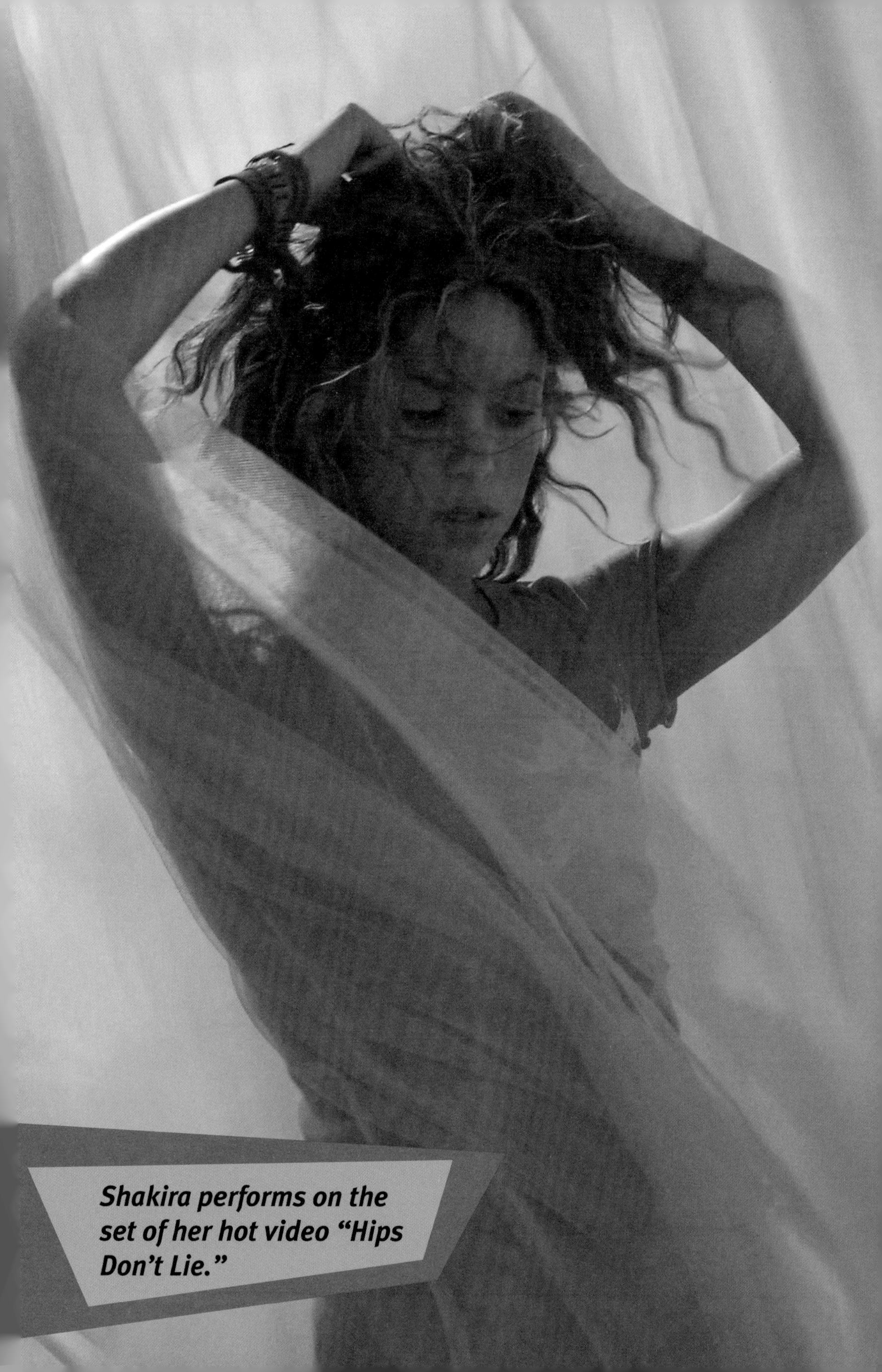

Shakira performs on the set of her hot video "Hips Don't Lie."

9 On the Big Screen

A Tragedy

Selena was a highly successful Mexican-American tejana singer. In 1995, at the age of twenty-three, Selena was murdered by the president of her fan club.

The movie *Selena—Live: The Last Concert* was released in 2003. It was filmed live at the Houston Astrodome in Texas in 1995. There were more than 64,000 fans at Selena's last concert.

Selena sings at a school in Texas in 1994, the year before she was killed.

Jennifer Lopez played Selena in a film about the real-life Mexican-American singer and her rise to success. The movie Selena was released in 1997.

A Comedy

Eva Longoria Parker costars in the 2008 romantic comedy *Over Her Dead Body*. She plays a woman who is killed by a falling ice sculpture before her wedding. The woman comes back as a ghost to haunt her former fiancé and his new girlfriend.

Parker works with a major Hispanic civil rights and advocacy organization to produce the American Latino Media Arts (ALMA) Awards. ALMA Awards go to Latin musicians, actors, and directors who show Latinos in a positive light. In Spanish, *alma* means "soul."

10 *First American Moments*

Years ago, a few big moments brought Latin music to the United States.

El Barrio

In 1919, a young Puerto Rican pianist named **Victoria Hernandez** arrived in New York City. She opened a grocery store in Spanish Harlem, called El Barrio. When she started selling records, local music fans flocked to her store.

Victoria's brother Rafael joined her a few years later after leaving the U.S. Army. Rafael started playing with African-American musicians in a local band called the **Hellfighters**.

The back room of Victoria's grocery store became a music center. Victoria gave piano lessons, and Rafael wrote songs. Victoria went on to create a record label called Hispano Records. She managed and promoted many Cuban and Puerto Rican musicians. Rafael became one of the most popular musical composers of his time.[12]

The *Mambo King*

Tito Puente was born to Puerto Rican parents in Spanish Harlem in 1923. He wanted to become a dancer, but an injury made him turn to playing music. With help from the GI Bill, Puente attended the well-known Juilliard School in New York City. A man of many nicknames, Puente has been called the Mambo King, the King of Latin Jazz, and el Rey del Timbal ("the King of the Timbales").

Puente's music appears in many movies, including *The Mambo Kings*. He guest starred on television shows such as *The Cosby Show* and *The Simpsons*.

Tito Puente is one of the best-known Latin music stars of all time.

11 Spreading Like Wildfire

After those first big moments, Latin music really got going in the United States. The music and personalities caught on from coast to coast.

Playing Music for Tacos

Carlos Santana's father was a mariachi violinist in Tijuana, Mexico. Santana talks about learning music from his dad when he was a kid. He says, "I played the songs he taught me on the street and people would give me 50 cents, and I could buy some tacos."[13]

During the 1960s, Santana played guitar for Tito Puente's song "Oye como va" ("Hey, How Are You?"). A few years later, Santana played congo drums on the hit Rolling Stones song "Sympathy for the Devil." He became wildly popular with rock and roll fans.

The legendary Carlos Santana plays with his band in 2007. His music has wowed fans for decades.

Do the Conga

As a college student, Cuban American **Gloria Estefan** met her husband **Emilio** in Miami, Florida. Emilio invited her to join his band, the **Miami Sound Machine**. The band's first smash hit was the Latin disco song "Conga," released in 1985. Miami Sound Machine went on to earn worldwide fame and success.

In 1990, Gloria Estefan was in a horrible tour bus accident. She was nearly paralyzed. She recovered ten months later and went right back to work. The song "Coming Out of the Dark" was inspired by the crash. It was the first song she performed after her recovery.

Boy Band!

The Puerto Rican band **Menudo** has been around since 1977. Talented Latino performers are invited to join the group when they are twelve years old. Each member leaves the group when he turns twenty. Megastar **Ricky Martin** got his start as a member of Menudo.

Menudo celebrated its thirtieth anniversary in November 2007. In that year, the reality television show *Making Menudo* aired on MTV.

A huge variety of sounds belongs to the family of Latin music. Pictured here are percussion players at a street festival in Cuba.

12 *Not So Simple*

Latin music is very diverse. Tito Puente once said, "Brazil has the samba, Cuba has the guaguanco—all the beautiful rhythms; Puerto Rico has the bomba and the plena, the Dominican Republic has merengue. Haiti has its rhythms; Jamaica has its reggae sound. All that comes from the Caribbean area and is considered Latin music."[14]

Samba music can be gentle or jazzy—but it always has a strong beat. Guaguanco is energetic and passionate. Bomba has a wild and crazy rhythm. Plena lyrics tell stories. Merengue music is full of joy.

Other styles of Latin music include bossa nova, conjunta, cumbia, guajira, mambo, ranchera, reggaeton, rumba, salsa, samba, tango, tejano, and vallenato. Are you overwhelmed yet?

Latino artists are also influenced by other types of music, such as pop, rock, jazz, hip-hop, and electronica. They blend different music with traditional Latin sounds to create Latin fusion.

*The young East Los Angeles band **Upground** sings in English and Spanish. Their music blends ska, reggae, rock, and cumbia. It is an example of the style called Latin fusion.*

Upground, a band from Los Angeles, mixes cultures and musical styles.

13 *The Studios*

Latin music artists record their songs at studios. Less famous artists use smaller recording studios, while superstars make albums at the bigger ones.

Moodswing Records in Los Angeles, California, is a small studio. **BigChris Flores** owns the place. The Mexican hip-hop group **Control Machete** recorded at Moodswing.

Reggaeton stars such as **Big Daddy** and **Los Benjamins** record at Más Flow Studios in San Juan, Puerto Rico. Producer Luny Tunes built this studio. It has nine places to record, a mastering suite, and lounge areas where the musicians hang out.

One of the biggest American studios is Sony BMG Music Entertainment in New York City. Sony BMG has recorded the albums of **Ricky Martin**, **Marc Anthony**, **Christina Aguilera**, **Jennifer Lopez**, **Carlos Santana**, and **Menudo**.

In 2006, reggaeton stars Wisin y Yandel established their own record company called WY Records. Gadiel, El Tio, and Franco "El Gorila" are some of the artists who have signed with WY Records.

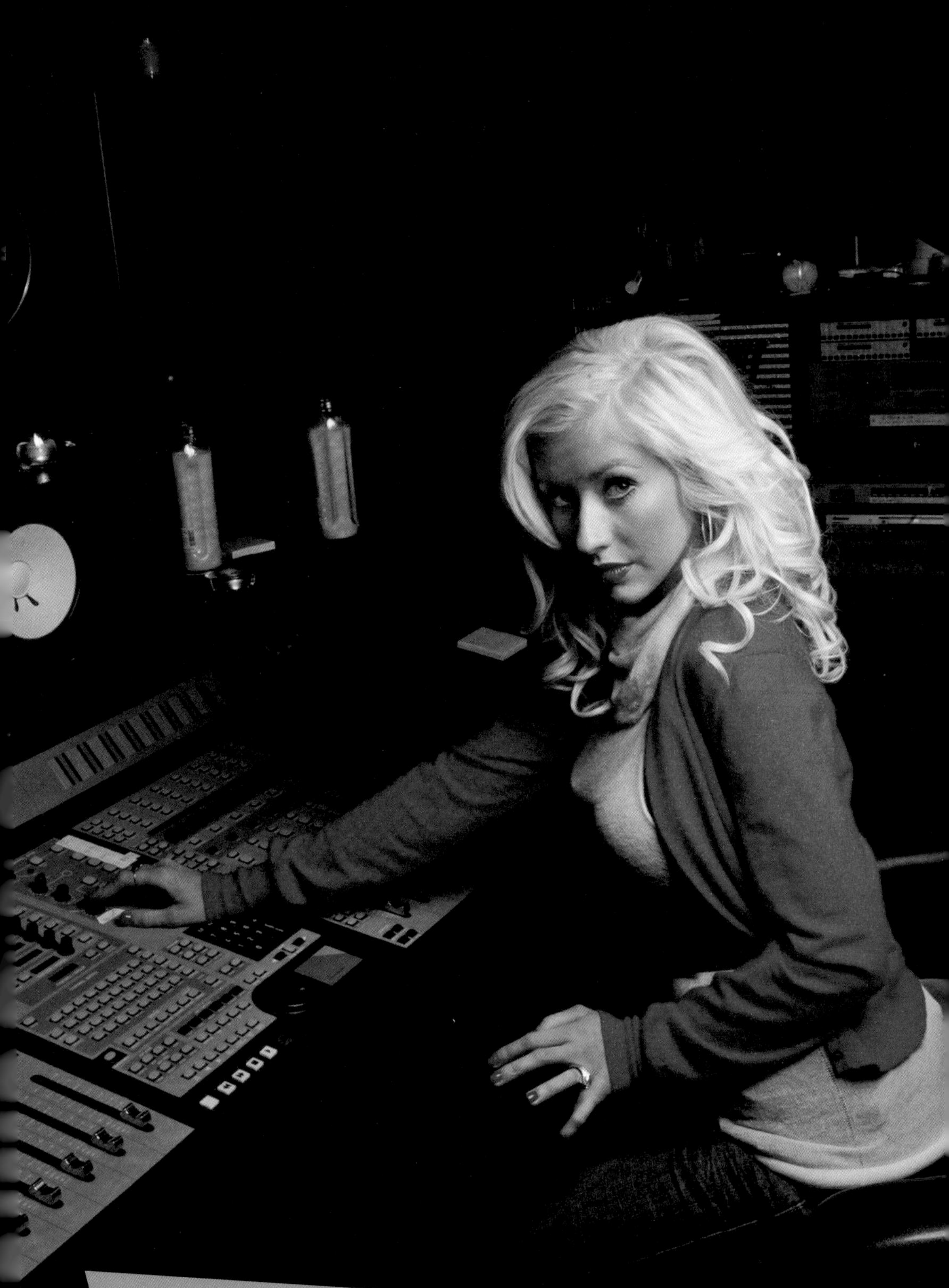

Christina Aguilera gets ready for the release of her album Back to Basics *at Sony Music Studios in New York City.*

14 *Tale of a Contract*

To win money and fame, every Latin music performer must sign a recording contract. In a contract, a record company legally agrees to make a recording of an artist's music. The record company works with a studio to do the recording. If the recording goes well, the record company sells it to stores and promotes the artist. Getting a recording contract is difficult because there is a lot of competition.

Daniel Discovered

Daniel René is a talented singer from Miami. He worked hard to get his first recording contract. He began his career as a child model. At the age of eleven, René was hired to sing for radio commercials.

One day René was in the studio recording a commercial. The famous music producer Emilio Estefan walked in. He thought René's voice was amazing. Estefan told the boy to call him when he got older and was ready to record music of his own.

A few years later, René auditioned for the boy band *Menudo*. He got into the group and sang with them until 1991. Then he decided to go out on his own as a solo artist. He would need a recording contract.

René remembered what Estefan had said to him years ago. He tried calling the producer for five months. Finally, he got through. Estefan invited René to audition at his studio. René was nervous, but he went anyway. Estefan gave René a recording contract on the spot.[15]

Like most artists, Latin sensation Daniel René worked for a long time to get a recording contract.

The Cuban band Los Van Van cuts an album in the studio.

15 Take One!

Recording just one song in a studio can take at least forty hours of work. This means artists have to pay close attention. They also must be willing to work hard. Before going into the studio, musicians must practice playing their songs over and over again.

On the first day in the studio, the recording engineer and music producer help record drum and bass tracks. The next day, the band, the engineer, and the producer get down guitar and keyboard tracks. The rest of the instruments are recorded in this way, one at a time.

As soon as all the instruments are recorded, it's time to get down the vocal tracks. Often the backup singers go on one track, and the lead singer goes on another. Singers take good care of their vocal chords. They drink hot tea and do vocal warm-ups before they begin to sing.

Studio professionals use sophisticated equipment to improve the sound of the final song. The engineer and producer work on one track at a time. They change the sounds of each track using compression and equalization. This means they brings low sounds up higher and high sounds down lower until the music sounds just right. Once every track is perfect, the tracks are blended together to create the song that will be released into the world.

BigChris Flores is a producer and engineer at his studio, Moodswing Records in Los Angeles. He says, "I do whatever it takes to get a song right. The musicians and I stay up all night if we have to."[16]

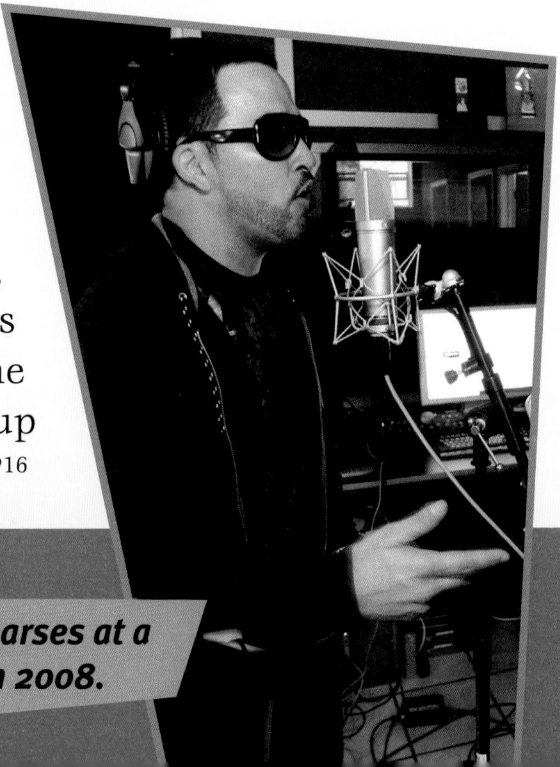

Latin artist Malverde rehearses at a private recording studio in 2008.

16 Latin Music in Action

Many Latin music stars use their fame to make a difference in the world. They hold concerts to raise money for important causes. They also create organizations to help the needy.

The Land of the Free and the Home of the Brave

In spring 2006, top Latin artists recorded a bilingual (English and Spanish) version of the U.S. anthem "The Star-Spangled Banner."

Grammy Award winner *Juanes* performed at the Nobel Peace Prize concert on December 11, 2007. Al Gore won the 2007 prize for his work educating people about climate change.

The artists wanted to show support for undocumented immigrants. Mexican pop diva ***Gloria Trevi***, Puerto Rican singer ***Carlos Ponce***, and Puerto Rican reggaeton star ***Don Omar*** were among the artists there.

Helping the Children

Shakira heads Fundación Pies Descalzos, or the Barefoot Foundation. It is a group that helps Colombian children who are victims of violence.

Shakira also started the Latin America Solidarity Action Foundation. It tries to end child poverty in Latin American countries. Shakira has gotten help from other stars such as ***Alejandro Sanz***, ***Daniela Mercury***, ***Maná***, ***Wyclef Jean***, ***Marc Anthony***, ***Jennifer Lopez***, and ***Miguel Bose***.[17]

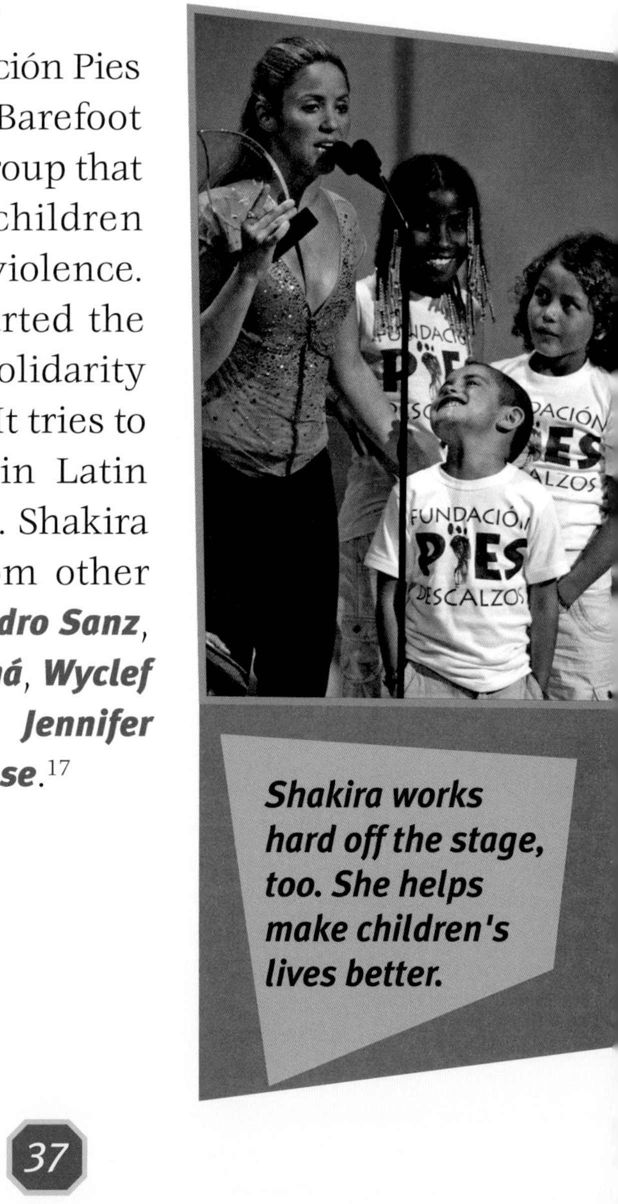
FUNDACIÓN
PIES
DESCALZOS

Shakira works hard off the stage, too. She helps make children's lives better.

The next star of Latin music could be you. Get your hands on a drum and start playing!

17 *Get into It*

Do you want to get into the Latin music scene? Many famous performers started making music at a young age. The time is now!

Practice Makes Perfect

One of the best ways to get started is to take instrument, voice, or dance lessons. Some common Latin instruments are the acoustic guitar, keyboard, and trumpet. Latin music is also known for its driving rhythm section.

Bongos, maracas, timbales, congos, claves, guiros, and agogo bells are only some of the common percussion instruments played.

Vocal lessons focus on proper posture and breathing for singing. Singers also learn how to project. This means they learn how to make their singing voices louder and stronger.

Salsa and merengue lessons are taught at many dance schools around the country. Community stores and online shops offer DVDs on how to dance in various Latin styles. Videos posted on the Internet are also sources for learning how to dance.

Marc Anthony's *career got off to an early start. He says, "I've been singing since I was three. I think I knew how to sing before I knew how to talk, so I felt totally comfortable expressing myself that way. I started singing at home with my dad. He would write his own songs and sing all night. I would sing first voice and he would sing second and we'd have a little show on the weekends." 18*

Young dancers perform the cumbia at a parade in Barranquilla, Colombia.

⬣18 *For a Living*

The Latin music recording industry offers jobs to people with many different skills, not just musicians. Here are two examples of people who make a living in the industry. You probably won't see their faces on TV, but these people are crucial behind the scenes.

Latin Music in Print

Rudolph Mangual is a former aerospace engineer and musician who lives with his wife Yvette in Los Angeles, California. In the late 1990s, Rudolph and Yvette felt there was no central place for people to get information about Latin music, so they founded *Latin Beat* magazine. Mangual still edits the magazine today. *Latin Beat* is read around the world, and it is used in schools to educate kids about Latin music.[19]

Reggaeton's Most Powerful Woman

Dominican-born **A. Ines Rooney** has been called "reggaeton's most powerful woman." Rooney was working as a financial analyst when she took over accounting work for Más Flow Records. Now she runs the entire studio! Rooney is also a great singer, and she has recorded songs of her own. On top of that, she speaks eleven languages and is the mother of three kids.[20]

The Future of Latin Music

Who will be the future of Latin music? You! From singers and instrumentalists to writers and fans, Latin music's next generation is reading this book.

Glossary

auditioned—Gave a test performance.

bachata—A style of music from the countryside of the Dominican Republic. The music tells stories of heartbreak.

beat—A rhythmic stress in music.

clave—A percussion instrument used in salsa music; the rhythm that claves create.

conga—A Cuban dance of African origin.

GI Bill—A law passed after World War II. It allows military veterans certain privileges such as a college education.

irreplaceable—Special; unable to be replaced.

mariachi—Relating to a Mexican musical group that performs on the streets. Musicians often wear silver-studded outfits and wide-brimmed hats.

mastering—Putting the final touches on a music recording.

merengue—A lively music and dance style that started in the Dominican Republic and Haiti.

music producer—A person who pays for or oversees the creation of a song or album.

paralyzed—Unable to move one's body.

promoted—Created public excitement about a musical artist or group.

recording engineer—A person in charge of recording equipment in a music studio.

reggaeton—A Latin music and dance style that started in Panama and gained popularity in the early 1990s.

remixed—Produced a new music recording by combining or changing already-recorded sounds.

rhythm—The regular repetition of strong beats.

salsa—A type of Latin American music with rhythm and blues, rock, and jazz influences; the dance that goes to the music.

solidarity—Togetherness or unity.

spiritual—Relating to religious values or strong beliefs.

tejano—A style of music from Texas that combines country music, rhythm and blues, and popular Latin music styles.

timbales—Drums shaped like cylinders and played with sticks.

tracks—Individual parts of a music recording. For example, the drums might be on one track, while the guitar might be on another.

undocumented—Without legal immigration papers.

Time Line

1919 Victoria Hernandez opens El Barrio grocery store. The store becomes a major music center for Latin artists.

1925 Celia Cruz, the Queen of Salsa, is born in Cuba.

1940 Desi Arnaz marries Lucille Ball, and they go on to create the hit TV show *I Love Lucy*.

1956 Johnny Ventura begins his career as a famous merengue player.

1968 Carlos Santana records congo drums on the Rolling Stones' famous song "Sympathy for the Devil."

1969 Marc Anthony is born in New York City.

1970 Jennifer Lopez is born in New York City.

1977 The band Menudo forms in Puerto Rico.

1985 Miami Sound Machine releases their hit single "Congo."

1988 Ricky Martin releases his debut solo album in English.

1992 Reggaeton begins to gain popularity.

1997 Shakira starts the Fundación Pies Descalzos (Barefoot Foundation) to help poor children in Colombia.

1999 Wisin y Yandel are signed to their first record label.

2002 David Bisbal presents his debut album.

2003 The movie *Selena—Live: The Last Concert* hits theaters.

2005 Paulina Rubio is named *People en Espanol*'s 2005 Star of the Year.

2006 Latin music stars release a bilingual version of "The Star-Spangled Banner."

2008 Jennifer Lopez and Marc Anthony have twins on February 22.

2009 Latin stars Wisin y Yandel and Juanes bring home Grammy Awards.

End Notes

1. Amy DuBois Barnett, "Jennifer's Latest Desire," *Bazaar.com*, February 2008, <http://www.harpersbazaar.com/magazine/cover/jennifer-lopez-0208-2> (January 11, 2009).

2. "Bio," *MarcAnthonyOnline.com*, n.d., <http://www.marcanthonyonline.com/> (January 11, 2009).

3. Mary Kent, *Salsa Talks: A Musical Heritage Uncovered* (Altamonte Springs, Florida: Digital Domain, 2005), p. 210.

4. Ibid, p. 170.

5. Shaheem Reid, "Daddy Yankee Describes Why Getting Shot Made Him the Man He Is," *MTV.com*, April 21, 2006, <http://www.mtv.com/news/articles/1529183/20060420/yankee_daddy.jhtml> (January 11, 2009).

6. "World Beater," *Observer Music Monthly*, July 15, 2007, <http://observer.guardian.co.uk/omm/story/0,,2123635,00.html#article_continue> (January 11, 2009).

7. "10 Questions for Jennifer Lopez," *Time.com*, October 18, 2007, <http://www.time.com/time/magazine/article/0,9171,1673250-1,00.html> (January 11, 2009).

8. "Columbian rock star Juanes, in interview," *Sound Generator*, April 20, 2006, <http://www.soundgenerator.com/viewArticle.cfm?ArticleID=7368> (January 11, 2009).

9. "GIJU Live on ESPN at World Salsa Championships," *mynewsletterbuilder.com*, December 2007, <http://www.mynewsletterbuilder.com/tools/published.php?action=view&newsletter_id=1409624804 > (January 11, 2009).

10. Julienne Gage, "The British *Invasión*," *Miami New Times Music*, May 17, 2007, <http://www.miaminewtimes.com/2007-05-17/music/the-british-invasi-oacute-n/> (January 11, 2009).

11. Jay S. Jacobs, "Shakira," *PopEntertainment.com*, n.d., <http://www.popentertainment.com/Shakira.htm> (January 11, 2009).

12. Sue Steward, *¡Musica!: salsa, rumba, merengue and more* (San Francisco: Chronicle Books, 1999), p. 47.

13. "Q&A with Carlos Santana," *Latina.com*, n.d., <http://www.latina.com/latina/entertainment/entertainment.jsp?genre=music&article=carlossantana> (November 15, 2008).

14. Mary Kent, p. 270.

15. José Dávila, "Pop, Into Your Head," *Miami New Times Music,* December 27, 2007, <http://www.miaminewtimes.com/2007-12-27/music/pop-into-your-head/full> (January 11, 2009).

16. Personal interview, BigChris Flores, December 14, 2007.

17. Juan Zamarano, "Shakira, Garcia Marquez Start Foundation," *Washintonpost.com*, December 12, 2006, <http://www.washingtonpost.com/wp-dyn/content/article/2006/12/12/AR2006121201294.html> (January 11, 2009).

18. Mary Kent, p. 202.

19. "Rudolph Mangual," *LBMO.org*, n.d., <http://www.latinbeatmagazine.com> (January 11, 2009).

20. "A. Ines Rooney, Reggaeton's Most Powerful Woman," *Latina.com*, n.d., <http://www.latina.com/latina/toolsforsuccess/toolsforsuccess.jsp?genre=travel&article=ainesrooney (January 11, 2009).

Further **Reading**

Books

Kallen, Stuart A. *The History of Latin Music.* San Diego: Lucent Books, 2006.

Krohn, Katherine. *Shakira.* Minneapolis: Twenty-First Century Books, 2007.

Mintzer, Richard. *Latino Americans in Sports, Film, Music, and Government.* Broomall, Pa.: Mason Crest, 2005.

Web Sites

Latina Magazine—Stories for Latin American Women
<*http://www.latina.com*>

Latin Heat Online—Latin American Culture, Business, and Events
<*http://latinheat.com*>

LBMO.com—A Magazine Focused on Latin Music and Media
<*http://latinbeatmagazine.com*>

Index